Nicholas Poppe

Grammar of Written Mongolian

PORTA LINGUARUM ORIENTALIUM

Neue Serie

Herausgegeben von Werner Diem und Lutz Edzard

Band 1

2006

Harrassowitz Verlag · Wiesbaden

Nicholas Poppe

Grammar of
Written Mongolian

5th unrevised printing

2006

Harrassowitz Verlag · Wiesbaden

Photo on the cover: Summary of Contents. Bičig of Busayid Baγatur Qan of 1320 (verso), Harvard Journal of Asiatic Studies 16 (1953), plate II close to p. 107.

Bibliografische Information Der Deutschen Bibliothek:
Die Deutsche Bibliothek verzeichnet diese Publikation in der Deutschen
Nationalbibliografie; detaillierte bibliografische Daten sind im Internet
über http://dnb.ddb.de abrufbar.

Bibliographic information published by Die Deutsche Bibliothek:
Die Deutsche Bibliothek lists this publication in the Deutsche
Nationalbibliografie; detailed bibliographic data is available in the
internet at http://dnb.ddb.de.e-mail: cip@dbf.ddb.de

For further information about our publishing program consult our
website https://www.harrassowitz-verlag.de
© Otto Harrassowitz KG, Wiesbaden 2006
Otto Harrassowitz GmbH & Co. KG, Kreuzberger Ring 7c-d,
D-65205 Wiesbaden, produktsicherheit.verlag@harrassowitz.de

ISSN 0554-7342
ISBN 978-3-447-00684-2

Contents

(The figures in parentheses refer to section numbers)

V. ACCIDENCE

NOUN:

Preface

The first scientific grammar of the Mongolian language, *Grammatik der mongolischen Sprache*, was published in St. Petersburg in 1831—more than one hundred and twenty years ago—by the German scholar Isaac Jacob SCHMIDT, a Member of the Imperial Russian Academy of Sciences. Since that time several other grammars have appeared, mainly in Russia, but there is no satisfactory grammar in any European language except Russian. I therefore hope that this book will be of use to all persons interested in the Mongolian language and Altaic studies generally.

This book deals with the Written Mongolian language, the earliest texts of which date from the first half of the thirteenth century. It is the written language of all Mongols of Inner and Outer Mongolia and prior to 1931, Written Mongolian was the only written language known to the Buriats in the USSR. Although a few years ago the Cyrillic alphabet was introduced in Outer Mongolia or the so-called Mongolian People's Republic, the old Mongolian script also is still used there.

The language written in the Mongolian script is not uniform, but varies greatly in different periods of history and in different types of literature. Therefore, I have considered it necessary to discuss the differences in the language of various periods and also the differences between the language of the religious and that of the secular literature. I have tried to make this grammar as complete as the present stage of research permits, and to give more attention to syntax than have the writers of the previous grammars.

I do not consider it necessary to enumerate my sources, but I may mention that I have used in the first place the classical grammar by Aleksei BOBROVNIKOV, *Grammatika mongol'sko-kalmyckago iazyka* (Kazan', 1849), G. J. RAMSTEDT's article, „Über die Konjugation des Khalkha-Mongolischen" (Helsingfors, 1903), and also my own grammar published in Russian in 1937.

The transcription used in this book is that found in most scientific works dealing with the Mongolian language. Since it is explained in the relevant sections, it needs no explanation here.

I take pleasure in expressing my cordial thanks to my friend, Professor Francis W. CLEAVES, of the Harvard University, for his help. He read the manuscript of this grammar, did the final editing of large portions of the manuscript, and made many valuable suggestions which contributed much to its improvement. In conclusion I should mention that this book owes it appearance to a generous financial contribution from the German *Forschungsgemeinschaft* and the University of Washington.

Nicholas Poppe
University of Washington.

Explanation of Some Signs

= is the same as, corresponds to

‖ parallel forms

∽ alternates with

/ appears in both forms according to general rules

> developed into

< developed from

* reconstructed form

- before a letter or a group of letters (e. g., -*n* or -*bar*) this indicates a suffix;
  before and after a letter or a group of letters (e. g., -*la*-) this indicates a verbal derivation suffix;
  after a word this indicates a verbal stem, e. g., *morila*-

id. — *idem*, the same

I. Introduction

Origin of the Mongolian Script

1. Written Mongolian is the written language of the Eastern Mongols. It is a language used only in texts, never spoken. The difference between this language and the numerous dialects spoken by various Mongolian peoples is greater than that between the written and spoken languages of most European peoples.

The Mongols got their script from the Uighurs, an ancient Turkic people, who did not invent their alphabet, but borrowed it from the Sogdians, an Iranian people, who, in turn, had taken theirs from an Aramaic script.

The introduction of script among the Mongols is supposed to have taken place in the twelfth century. The most ancient monument of Written Mongolian is an inscription on a stone erected in honor of Chinggis Khan's nephew, Yisüngge, in about 1225.

The language of the Mongolian script differs fundamentally from all spoken Mongolian languages and dialects and, so far as we know, it differed from contemporaneous Mongolian dialects even in the thirteenth century. The history of the Mongolian dialects can be divided into three main periods: ancient, middle, and modern. Accordingly, science recognizes Ancient Mongolian, Middle Mongolian, and Modern Mongolian.

2. Ancient Mongolian possessed an initial, voiceless, bilabial consonant *p or *f which developed into h in Middle Mongolian and has vanished in Modern Mongolian. Actually this sound still exists in certain positions in the Monguor language in the Kansu province in China: *fuguor* (ox) = Mo. *üker*, Kh. *üxür* (*id.*).

Ancient Mongolian possessed the intervocalic, voiced, velar consonants *γ and *g which vanished in Middle Mongolian: *$a\gamma ula$ (mountain) = Mid. Mong. *aula* (*id.*).

In Ancient Mongolian the vowels i and e were maintained in all positions, whereas in the modern dialects they have developed under the influence of the vowel of the following syllable, into other vowels: $i > a$ under the influence of a following a, e. g., *miqan* (flesh, meat) = Kh. *maxa* (*id.*); *ebül* (winter) = Kh. *öwöl* (*id.*).

In Written Mongolian the intervocalic consonants γ and g and the vowels i and e are maintained in all positions. From the point of view of its phonetic development, Written Mongolian is a language which has retained some Ancient Mongolian features. Only the initial *p or *f has vanished in Written Mongolian; in all other respects it is the most archaic Mongolian language which has preserved some features of Ancient Mongolian.

3. The middle period of the history of the Mongolian languages extends from the thirteenth century to the end of the sixteenth century. Middle Mongolian is well represented by numerous texts, of which the most important are the following:

(a) The most ancient text of Mongolian literature, *Mongγol-un ni'uča tobča'an* (*The Secret History of the Mongols*), *Yüan-ch'ao pi-shih* in Chinese, written in 1240 in a Mongolian dialect and later transcribed with Chinese characters.

(b) The ḥP'ags-pa script or the so called square script, invented in 1269 and used until the collapse of the Yüan dynasty in China in 1368.

(c) Numerous Arabic-Mongolian, Persian-Mongolian, Georgian-Mongolian, and Armenian-Mongolian dictionaries and glossaries of the thirteenth and fourteenth centuries.

The languages of the Dagurs in Manchuria and the Moghols in Afghanistan have preserved some Middle Mongolian features. Middle Mongolian is characterized by the following phonological peculiarities:

The initial **p* or **f* has developed into *h*, e. g., *hüker* (ox) < **püker* or **füker id.*

The intervocalic **γ* and **g* no longer exist, but the vowels have not as yet contracted, e. g., *aula* (mountain) < **aγula id.*

The vowels *i* and *e* are maintained in all positions, e. g., *miqan* (flesh), *ebüdüg* (knee).

The affricates *č* and *ǰ* are still pronounced as sibilant sounds in all positions, while in certain modern languages they have developed into *ts* and *dz*.

4. The modern period started at the end of the sixteenth century. By that time the following changes had occurred in most of the colloquial languages:

The initial *h* < **p* or **f* had vanished: Kh. *üxür* < **hüker* < **püker* or **füker*.

The vowels between which the ancient velar consonants **γ* and **g* occurred had been contracted into a single long vowel: Kh. *ūla* < **aula* < **aγula* (mountain).

The vowels *i* and *e* of the first syllable had developed into other vowels: Kh. *maxa* < **miqan* (flesh, meat), Kh. *öwöl* < **ebül* (winter).

The following Mongolian colloquial languages represent the modern stage of development: East Mongolian (Buriat, Khalkha, Chakhar, Urat, Ordos or Urdus, Kharchin) and West Mongolian (all the Oirat dialects and among them the Kalmuk language).

As Written Mongolian is close to Ancient Mongolian language and the extant colloquial languages stand either at the Middle or at the Modern stage of their development, there are great differences among them. Yet, though Written Mongolian is not spoken, it is not a dead language.

5. The history of Written Mongolian, too, can be divided into three periods: the pre-classical, the classical, and the modern.

The pre-classical period extends from the very beginning to the seventeenth century. Both the script and the language of the pre-classical period differ from those of the succeeding periods. The shape of the letters strongly resembles that of the Uighur and Sogdian letters. The diacritical marks on such letters as *n*, *γ*, *š* are used either not at all or rarely. The sounds *č* and *ǰ* in medial positions are rendered by the same characters. As to the language of the pre-classical period, it manifests numerous inconsistencies in its grammar and orthography. Many words differ in their spelling from their equivalents in the classical language. The pre-classical vocabulary strongly differs from that of the classical period.

The most ancient loan words in Written Mongolian are of Chinese origin. There are also old Indo-European loan words: Mo. *esrua* < Sogd. *$z^arw\bar{a}$ (Zerwan) (an Iranian Mazdaic god), Mo. *šijir* (a weight) < Sogd. *$s^it\check{e}r$ < Greek στατήρ (stater). Most Indo-European loan words penetrated through the Uighur: Mo. *nom* (doctrine, Buddhist dharma) < Uigh. *nom* < Sogd. *nom* < Greek νόμος. These and many other loan words are older than the twelfth century.

There are many Uighur loan words which spread with the Buddhist literature in the fourteenth and fifteenth centuries.

6. The spread of Buddhism made good progress in the sixteenth and seventeenth centuries. This new period of history, called the Buddhist Renaissance of Mongolia, coincides with the beginning of a new period in the history of the Mongolian script. The mighty progress of Buddhism enriched Written Mongolian with numerous Buddhist philosophical and religious terms of Tibetan and Sanskrit origin. Obsolete and incomprehensible ancient words, originally Uighur loan words, were replaced by new expressions. As the Mongols became familiar with the art of printing and xylographs were published in hundreds of copies, the orthography depended no longer upon the skill of the copyists. A unified orthography was introduced, the grammar of the written language was purged of colloquial elements, and all inconsistencies were eliminated. The letters acquired their present form, and some new letters were invented to transcribe Tibetan and Sanskrit sounds. Thus there arose a new language which we call Classical.

Classical Written Mongolian failed to dominate all the literary activities; it was used only in the xylographic editions of Buddhist works, while secular literature continued to be influenced by the dialects.

7. The latest period of the history of the written language began in the first years of the twentieth century as a phenomenon simultaneous with the awakening of the national self-consciousness of the Mongols and their struggle for liberation from Chinese domination. In the first years of the present century there were established the first printing offices provided with modern European equipment. The first magazines and newspapers were published. Afterward, in the early twenties, a Mongolian publishing house was established in Peking and another one in Ulan Bator (former Urga) in Outer Mongolia. A scientific committee was organized in Ulan Bator. All these and other publishing houses printed many books of various kinds: tales, stories, manuals, dictionaries, political pamphlets, and so on.

Though the orthography and grammar of the language of the new editions do not differ from those of the classical period, the language is quite different because of numerous new expressions in politics, economics, and technology.

Written Mongolian is used by all East Mongols, i. e., Chakhars, Ordos, Urat, Kharchin, Bargut, and all other groups of Inner Mongolia and Manchuria, and by the Mongols of Outer Mongolia (mainly Khalkha). The government of Outer Mongolia or the Mongolian People's Republic abandoned Written Mongolian in 1941, introduced the Russian alphabet,

Vowels

᠌ᠠ		—		a
᠊ᠣ	᠊ᠣ᠌	᠌ᠥ	᠌ᠥ᠌	o
᠊ᠣ᠋		᠌ᠤ		u
᠊ᠡ		ᠡ		e
᠊ᠢ	᠊ᠢ᠌	᠊ᠥ	᠊ᠥ᠌	ė
᠊ᠥᠡ	᠊ᠥᠡ᠌	᠊ᠥᠣ	᠊ᠥᠣ᠌	ö
᠊ᠥᠣᠡ		᠊ᠥᠣᠡ		ü
᠊ᠢ		᠊ᠢ		i

and adopted the colloquial language as the literary language. Yet all literate people still use Written Mongolian in private life, and the complete disappearance of Written Mongolian will not take place there soon.

The Buriats, too, used Written Mongolian and developed an interesting literature in this language. The Buriats officially abandoned Written Mongolian in 1931 and introduced the Latin alphabet, which was, in turn, replaced by the Russian alphabet in 1937. Yet even the Buriats still privately use Written Mongolian and there still are many people who know this language well.

8. The Western Mongols, the so-called Oirats, adopted an alphabet of their own in 1648. A learned Buddhist priest, Zaya Pandita, created it on the basis of the Mongolian script. This Oirat script was used by all Oirats, among them the Kalmuks. The latter abandoned it in the early 1920's and introduced the Russian alphabet; later on, they replaced it with the Latin alphabet, but ultimately, in 1937, they reintroduced the Russian alphabet.

The ḥP'ags-pa Script

Consonants

ㄹ	p	ᐷ	$\check{c}^{\iota}$
ㄹ	b	ᗓ	$\check{j}$
ᄯ 匼	v	ᑕ	$\check{s}$
ᴣ	m	ᖉ	$\check{z}$
ᅚ	t	ᵾ	y
ᴣ	t^{ι}	ᵯ	k
ᴢ	d	ᖆ	k^{ι}
ᴐ	n	ᵰ	g
ᴛ	r	ᵯ	q
ᗕ	l	ᗓ	γ
ᗔ ᗔ	c^{ι}	ᴢ	η
ᗗ ᗗ	j	ᵽ	h
ᴣ	s	ᗕ	$\cdot$
ᴟ	z	ᵲ	^{y}
ᗩ	$\check{c}$	◢	$\underset{\wedge}{\underset{\cdot}{u}}$

9. The Emperor Khubilai of the Yüan dynasty ordered the learned Buddhist priest ḥP'ags-pa to invent a new script to replace the old Uighur script used by the Mongols. This script was invented and officially introduced in 1269. Despite great efforts to replace the old script then being used in the Mongolian empire, the new script spread slowly and made no perceptible progress. It was in official use until the collapse of the Yüan dynasty (1368).

Because of the square shape of the letters it is also called the square script. The new alphabet was a remodeled Tibetan alphabet. As to the language of this script, it was a Middle Mongolian dialect, differing considerably from Written Mongolian. Since the language of the ḥPʽags-pa is different from Written Mongolian, it cannot be discussed in this grammar. Therefore, only tables of the ḥPʽags-pa characters are given on p. 4—5.

Colloquial Mongolian

10. There is no uniform Mongolian colloquial language; there is a group of languages and dialects more or less differing from each other and spoken by some three million Mongols.

The Mongolian languages are classified into two main groups: the eastern and western. In addition there are numerous small insular languages not belonging to either of these groups. Both the East and West Mongolian are Modern Mongolian languages, while the insular languages are remnants of Middle Mongolian.

11. The eastern group consists of the languages of Inner and Outer Mongolia, Manchuria, and East Siberia.

The most important Inner Mongolian languages are the following: (a) Kharchin in the Jehol province, (b) Tumut, (c) Chakhar in the Chakhar province and in the territory of the Shilin Gol League, (d) Urdus or Ordos in the Suiyuan province (Yeke Ju League), and (e) Urat in Ulan Tsab. These languages do not differ much from one another. The difference is merely in the pronunciation. Therefore, mutual understanding among those tribes is easy.

In Manchuria, the language of the Khuchin Bargu (or Chipchin) and that of the Khorchin are the most important. They differ but slightly from each other and from the Inner Mongolian languages. Together with the latter, they constitute the southern branch of East Mongolian.

In Outer Mongolia the greater part of the population, almost 800,000 people, speak Khalkha-Mongolian, which consists of two main dialects: Khalkha proper and, in the western part of the Mongolian Republic, the Khotogoitu dialect. In the area around Lake Kossogol (Köbsögöl Dalai) live the Darkhat, who speak a mixed dialect consisting of Khalkha, Oirat, and Buriat elements. These languages and their dialects constitute the central branch of East Mongolian.

The Buriat-Mongolian Autonomous Soviet Republic, which is part of the Soviet Union, is situated north of Outer Mongolia. This republic is mainly populated by Buriats (almost 300,000 people). The Buriat language represents the northern branch of East Mongolian.

The Buriat language consists of three dialects: the western (west and north of Lake Baikal), the eastern (east and south of Lake Baikal), and the Selenga in the Selenga valley. These dialects consist of numerous sub-dialects. One of them is the Bargu Buriat in northwest Manchuria. The Tsongol and Sartul sub-dialects of the Selenga dialect are transitional dialects between the Buriat and Khalkha languages.

All eastern Mongols, among them all Buriats except those speaking the West Buriat dialect, use or, until recently, have been using Written Mongolian.

12. West Mongolian, otherwise called the Oirat language, is spoken in various parts of Outer Mongolia (in northwest Mongolia), in China, Tibet, and even in European Russia. The following languages and dialects belong to the Western group:

The Kalmuk language is spoken by almost 150,000 people in the former Autonomous Kalmuk Soviet Republic on the lower course of the Volga River. This language comprises the Dörbet, Torgut, and Buzava dialects. The Kalmuks came to the Volga River in the seventeenth century from Central Asia, but the greater part of them left their new home at the end of the eighteenth century and returned to Central Asia. The descendants of those who returned, the Dörbet and Torgut tribes, still live in Outer Mongolia. In the northeastern part of Outer Mongolia live the Dörbet, Bayit, Torgut, Uriankha, Dzakhachin, Mingat, and Dambi-Ölet tribes, each speaking its own dialect.

Numerous Oirats, mainly Torguts, live in various countries of Central Asia: in Alashan, in the Chinese Ch'inghai (Kökö Nur) province, in Northern Tibet, and so on.

All Oirats except the Kalmuks use the Oirat script. The Kalmuks, too, used it until the Russian revolution, but later on they abandoned it and adopted the Russian alphabet.

13. The insular Mongolian languages cannot be placed in any group. One of the best known of these is the Monguor language spoken in Kansu. Another is the Dagur language spoken in Manchuria (near Khailar and in the Nonni valley). In Afghanistan live the so-called Moghols, the descendants of the Mongolian invaders of the thirteenth and fourteenth centuries, speaking the Moghol language. Besides these, there are various other Mongolian tribes in northern Tibet which as yet have not been investigated.

Written Mongolian is unknown to those insular tribes. A few Dagurs use it, though the majority of them use either the Manchu language or the Chinese. The Moghols are illiterate, though a few of them can write either in Arabic or in Pushtu.

14. The Mongolian languages belong to the Altaic family and are closely related to the Manchu-Tungus and Turkic languages and to Korean. These languages possess a common grammatical system and a common vocabulary.

II. Phonetics

Accent

15. The accent is an expiratory stress always falling upon the first syllable regardless of vocalic length. Therefore, there is no need of marking the stressed syllable.

Vowels

Description of the Vowels

16. In treating of general phonetics, vowels are classified into front, middle, and back, but since the phonetic classification has no meaning for Written Mongolian grammar, a classification into front and back vowels alone has been adopted in line with the vocalic harmony which characterizes the Written Mongolian language. The front vowels are *e*, *ö*, *ü*; the back vowels are *a*, *o*, *u*. The vowel *i* is neutral, being classified with neither.

For a discussion of vocalic harmony, see sections 32—34.

17. The vowel *a* is a low-back-wide sound more or less similar to the "pure" Italian *a* in *padre* or English *father*.

mal cattle	*ala* kill!
bal honey, mead	*sara* moon

18. The vowel *o* is a mid-back-round sound more or less similar to the English *oo* in *door* (pronounced short).

olan many	*bos* rise!
on year	*bolba* he became

19. The vowel *u* is a back sound articulated deep in the oral cavity with the larynx lowered. This gives the acoustic impression of a dull sound similar to that between the English *oo* in *door* and *oo* in *foot*.

usun water	*urtu* long
uran skilful	*unu* ride horse-back!

20. The vowel *e* is a mid-front-wide sound more or less similar to the English *e* in *set*.

ene this	*tende* there
tere that	*eke* mother

21. The vowel *ö* is the French *eu* in *peu* (little) or German *ö* in *Körper* (body). As pronounced by the Khalkha-Mongols in Outer Mongolia, the Buriats, and even other Mongols, it is a sound which falls between the high-mixed-wide-round and the mid-mixed-narrow-round vowels, resembling the *u* in the South Swedish pronunciation of *lund*.

köl foot	*köke* blue
ög give!	*bös* cotton-stuff

22. The vowel *ü* is the French *u* in *lune* (moon) or the German *ü* in *dünn* (thin). The Khalkha-Mongols and many other groups pronounce this

as a high-mixed-narrow-round sound similar to the Norwegian *u* in *hus* (house).

üsün hair	*küčün* strength
ünen truth	*ükül* death

23. The vowel *i* is similar to the English *i* in *pin*.

Long Vowels

24. In the Mongolian orthography, the length of the vowels is not marked, though, in the traditional pronunciation of Written Mongolian, there is a perceptible difference between the long and short vowels. In scientific works on Written Mongolian the length is not marked.

The long vowels are *ā, ō, ū, ē, ȫ, ǖ, ī*:

$ā$ = English *a* in *far*
$ō$ = English *aw* in *awful*
$ū$ = English *u* in *rule*
$ē$ = English *ai* in *air* or German *e* in *Ehre* (honor)
$ȫ$ = German *ö* in *Höhle* (cave)
$ǖ$ = German *ü* in *kühn* (bold)
$ī$ = English *ee* in *bee*

25. Vowels immediately preceded by the combination *iy-* are always long. This means that the combinations *iya, iye* are to be pronounced as *iyā, iyē*.

tariyan = *tariyān* seed, field *eliye* = *eliyē* vulture

26. In many words, though not in all, vowels immediately following the combination of any vowel + *γ* or *g* are long. This means that in such cases the second vowel of the combinations *aγa, aγu, ege, egü*, and so on, is long.

qaγalγa = *qaγālγa* gate	*aγula* = *aγūla* mountain
niγur = *niγūr* face	
degere = *degēre* above	*segül* = *segǖl* tail

27. All vowels represented in Mongolian spelling by two vowels of the same quality are pronounced as one long vowel. Exceptions to this rule will be discussed in section 90.

buu = *bū* gun, rifle *γajiiqu* = *γajīqu* to incline

28. In certain words single vowels are pronounced long.

kümün = *kümūn* man	*kemekü* or *gemekü* = *kemēkü* or *gemēkü* to say
gere = *gerē* treaty	*tuya* = *tuyā* ray

Diphthongs

29. There are two kinds of diphthongs: those of which the first component is a syllabic element and those of which the second component is a syllabic element.

The diphthongs formed with a non-syllabic *i*, i. e., *i̯*, belong to the first category; the syllabic element, that is to say, the first component of these diphthongs, is pronounced long.

The diphthong $a\underset{\ }{i}$ is pronounced as the English *i* in *dice;* $o\underset{\ }{i}$ is similar to the English *oi* in *oil* or *oy* in *boy;* $e\underset{\ }{i}$ as English *ey* in *obey*. The remaining Mongolian diphthongs $u\underset{\ }{i}$ and $\ddot{u}\underset{\ }{i}$ have no equivalents in English.

noqai̯ = noqāi̯ dog	*široi̯ = širōi̯* earth, dust
moyai̯ = moyāi̯ snake	*qarangγui̯ = qarangγūi̯* darkness
menekei̯ = menekēi̯ frog	*tedüi̯ = tedǖi̯* so much

30. The diphthongs *ua, au, eü* belong to the second category. Here the last component is a syllabic element. The non-syllabic element of these diphthongs bears resemblance to the English *w* in *watch* or *u* in *out*.
The syllabic element of the diphthong *ua* is long in most words but in a few words the syllabic element of *ua* is short.

lingqua = lingquā lotus	*qua = quā* chestnut-colored (horse)
	γua = γuā beautiful (woman)
činua = činua wolf	*irua = irua* omen

31. In the diphthongs *au* and *eü* the second component is always long.

taulai̯ = taūlai̯ hare	*auya = aūya* strength
keüken = keǖken child	*teüke = teǖke* history

Vocalic Harmony

32. A word can contain only back vowels (*a, o, u*) or only front vowels (*e, ö, ü*). Back and front vowels do not occur together in any words except loan words.
The vowel *i*, however, though pronounced as a front vowel, does occur in both types of words and is, therefore, considered a neutral vowel. The explanation is that in Proto-Mongolian there were two vowels: *ï* which occurred in back vocalic words and *i* which occurred in words with front vowels only. Thus in Proto-Mongolian there were no neutral vowels at all and all vowels were subject to the rules of vocalic harmony. In Written Mongolian and in the existing Mongolian languages, the *ï* and *i* have converged into one sound which is *i*.
A Mongolian word can have either back or front vowels but not both, with the exception of *i*, which is not subject to these restrictions. This constitutes vocalic harmony.
Vocalic harmony affects the use of endings: words with back vowels require endings with back vowels, but words with front vowels can only take endings with front vowels. Endings of which *i* is the only vowel can be taken by all words.
Words with *i* in all syllables are front vocalic words and require endings with front vowels.

33. The vowel *o* does not occur in the medial or in the final syllables of words of which the first syllable is formed by *a* or *u*. The vowel *o* occurs only in the non-initial syllables of words of which the first syllable contains *o* or, rarely, *i*.
The vowel *ö* occurs in the non-initial syllables of words of which the first syllable contains *ö*.

34. The dependence of the vowels of non-initial syllables upon the vowel of the first syllable can be demonstrated in the following table:

first syllable	non-initial syllables	
a or *u*	*a* *u*	
o	*a* *o* *u*	
e or *ö* or *ü*	*e* *ü*	*i*
i	*a o u e ü*	

aqa elder brother	*eliye* vulture
utasun thread	*ünen* truth
bariqu to seize	*üsün* hair
uriqu to invite	*üniye* cow
usun water	*öngge* color
qola far	*öndür* high
oron < **oran* place	*öšiye* hatred
mongγol < **mongγal* Mongol	*miqan* flesh, meat
oroį < **oraį* top	*široį* earth, dust
qorin twenty	*niyur* face
ene this	*irekü* to come
ebüdüg knee	*jigšikü* to loathe

Consonants

Description of the Consonants

35. The consonants are classified into labial, dental & alveolar, palatal, velar, and laryngal consonants.

Labial consonants: *p, b, v, m*
Dental & alveolar consonants: *t, d, č, j, s, š, l, r, n*
Palatal consonants: *y*
Velar consonants: *q, γ, k, g, ng*
Laryngal consonants: *h*

36. The sound *p* is an aspirated bilabial strong consonant which can be otherwise transcribed as *ph*. This consonant occurs both initially and medially in foreign words.

pürbü Thursday < Tibetan
yampai pavilion, a gate with a roof < Chinese

37. The weak bilabial *b* is similar to the English *b*.

bal honey, mead	*keb* model
tabun five	*eb* peace, unanimity

38. The voiced spirant *v* is pronounced as the English *w*. This sound occurs at the beginning and the middle of loan words.

vivangkirid prophecy < Sanskrit *vyākṛti*

39. The consonant *m* is the same as the English *m*.

mal cattle	*aman* mouth
em medicine	*naγadum* play, game

40. The sound *t* is an aspirated, strong dental plosive consonant differing from the English *t*, which is unaspirated. This consonant occurs only at the beginning of words or in intervocalic position, never at the end of syllables or words.

tende there	*tataqu* to pull
ta you	*qota* town

41. The sound *d* is a weak dental plosive; it differs from the English *d* in being voiceless, giving the acoustic impression of something between the English *d* and *t*.

duran desire	*odqan* the youngest son
ede these	*bolod* steel

42. The sound *č* is an aspirated strong dental affricate corresponding to the English *ch* in *church* but differing from the latter by its aspiration and dental articulation. This consonant does not occur at the end of syllables or words.

či thou, you (singular)	*čaγan* white
ači grandson	*qačar* cheek

43. The sound *ǰ* is a weak dental affricate more or less similar to the English *j* in *journey*. This consonant does not occur at the end of syllables or words.

ǰiγasun fish	*ǰegün* left
γaǰar country	*aǰirγa* stallion

44. The alveolar voiceless spirant *s* corresponds to the English voiceless *s* in *song* or *c* in *ceiling*.

sara moon, month	*bosqu* to rise
nasun age	*ulus* people

45. The voiceless spirant *š* corresponds to the English *sh*. This sound does not occur at the end of words but does occur at the end of syllables.

šira yellow	*bošuγ* prophecy
öšiye hatred	*aγuški* lung

46. The alveolar *l*, before back vowels, more or less corresponds to the English *l* in *all* or to the Polish *ł*. Before front vowels—*e, ö, ü, i*—and before the consonants *č* and *ǰ* it is pronounced as the French *l* in *le, elle*, and so on.

luu dragon	*mongγol* Mongol
qola far	*kelen* tongue
altan gold	*elǰigen* donkey

47. The consonant *r* is a strongly rolled alveolar sound differing from the English, French, or German *r*, and corresponding to the Russian,

Italian, or Finnish *r*. This consonant occurs initially only in loan words and occurs in genuine Mongolian words only medially or finally.

> *rašiyan* nectar < Sanskrit *rasāyana*   *arban* ten
> *aru* the northern slope of a mountain   *edür* day

48. The mediolingual *y* is the English *y* in *year*.

> *yabu* go!   *eye* peace
> *eliye* vulture   *bayan* rich

49. The deep-velar consonant *q* was in Ancient Mongolian a plosive but now is pronounced as a deep-velar spirant corresponding to what in English is transcribed with *kh* in *khaki* or to *ch* in Scottish *loch*. This consonant occurs only before back vowels, and does not occur at the end of syllables or words. Nor does it occur before *i*, although in the language of the fourteenth to the sixteenth centuries *q* did occur before *i* in words with back vowels. Since *q* is now pronounced as a spirant, it is sometimes transcribed as *x*.

> *qayan* khan, emperor   *aqa* the elder brother
> *qara* black   *saqiqu* (fourteenth century) to watch

50. The deep-velar consonant *γ* is a plosive. It is articulated further back than the English *g* in *gun*. The consonant *γ* occurs before or after back vowels, at the beginning and in the middle of words, and at the end of syllables or words. Both in the classical and in the modern language, *γ* occurs before *i* only if the latter belongs to a suffix and *γ* belongs to the end of the stem. In the preclassical language it occurred before *i* of all origins in back vocalic words.

> *γajar* country, place   *aday* end
> *aγula* mountain   *aday-i* the end (accusative)
> *maγtaqu* to praise   *jangγi* (fourteenth century) news
>   (modern *janggi* news)

51. The velar strong plosive consonant *k* corresponds more or less to the English *c* in *cat*. This sound occurs in words with front vowels but in back vocalic words it occurs only before *i*, where it has replaced the ancient *q*. The consonant *k* does not occur at the end of syllables or words. In loan words *k* may occur with *a* and other back vowels.

> *kelen* tongue   *ekin* beginning
> *eke* mother   *irekü* to come
> *sakiqu* to watch   *kunda* jasmin < Sanskrit

52. The velar *g* is a weak plosive more or less similar to the English *g* in *goat*. This sound occurs in all positions in words with front vowels. In words with back vowels it occurs only before *i*, in which position it has replaced the ancient *γ*. In loan words *g* occurs before *a* and other back vowels.

ger house

degere above

degdekü to rise

körüg picture

agi absinthium (Artemisia absin-thium)

gašib Kaçyapa (the name of a Buddha) < Sanskrit

53. The velar *ng* corresponds to the English *ng* in *song*. This sound does not occur at the beginning of words.

engke peace

ang deer, game

qongšiyar snout

jobalang pain, suffering

54. The laryngal spirant *h*, similar to the English *h* in *hand* or German *h* in *heben* (to lift, to raise), occurs in loan words.

hari green < Sanskrit

Summarizing Remarks on the Consonants

55. Only a few loan words begin with or end in two or more consonants. There are no original Mongolian words of this kind.

blama lama < Tibetan *bla-ma*

bodisdv Bodhisattva < Sanskrit

56. As stated above, the consonants *q*, *γ*, *k*, and *g* are joined with only certain vowels. Thus only the following syllables are possible:

qa, qo, qu (and *qi* only in the pre-classical language)

γa, γo, γu (and *γi* if *γ* belongs to the stem and *i* to the suffix)

ke, kö, kü, ki

ge, gö, gü, gi

57. The consonants *p*, *t*, *č*, *ǰ*, *q*, and *k* do not occur either at the end of syllables or at the end of words.

The consonant *š* does not occur at the end of words, but does occur at the end of syllables.

III. Script

58. The old script is written or printed vertically from left to right. Most letters have three different forms according to their position in the word: an initial one used at the beginning of words, a medial one used in the middle of words, and a final one used at the end of words. The letters will be discussed in the Mongolian alphabetic order.

59. The letters are given in the following table.

Letters of the Mongolian Alphabet

Number	Transcription	Characters		
		Initial	Medial	Final
1	a			
2	e			
3	i			
4	o u			
5	ö ü			
6	n			
7	ng			
8	q			
9	γ			
10	b			
11	p			
12	s			
13	š			
14	t d			
15	l			
16	m			
17	č			
18	ǰ			
19	y			
20	k g			
21	k			
22	r			
23	v			
24	h			

60. The initial forms of the vowels differ from the medial forms in that they have an additional stroke at the top. The final forms of *a* and *e* have an extension to the right in the shape of a slightly curved stroke. The vowels *i, o, u, ü* at the end of words have extensions in the shape of tails curved downward to the right. The final forms of the vowels *a* and *e*, in certain cases, have extensions to the left.

61. Four forms of the letter are used to represent the sound *a*. The initial form is used at the beginning of words and in enumerations as Europeans use *a), b),* and so on.

In ancient manuscripts and xylographs, the final form, when written apart from the word, is extended to the left (see the final form under 1 in the table).

The final form of the letter for *a*, as remarked above, is extended either to the right or to the left. The extension to the right is used after all consonants except *b, p,* and, in foreign words, *k*. After these consonants the extension to the left is used. This extension is also used if the letter is separated from the word.

	alaɣ dapple		*qoyina* after
	qaraɣul guard		*činu-a* wolf
	dabaɣa mountain pass		*altan* gold
	qoršiy-a corporation		*qaɣas* half

62. The sound *e* is represented in the middle and at the end of words by the same letters as *a*. There are two final letters, one of which is written after all consonants except *b, p, k,* and *g* and the other after these four consonants or when written apart from the word.

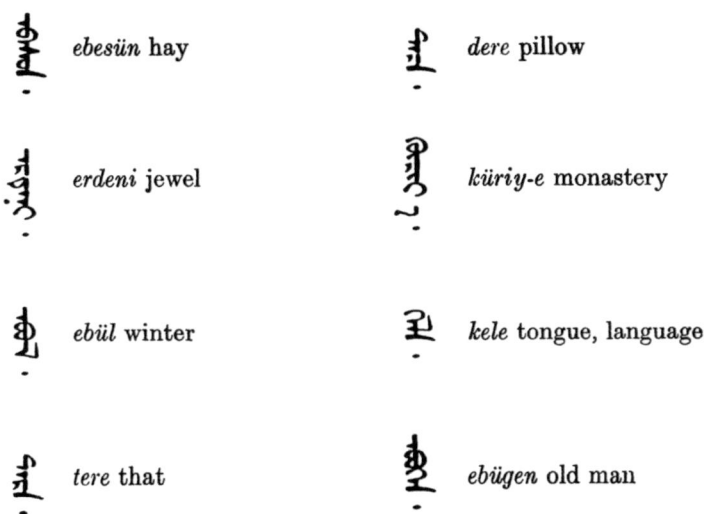

	ebesün hay		*dere* pillow
	erdeni jewel		*küriy-e* monastery
	ebül winter		*kele* tongue, language
	tere that		*ebügen* old man

63. There are three forms of the letter for *i*, of which the final one is used when written separately from the word.

In ancient books there occurs a special letter representing the sound *i* not belonging to any word, e. g., in enumeration corresponding to *i*) in European books. This is a combination of the final *i* with the head of initial letters.

	imaɣan goat		*čimadur* to you
	mingɣan thousand		*ǰil* year
	egüni him (accusative)		*či* you

64. The sounds *o* and *u* are not distinguished in the script. The fina· letter is also used if separated from the word.

In ancient books there is a special letter representing the sound *o* or *u* not belonging to any word This is a combination of the final letter with the head of the initial letter for *o* or *u*.

2•

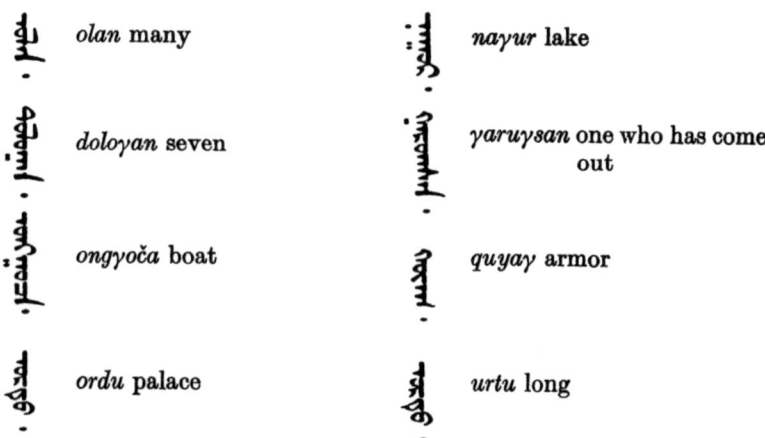

olan many

nayur lake

doloyan seven

yaruysan one who has come out

ongyoča boat

quyay armor

ordu palace

urtu long

65. The sounds *ö* and *ü* are represented by the same letters. In the body of a word two letters are used: one, only in the first syllable, and the other in the non-initial syllables. The former letter is the initial *ö* or *ü* without its head and the latter is the letter also representing the sounds *o* and *u* as well as *ö* and *ü*.

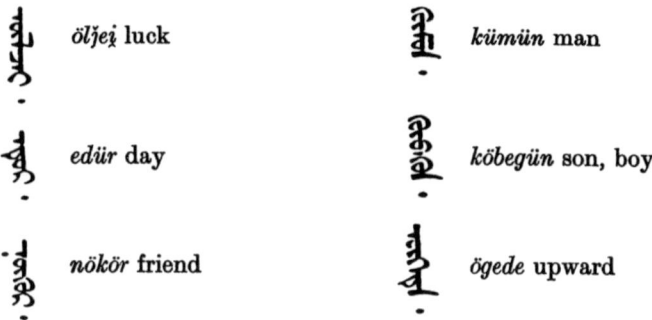

ölǰeǐ luck

kümün man

edür day

köbegün son, boy

nökör friend

ögede upward

66. The consonant *n* has two forms in the middle of words: one with a point and another one without a point. The former is used in prevocalic positions and the latter before consonants. At the end of words the form of the letter does not differ from that for *a* or *e*. In manuscripts the final form sometimes has a point on its left.

In ancient manuscripts no points are used and even the initial and medial forms lack their point.

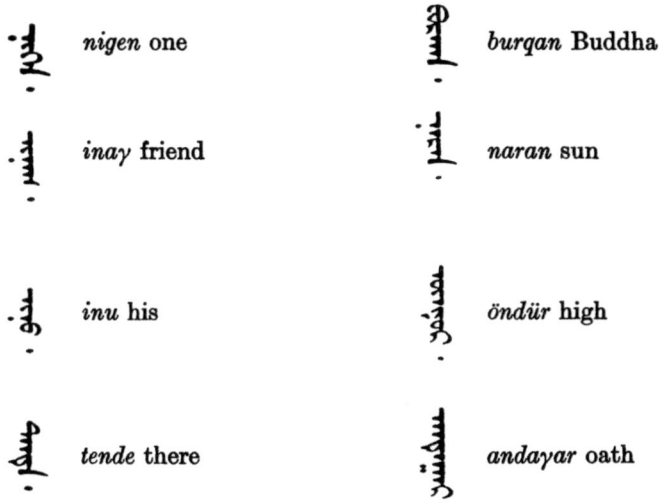

nigen one		*burqan* Buddha	
inaγ friend		*naran* sun	
inu his		*öndür* high	
tende there		*andaγar* oath	

67. The consonant *q* does not occur at the end of syllables or words, but if the final *a* is separated from the word, the consonant *q* of the last syllable is rendered by the letter given in column 3 of the above table. In ancient manuscripts the combination *qi* occurs in words with back vowels instead of the modern *ki*.

In ancient manuscripts the initial *q* is sometimes represented by the medial form.

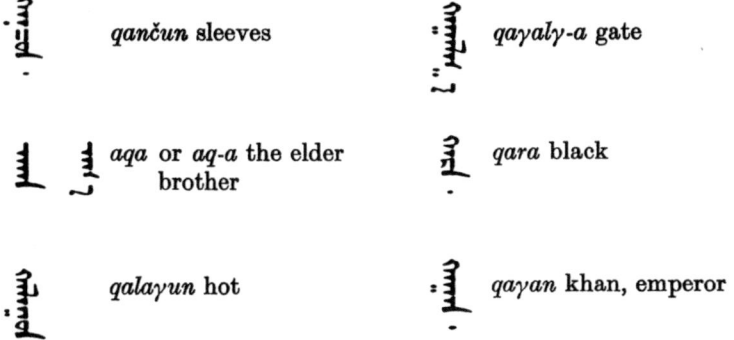

qančun sleeves		*qaγalγ-a* gate	
aqa or *aq-a* the elder brother		*qara* black	
qalaγun hot		*qaγan* khan, emperor	

68. The consonant *γ* is represented at the very end of words by the final form without points. Before *a* written separately from the word the final form with points is used.

In the intervocalic position the medial form has points but before consonants there are no points.

In ancient manuscripts the points are usually omitted and the forms of *γ* do not differ from those of *q*.

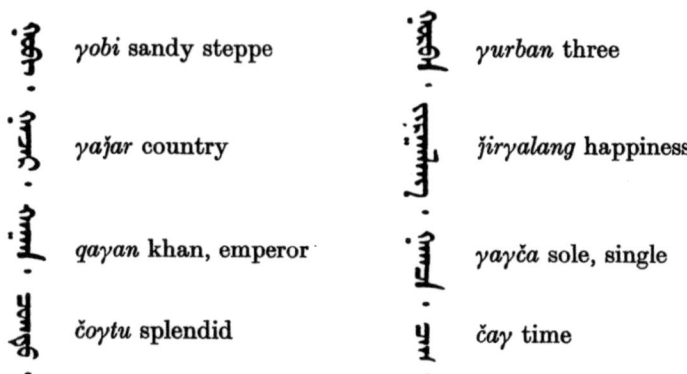

ɣobi sandy steppe		ɣurban three	
ɣaǰar country		ǰirɣalang happiness	
qaɣan khan, emperor		ɣaɣča sole, single	
čoɣtu splendid		čaɣ time	

69. The letter for *b* forms, together with vowels, special combined forms or ligatures demonstrated in the following table:

Syllables	Ligatures		
	Initial	Medial	Final
ba *be*	?	?	?
bi	?	?	?
bo *bu*	?	?	?
bȫ *bü*	?	?	?

baɣ-a little, small		ba and	
belge sign		irebe he came	
bilegüü whetstone, hone		bi I	
bosba he rose		yabuba he went	
böke wrestler		ebügen old man	

70. The sound *p* is rendered by letters differing from those for *b* in that they have an additional element to the left. The syllables *pa, pe, pi,* and so on, are rendered by ligatures similar to those for *ba, be, bi,* and so on, differing from the latter only in having that additional element.

71. The consonant *s* at the end of words can be rendered by either of the two letters given in the third column of the table. Of these the former is the current one and the latter is used in ancient books. Before an *i* belonging to the stem, *s* is pronounced *š*, but the final *s* of the stem before *i* belonging to a suffix is pronounced *s*.

𐄣	*sara* moon, month	𐄣	*šidün* tooth
	usun water		
	ulus state		*ulus-i* the state (accusative)

72. The letter for *š* differs from that for *s* in that it has points to the right. Before *i* the points are omitted.

73. The consonants *t* and *d* are not distinguished in the script. Therefore, unless the exact pronunciation of a word is known, it is difficult to read the respective letters correctly.

The sound *t* does not occur at the end of words or syllables. There are two medial forms for the consonant *d*. One of them is used before vowels and the other before consonants.

In foreign words and in proper names the sounds *t* and *d* are sometimes distinguished: *t* is represented in such cases by the initial and *d* by the medial form, independently of their position in the word. In the suffixes of the dative-locative *-tur* and *-dur*, which are always written separately from the word to which they belong, the sound *t* is represented by the initial form, while the sound *d* is represented by the medial form.

	tarbaɣan marmot		*ende* here
	toɣus peacock		*modun* tree
	baɣatur hero		*šidam* stick
	toqoqu to saddle		*saɣuɣad* after sitting

74. The medial form for *m*, together with the letter for *l*, forms a ligature.

    emlekü to cure, to treat   *nomlaqu* to preach

75. The consonants *ǰ* and *y* at the beginning of words are not distinguished, being represented by the same letter. But in manuscripts they are distinguished; the initial form for *y* differs from that for *ǰ* in that it has a small hook turned upward.

In the middle of words the consonants *ǰ* and *y* are represented by different forms.

At the end of words there is no *ǰ*. Before the vowel *a* written separately from a word, the consonant *ǰ* of the last syllable is represented with the final form for *i*.

	ǰabsar interval, space between		*ǰil* year
	ǰun summer		*aǰiry-a* stallion
	baǰa husbands of two sisters		*ǰisün* color of animals
	ǰ-a well, allright		*ǰida* spear
	yabuqu to go		*yabuǰuqui* he went
	qayaqu to throw		
	bey-e body		*bayan* rich

76. The consonants *k* and *g* are represented by the same letters. The correct reading is, therefore, possible only if the word is known.

The sound *k* does not occur at the end of words or syllables. The letter for *k* or *g* forms, together with the vowels, the ligatures given in the following table:

ke ge	?	?	?
ki gi	?	?	?
kö gö kū gü	?	?	?

keseg piece

eke mother

ger house

kituɣ-a knife

eki beginning

köbegün boy

bügüde all

ükükü to die

bilig intellect

77. The syllables *go, gu, ko, ku* in foreign words are rendered with ligatures.

kunda jasmin < Sanskrit

goši teacher < Chinese *kuo-shih*

78. The consonant *k* of the Written Mongolian is pronounced by many Mongols as a velar spirant similar to the Scottish *ch* in *loch*. Such is the pronunciation in Outer Mongolia, in Buriat-Mongolia, and so on. To represent the plosive velar consonant in foreign words the Mongols use the letter given in the table under No. 21. These letters, together with the vowels, form ligatures similar to those in section 76.

Palaeographic Remarks

79. In ancient manuscripts and in old xylographic editions of the preclassical period, the letters differ from their present equivalents. Final *a, e, n,* and *d,* in cases where there remains too little space in the line for the following word but too much for the word terminating in any of these, are represented by the final forms occupying the entire space left in the line. These can be seen in the table given in section 82.

80. The points of the letters representing the sounds *n*, *γ*, and *š* are omitted. The sounds *q* and *γ* at the beginning of words are sometimes represented by the medial forms. The sound *t* in the middle of certain words is sometimes represented by the medial form for *d* which is used before consonants.

81. The final *d* in manuscripts is sometimes represented by the final form for *a* or *n* with a small circle to the left.

The sounds *č* and *ǰ* in the middle of words are not distinguished and both of them are represented by the medial form for *ǰ*.

82. In new manuscripts of the nineteenth and twentieth centuries there is a tendency to distinguish *t* and *d*, especially in foreign words and in proper names. The sound *d* is frequently marked with a point to the right.

Table of Mongolian Letters of the Pre-classical Period

Initial	Medial	Final	Transcription	Initial	Medial	Final	Transcription
			a				*s*
			e				*š*
			i				*t d*
			o u				*l*
			ö ü				*m*
			n				*č ǰ*
			ng				*ǰ y*
			q				*k g*
			γ g̠				*r*
			b				*v*

Transcription of Tibetan and Sanskrit

83. Both Tibetan and Sanskrit are phonologically quite different from Mongolian. To transcribe Tibetan and Sanskrit sounds the Mongols use a special system.

Transcription of Tibetan Letters

84. The Tibetan letters and their transcription are given in the Tibetan alphabetic order.

a	*i*	*u*	*e*	*o*	*ka*	*kha*	*ga*	*ṅa*	*ča*	*čha*	*ja*	*ña*	*ta*	*tha*	*da*	

na	*pa*	*pha*	*ba*	*ma*	*ca*	*cha*	*ja*	*va*	*ža*	*za*	*'a*	*ya*	*ra*	*la*

ša	*sa*	*ha*	*kya*	*khya*	*gya*	*pya*	*phya*	*bya*	*mya*	*kra*	*khra*	*gra*	*tra*	*dra*

pra	*phra*	*bra*	*mra*	*sra*	*hra*	*kla*	*gla*	*bla*	*zla*	*rla*	*sla*	*kva*	*khva*	*gva*

grva	*ñva*	*dva*	*rcva*	*rchva*	*žva*	*zva*	*lva*	*šva*	*hva*	*rka*	*rga*	*rṅa*	*rja*	*rña*

rta	*rda*	*rna*	*rba*	*rma*	*rca*	*rja*	*rla*	*lka*	*lga*	*lṅa*	*lča*	*lja*	*lta*	*lda*	*lpa*

lba	*lha*	*ska*	*sga*	*sṅa*	*sña*	*sta*	*sda*	*sna*	*spa*	*sba*	*sma*	*sca*	*sla*	*rkya*	*rgya*

rmya	*skya*	*sgya*	*spya*	*sbya*	*smya*	*skra*	*sgra*	*snra*	*spra*	*sbra*	*smra*

Transcription of Sanskrit Letters

85. The Sanskrit letters and their Tibetan equivalents with transcription are given in the Sanskrit alphabetic order.

a ā i ī   u ū ṛ ṛi   ḷ ḷi e ē   o   au am aḥ

ka kha ga gha ṅa   tsa tsha dsa dsha ña   ṭa ṭha ḍa ḍha ṇa   ta tha da dha na

pa pha ba bha ma   ya ra la va   ça ṣa sa ha   kṣa

Punctuation

86. There are no fixed rules of punctuation and often signs of punctuation are used at random.

Groups of words are separated from each other by the dot or so-called *čeg* (·). This sign corresponds more or less to the comma.

At the end of sentences the *dabqur čeg* "the double point" (:) is used. This corresponds to the period.

At the end of paragraphs or chapters the *dörbelǰin čeg* "the square čeg" (·:·) is used.

At the beginning of books or chapters, at the top of the first line, the so-called *birya* ۔۔۔ is used.

All of the above-mentioned signs can be seen in the following text:

Orthography

General Rules

87. The spelling rules will be given according to those of the classical language.

All words are written with all letters connected, but in cases where the consonant of the last syllable is *q*, *γ*, *s*, *l*, *m* or *r* the final vowel *a* is usually written separately and the respective consonants are represented by final forms.

This rule applies also to the final syllables *se*, *le*, *me*, and *re*.

88. The case suffixes are always written separately. If the suffix starts with a vowel, the latter is represented by the medial form. If the suffix consists of but one vowel, the latter is represented by the final form. The initial consonant of the suffix of the dative-locative *-tur* is represented by the initial form for *t*; the consonant of the dative-locative suffix *-dur* is represented by the medial form for *d* so as to distinguish them.

Plural suffixes forming a syllable or two syllables are also written separately, but those consisting of but one consonant are connected to the stem.

Compound words are written separately from each other, but compound proper names in the modern language are usually connected, e. g., *ulaγanbaγatur* "Ulan Bator" (the capital of Outer Mongolia).

Long and Short Vowels

89. The long vowels *u*, *ü*, and *i* are rendered with doubled letters.

buu = *bū* rifle	*degüü* = *degṻ* the younger brother
uul = *ūl* genuine	*bilegüü* = *bilegǖ* hone
aγuu = *aγū* large	*γaǰiiqu* = *γaǰiqu* to incline, to deviate

90. In a few words the short *o* is represented by reduplication. Such a spelling distinguishes words with the short *o* vowel from words with the vowel *u*.

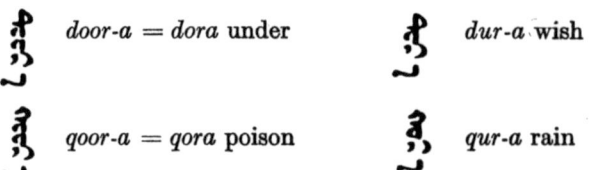

	door-a = *dora* under			*dur-a* wish
	qoor-a = *qora* poison			*qur-a* rain

Omission of Vowels

91. In certain words the vowels are usually omitted. These are

tngri = *tengri* heaven, deity   *včir* = *vačir* thunderbolt

Diphthongs

92. The diphthongs *ai̯*, *ei̯*, *oi̯*, *ui̯*, as transcribed here, are so represented only at the end of words. At the beginning and in the middle of words they are represented by combinations of the forms for *ayi* (an exception is *nai̯man* "eight"), *eyi*, *oyi*, and *uyi*. The diphthongs *oyi* (*oi̯*), *uyi* (*ui̯*), and *üi̯* are represented by the same forms so that, without knowing the pronunciation of a given word, it is impossible to distinguish them from one another.

The diphthongs are demonstrated in the table.

Transcription	Spelling		
	Initial	Medial	Final
ayi *ai̯*			
eyi *ei̯*			
oyi *oi̯* *uyi* *ui̯* *üi̯*			

ayil Mongolian tent

sayin good

nai̯man eight

dalai̯ sea

qoyitu northern

uyilaqu to weep

qarangγui̯ darkness

ǰüi̯tei̯ just

deyilekü to vanquish

eyimü such one

demei̯ useless, in vain

oroi̯ top

93. The diphthongs *ua* and *uua* are represented by

	quu-a isabel		*lingqu-a* lotus
	iruu-a omen		*činu-a* wolf

94. The diphthongs $au = a\bar{u}$ and $e\ddot{u} = e\ddot{\bar{u}}$ are represented by the letters for *a* (or *e*) and *u* (or *ü*).

	taulaį hare		*keüser* sterile
	auy-a strength		*teüke* history
	γauli brass		*keüken* child, girl
	qauli law		

Consonants

95. At the beginning of a few words there are two consonants:

blam-a = lama lama < Tibetan *bla-ma*

kšan moment < Sanskrit *kṣana*

96. The word *ed* "goods, property" < Uigur *ed* is always written with the medial prevocalic form of *d*. This distinguishes it from *on* "year". The derivatives of *ed*, the words *edlekü* "to possess", *edlel* "possession", and others, are written with the same form of *d*.

97. Although, as a general rule, there are no geminated consonants in Written Mongolian, there is a gemination of the final *d* and *g* of verbal stems before the vowel of suffixes.

     üįled- to work, to do   *üįleddümüį* he works, he does
     ög- to give   *öggümüį* he gives

Reading Rules

98. As certain letters or combinations thereof represent different sounds, it is sometimes difficult to decide how the letter in question should be read. The following synoptical table will demonstrate that, in reality, but very few letters can be mistaken, since most letters represent different sounds only in different positions, e. g., the final form of *a* or *e* which is also the final form of *n*. It is not difficult to decide when this is to be read *a* and when this is to be read *e* or *n*. First, the vowel *a* occurs only in words with back vowels. If the first vowel is *a* or *u*, the final sound cannot be *e*. Thus there is a rule stating in what words the final sound can be *a*. Second, if the sound immediately preceding the final sound is a consonant, the final sound cannot be the consonant *n* as there are no words ending in *ln*, *rn*, *gn*, and so on. But if the sound preceding the final sound is a vowel, the final sound cannot be *a* or *e*, since, except for the diphthong *ua* which is written in an unmistakable way, there are no combinations of two vowels at the end of words. This is but one example. The table will show that almost all dubious cases can be solved without difficulty.

Letters	Explanation
ᠠ	1. Initial *a* 2. Medial *q*; before consonants *γ*
ᠡ	1. Initial *e* 2. Medial *a* or *e* according to vocalic harmony 3. Medial *n* in postvocalic and pre-consonantic position
᠊	1. After a consonant final *a* or *e* 2. After a vowel final *n*
᠊ᠵ	Separate from a word *a* or *e*
ᠢ	Initial *i*
ᠶ	1. Initial *y* or *ǰ* 2. Medial intervocalic *y*; between consonants *i*
ᠥ	1. After a consonant final *i*; after a vowel final *ị* 2. Separate from a word *ǰ* or *y*
ᠤ	Initial *o* or *u*
ᠣ	Medial *o* or *u*; in non-first syllables also *ü* (vocalic harmony)
ᠥ	1. Final *u* (*o*) or *ü* 2. Initial or medial *b*
ᠦ	Initial *ö* or *ü*
ᠧ	Medial *ö* or *ü* (in the first syllable)
ᠨ	Initial and medial (in ante-vocalic position) *n*
ᠩ	Medial *ng*

	Final *ng*
	Initial *q*
	1. At the absolute end of words *γ* 2. Before *a* written separately *q*
	Initial *γ*
	Medial *γ*
	Before *a* written separately *γ*
	Final *b*
	Initial or medial *p*
	Initial or medial *s*; before *i* this is *š*
	Final *s*
	Initial and medial *š*
	Before a final vowel written separately *š*
	Initial *t* or *d*
	Medial *t* or *d*
	1. Medial *d* before a consonant 2. Medial syllable *on* or *un* (in front vocalic words *ün*) before a consonant
	Final *d* after a vowel; after a consonant final *un* or *ün*
	Initial or medial *l*
	Final *l*
	Initial or medial *m*
	Final *m*
	Initial or medial *č*
	Medial *ǰ*
	Initial or medial *k* or *g*; before consonants only *g*

ﺟ	Final *g*
ﻥ	Initial or medial *r*
ﺭ	Final *r*
ﺍ	In all positions *v*

99. Vocalic harmony is an important aid, as there cannot be any doubt about the correct reading of a letter, if the word in question contains, in other syllables, vowels which are unmistakably back or front sounds. For instance, if the initial sound is *a* or *o* (*u*), there cannot be *e* or *ü* in the other syllables.

Another important indication is the presence of the consonants *q* and *γ* which occur only with back vowels. On the other hand, *k* or *g* do not occur with *a* or *u* except for a very few foreign words, although they occur before *i* even in words with back vowels.

100. The peculiarity of the Mongolian script is that the letters have no constant phonetic value. The latter depends on the position in the word or on the general nature of the word (back vocalism or front vocalism). The Mongols call the back vocalic words "male" and the front vocalic words "female". Reading, therefore, requires the taking into consideration of the "male" or "female" nature of the word in question and many other factors.

101. Yet, in certain cases, it is impossible to guess the correct reading, as certain sounds are represented by the same letters in the same positions.

These are: 1) *o* and *u*, 2) *ö* and *ü*, 3) *t* and *d*, 4) the initial *y* and *ǰ*. As the reading is indicated in dictionaries, the latter should be consulted in all such cases.

Besides, there are words containing no letters hinting at what their general nature is from the point of view of vocalic harmony. Therefore, the following, and many other words, can be read in different ways as there are many homographs:

	unuqu to ride horseback		*yaγun* what
	onoqu to understand		*ǰaγun* hundred
	ger house		*urtu* long
	ker how		*ordu* palace
	ende here		*tere* that
	ada devil		*dere* cushion

The same circumstances obtain in the case of the following and still other words:

bal honey
bel waist, slope of a hill
döši anvil
tüši lean!
nisun snivel
nisün flying
nuγusun duck
noγosun wool

önör having a large family
ünür smell
qola far
qula dark brown (a horse)
sam comb
sem secret
törökü to be born
dürükü to push into

Colloquial Pronunciation of Written Mongolian

102. The Mongols usually pronounce Written Mongolian words according to the pronunciation in their local dialects and substitute for the sounds or groups of sounds of the written language sounds of the colloquial language.

In general, the colloquial languages differ from the written language in the following respects:

1. The vowel *i* of the first syllable of the written language is replaced by the vowel of the second syllable:

Written Language	Colloquial
miqan flesh, meat	*maxa*
nidurγa fist	*nudurγa*
šira yellow	*šara*
nidün eye	*nüdü*
nilmusun tear	*nulmusu*
čisun blood	*čusu*

2. The vowel *e* of the first syllable of the written language is replaced by *ö* before a syllable with *ü* or before *be*:

Written Language	Colloquial
edür day	*ödür*
emüs- to put on	*ömüs-*
ebesün hay	*öbösü*
ebedčin illness, disease	*öbödčin*
ebüdüg knee	*öbödüg*

3. The groups *aγa, aγu, ege, egü,* and so on have become long vowels:

Written Mongolian and Colloquial	Examples
aγa > ā	*qaγalγa = xālγa* gate
aγu > ū	*aγula = ūla* mountain
oγa > ō	*toγa = tō* number
oγo > ō	*qoγolai = xōloi* throat
uγa > ō	*ǰiluγa = ǰolō* reins
uγu > ū	*buγura = būra* a male camel
ege > ē	*degere = dēre* on, above
egü > ü	*egür = ǖr* nest
öge > ȫ	*bögere = bȫrö* kidney

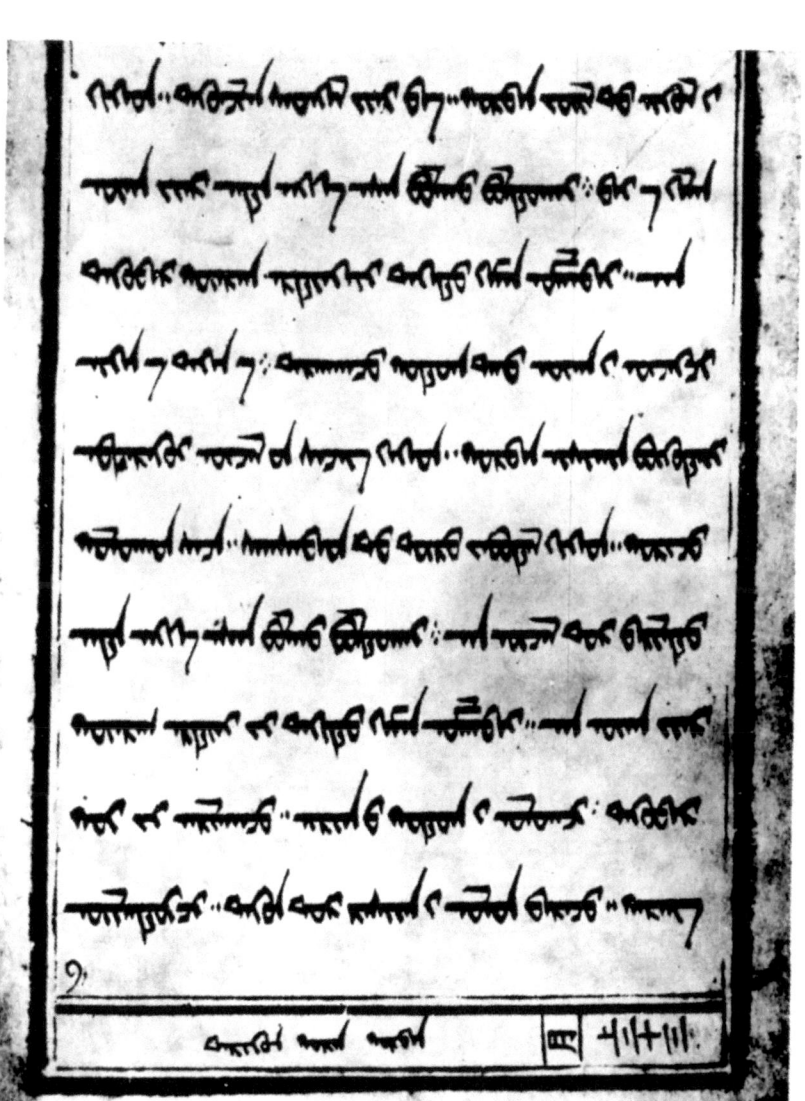

Page from a xylograph of the XVII century

üge $> \check{o}$	*čilüge* $= \check{c}\ddot{o}l\check{o}$ crack
ügü $> \ddot{u}$	*küjügün* $= k\ddot{u}j\ddot{u}$ neck
iya $> \bar{a}$	*niya-* $= n\bar{a}$- to glue
ige $> \check{e}$	*jige* $= j\check{e}$ nephew (son of the sister)
igi $> \bar{i}$	*čigig* $= \check{c}\bar{i}g$ damp
iyu $> \bar{u}$	*niyu-* $= n\bar{u}$- to hide
igü $> \ddot{u}$	*šigür* $= \check{s}\ddot{u}r$ broom

4. The groups *iya* and *iye* have become $\bar{a}$, $\check{e}$:

     ačiyan load $= a\check{c}\bar{a}$ *üniye* cow $= \ddot{u}n\check{e}$

5. The final *n* is often omitted:

     modun tree $= modu$ *morin* horse $= mori$

These are general rules. In particular cases many other changes occur.

IV. Derivation

General Remarks

103. Written Mongolian is an agglutinative language. This means that words are derived from other words by adding suffixes to invariable primary stems. There are no alternations of sounds as in Indo-European languages.

From the morphological point of view all words can be divided into two classes: 1) those of which the stem is primary and 2) those of which the stem is secondary. The primary stems cannot be further broken down, e. g., *eke* "mother". The secondary stems are derived from primary stems by means of suffixes, e. g., *temürči* "smith" < *temür* "iron" + suffix *-či*.

The stem of a noun is the nominative case. The stem of a verb is the imperative.

The suffixes are added mechanically; they do not produce any changes in the sounds of the stem. Nouns ending in an *n* which disappears before derivative suffixes are exceptions: *modun* "wood" + suff. *-či* is *moduči* "carpenter". Besides, there are several suffixes before which all final consonants of the stems disappear.

104. The suffixes are subject to the rules of vocalic harmony, that is, all suffixes appear in two forms: 1) with a back vowel when attached to stems with back vowels and 2) with a front vowel when attached to stems with front vowels.

	On stems with back vowels	On stems with front vowels
Suffix	*a*	*e*
vowel	*u*	*ü*

Comitative case: *qayan-luya* with the khan   *eke-lüge* with the mother

Dative-Locative: *yajar-a* to the country   *edür-e* on the day

105. If the stem ends in a consonant and the suffix consists only of a consonant (e. g., the suff. *-n*) or if the suffix has two initial consonants (e. g., the suff. *-ysan*), between the stem and the suffix a vowel *u* (in words with back vowels) or *ü* (in words with front vowels) is inserted.

There are a few suffixes requiring such a connective vowel even though the suffix concerned consists of a consonant and a vowel; e. g., the suffix of the present tense *-muį*: *ol* "find!" + suff. *-muį* is *olumuį* "he finds". But such suffixes are few. The general rule is that formulated above; e. g., stem *yar-* "to go out" + suff. *-n* is *yarun* "going out", the same stem + suff. *-ysan* is *yaruysan* "(a person) who has come out".

Parts of Speech

106. There are the following parts of speech: nouns, pronouns, numerals, postpositions, adverbs, verbs, conjunctions, particles, and interjections.

There is no morphological difference between substantives and adjectives; all adjectives occur in only one constant form. All words expressing things can function as adjectives and all words expressing qualities can function as substantives, e. g., *modun* "tree" and "wooden", *mayu* "bad" and "evil". Therefore, instead of the misleading terms "substantives" and "adjectives" the term "noun" will be used here.

Nouns

General Remarks

107. There are denominal and deverbal nouns. The former are derived from primary nouns, the latter from primary verbs. There are also nouns derived from adverbs.

Denominal Nouns

108. Suffix *-bči* with final *n* dropped. Function: to form nouns designating covers of objects.

čikibči cover for ears	< *čikin* ear
dalubči wing	< *dalu* scapula
quruyubči thimble	< *quruyun* finger
eligebči type of waist-coat	< *eligen* liver
küjügübči collar	< *küjügün* neck
nidübči cover for eyes, eye flap	< *nidün* eye

109. Suffix *-bir* with the final *n* dropped. Function: to form nouns designating slight shades of colors.

čayabir whitish	< *čayan* white
ulayabir reddish	< *ulayan* red

110. Suffix *-bki* with the final *n* dropped.

usubki watery	< *usun* water
idebki energy, energetic	< *ide* ability

111. Suffix *-btur/-btür* with the final *n* dropped. Function: to form nouns designating slight shades of colors.

qarabtur blackish	< *qar-a* black
širabtur yellowish	< *šir-a* yellow
ulayabtur reddish	< *ulayan* red
kökebtür bluish	< *köke* blue

112. Suffix *-bur/-bür* with the final *n* dropped. Function: = *-bir*, *-btur/-btür*.

ulayabur reddish	< *ulayan* red
noyuyabur greenish	< *noyuyan* green

113. Suffix *-čar/-čer*. Meaning: slight shades of colors (cf. § 207).

qaračar blackish	< *qar-a* black

114. Suffix *-či* with the final *n* dropped. Function: to form nouns designating names of vocations.

qoniči shepherd	< *qonin* sheep
aduγuči horsegroom	< *aduγun* herd of horses
ükerči cowherd	< *üker* ox
malči herdsman	< *mal* cattle
altači goldsmith	< *altan* gold
emči physician	< *em* medicine

115. Suffix *-ču*. Function: to form nouns designating social groups.

qaraču vulgar people, ordinary man	< *qar-a* black
boroču ordinary man	< *boro* gray

116. Suffix *-daki/-deki* attached to stems ending in *n* (which is retained), *ng*, *l*, *m* or vowels or diphthongs; suffix *-taki/-teki* attached to stems ending in *γ*, *b*, *s*, *d*, *g* or *r*. Function: to form nouns designating the fact of being in or belonging to something.

usun-daki aquatic, being in water	< *usun* water
delekeị-deki living in the world, inhabitant of the world	< *delekeị* world
γaịar-taki being in a country, being on the earth, terrestrial	< *γaịar* earth, country
ger-teki living in a house, belonging to the house	< *ger* house

117. Suffix *-du/-dü* with the final *n* dropped. Function: to form nouns designating qualities.

amidu living, live	< *amin* life
dumdadu central	< *dumda* center

118. Suffix *-γali/-geli*. Function: to form nouns designating names of distant degrees of relationship.

qayaγali second cousin	< *qay-a* distant relationship
üyegeli cousin	< *üy-e* generation

119. Suffix *-γana/-gene* with the final *n* dropped. Function: to form nouns designating names of plants and animals.

qulaγana mouse	< *qula* dark brown, dark gray
altaγana kind of plant	< *altan* gold
qaraγana kind of plant	< *qara* black

120. Suffix *-γčin/-gčin* with all final consonants of the stem dropped. Function: to form nouns designating colors and names of female animals.

širaγčin yellow (e. g., of a cow)	< *šir-a* yellow (e.g., of a bull)
čaγaγčin white	< *čaγan* white
qongγoγčin brown (e.g., of a mare)	< *qongγor* brown (e. g., of a stallion)
ịaγaγčin brown with a dark strip on the spine (of a female)	< *ịaγal* brown with a dark strip on the spine (of a male)
ölögčin bitch	< *ölö* gray

121. Suffix *-ɣtai̯/-gtei̯* with the final *n* dropped. Function: to form nouns designating the sex of human beings.

eregtei̯ male	< *er-e* man
emegtei̯ female	< *em-e* woman
qatuɣtai̯ female	< *qatun* lady, queen

122. Suffix *-ɣui̯*. Function: to form nouns designating female beings.

quduɣui̯ (< *qudaɣui̯*) the mother of the son-in-law	< *quda* the father of the son-in-law

123. Suffix *-qai̯/-kei̯*. Function: to form nouns designating qualities.

balarqai̯ dark	< *balar* dark
qongqorqai̯ uneven	< *qongqor* hole

124. Suffix *-qan/-ken* with the final *n* dropped. Function: to form nouns designating diminutives, sometimes female beings (cf. also § 203).

qaraqan black (of small or lovely beings, e.g., of small horses or birds)	< *qar-a* black
ulaɣaqan red (of nice little objects, e.g., a red flower)	< *ulaɣan* red
noyiqan princess	< *noyan* prince
keüken girl, daughter, child	< *keü* son
eneken this	< *ene* id.

125. Suffix *-ǰin* with the final *n* dropped. Function: to form nouns designating female beings.

mongɣolǰin Mongolian woman (name of a river)	< *mongɣol* Mongol
barɣuǰin Bargujin (name of a river and a country in Transbaikalia)	< *barɣu* (name of a tribe and country in Northwestern Manchuria)
ɣunaǰin three-year-old (female)	< *ɣunan* three-year-old (male)
döneǰin four-year-old (female)	< *dönen* four-year-old (male)

126. Suffix *-lang/-leng* with the final *n* dropped.

soyuɣalang a domestic animal at the age of growing new eyeteeth	< *soyuɣ-a* eyetooth
šidüleng a domestic animal at the age of growing new teeth	< *šidün* tooth
tariyalang field	< *tariyan* seed

127. Suffix *-liɣ/-lig* with the final *n* dropped. Function: to form nouns designating abundance of something.

čečeglig or *čečerlig* flower garden	< *čečeg* flower
ǰimislig orchard	< *ǰimis* fruit
temürlig metal (the basic qualities of iron)	< *temür* iron
miqaliɣ corpulent	< *miqan* flesh
bayaliɣ rich, riches	< *bayan* rich

128. Suffix *-ljin* with the final *n* dropped. Function: to form nouns designating birds, insects, and geometric figures.

širaljin name of a species of absinthium	< *šir-a* yellow
boroljin name of another species of absinthium	< *boro* gray
temegeljin dragon-fly	< *temegen* camel
yurbaljin triangle	< *yurban* three
dörbeljin square	< *dörben* four

129. Suffix *-lun/-lün* with the final *n* dropped. Function: to form nouns designating proper names of women in ancient texts.

altalun Altalun	< *altan* gold
mönggülün Mönggülün	< *mönggün* silver

129a. Suffix *-mad/-med*. Function: to form collective nouns (nouns designating groups of people) and adjectives (cf. § 263).

aqamad elder, senior; authorities	< *aq-a* elder brother
egečimed elder (daughter etc.)	< *egeči* elder sister
alimad whoever, whatever	< *ali* what, which

130. Suffix *-may*. Function: this suffix occurs in few words and these are diminutives.

nayurmay pool	< *nayur* lake

131. Suffix *-msuy/-msüg*. Function: to form nouns designating exaggerated qualities.

yoyimsuy dressy, conceited, coquette	< *yoyi* pretty
yekemsüg haughty, proud	< *yeke* big, great

132. Suffix *-nčar/-nčer*. Function: to form nouns designating names of degrees of relationship.

üyenčer nephew twice removed	< *üy-e* generation
yučinčar great-great-great-grandson	< *yuči* great-great-grandson

133. Suffix *-ngyui̧*.

qarangyui̧ darkness	< *qar-a* black

134. Suffix *-rqay/-rkeg*. With all final consonants of the primary stem dropped. Function: to form nouns designating abundance of something.

ayularqay mountainous	< *ayula* mountain
čilayurqay stony	< *čilayun* stone
bayarqay boasting of his wealth	< *bayan* rich
noyarqay tyrannic	< *noyan* prince
omorqay proud	< *omoy* pride

135. Suffix *-say/-seg* with the final *n* dropped. Function: to form nouns designating penchant for or fondness of something.

eligeseg friendly to his relatives	< *eligen* liver
miqasay fond of meat	< *miqan* meat
arakisay drunkard	< *araki* liquor
emeseg lady's man	< *em-e* woman

136. Suffix *-sar/-ser*. Function: to form nouns designating lack or absence of something (= English "-less").

    keüser sterile (woman)   < *keü* son

137. Suffix *-sun/-sün* with the final *n* dropped. Function: to form nouns of which the meaning is usually the same as that of the primary word.

    aɣurasun household equipment   < *aɣur-a* id.
    aduɣusun animal   < *aduɣun* herd of horses

138. Suffix *-tai̯/-tei̯* with the final *n* dropped. Function: to form nouns designating possession, connection with, or containment in something (Cf. § 296).

    moritai̯ having a horse, horseman   < *morin* horse
    surɣaɣulitai̯ learned, educated   < *surɣaɣuli* school
    ayaɣatai̯ čai̯ a cup of tea (lit., tea   < *ayaɣ-a* cup
       in a cup)
    arbatai̯ ten-year-old   < *arban* ten

139. Suffix *-tan/-ten* with the final *n* dropped. Function: to form collective nouns, plural of words ending in *-tai̯* or *-tu* (Cf. § 271).

    albatan subjects   < *alban* tribute
    ariyatan wild animals   < *ariy-a∾aray-a* grinder
    erdemten learned people   < *erdem* science
    körönggeten bourgeoisie   < *köröngge* capital

140. Suffix *-tu/-tü* with the final *n* dropped. Function: to form nouns designating possession of or containment in something.

    moritu horseman   < *morin* horse
    ǰebsegtü armed   < *ǰebseg* weapon
    ayaɣatu čai̯ a cup of tea   < *ayaɣ-a* cup
    arban nasutu ten-year-old   < *nasun* age

Deverbal Nouns

141. Suffix *-buri/-büri;* sometimes also *-muri/-müri* in the case of stems ending in *l*. Function: to form nouns designating, in general, the process or the aim of an action.

    aburi manner, temper   < *a-* to be
    bolburi ripening   < *bol-* to ripen
    tayilburi comment, explanation   < *tayil-* to explain
    kötelbüri instruction   < *kötël-* to guide, to lead
    ködelmüri work   < *ködel-* to work

142. Suffix *-ča/-če*. Function: to form deverbal nouns.

    ǰaruča servant   < *ǰaru-* to employ
    yabuča course   < *yabu-* to go

143. Suffix *-dal/-del;* always *-tal/-tel* in the case of stems ending in *r*. Function: to form nouns designating abstract ideas or the results of actions.

bayidal life, existence	< *bayi-* to be
yabudal deed	< *yabu-* to go, to act
üküdel corpse	< *ükü-* to die
oyudal seam	< *oyu-* to sew
surtal doctrine	< *sur-* to learn

144. Suffix *-dasun/-desün*. Function: to form deverbal nouns.

ugiyadasun swill, dirty water	< *ugiya-* to wash
ǰarudasun servant	< *ǰaru-* to employ

145. Suffix *-dun/-dün*. Function: to form nouns designating bodily conditions.

qaniyadun cough	< *qaniya-* to cough
iniyedün laughter	< *iniye-* to laugh

146. Suffix *-γ/-g*. Function: to form nouns designating results of actions, abstract ideas.

ǰiruγ picture	< *ǰiru-* to draw, to paint
bičig letter	< *biči-* to write
ǰoriγ intention	< *ǰori-* to intend
qoriγ forbiddance	< *qori-* to forbid
büǰig dance	< *büǰi-* to dance
ideg bribe	< *ide-* to eat

147. Suffix *-γači/-geči*. Function: to form nouns designating names of vocations.

ǰiruγači painter	< *ǰiru-* to paint
bičigeči writer, clerk	< *biči-* to write
alaγači murderer, killer	< *ala-* to kill
barilduγači wrestler	< *barildu-* to wrestle

148. Suffix *-γai̯/-gei̯* on stems ending in *-yi-* with the latter dropped; *-qai̯/-kei̯* on stems ending in *-ra-/-re-* with the final *a/e* dropped. Function: to form nouns designating qualities resulting from the action.

qaǰayai̯ curved, oblique	< *qaǰayi-* to bend
qabtayai̯ flat	< *qabtayi-* to become flat
keltegei̯ oblique	< *kelteyi-* to wry
butarqai̯ dismembered	< *butara-* to fall to pieces
tasurqai̯ rent, torn	< *tasura-* to rend

149. Suffix *-γan/-gen*. Function: to form deverbal nouns.

utaγan smoke	< *uta-* to smoke
idegen food	< *ide-* to eat
qaraγan sight	< *qara-* to look at
bayilduγan battle	< *bayildu-* to fight
barilduγan wrestling match	< *barildu-* to wrestle
qubilγan reincarnation	< *qubil-* to change
udaγan slow, lasting for a long time	< *uda-* to hesitate, to tarry
ködelgegen movement	< *ködelge-* to move

150. Suffix *-γar/-ger* added to verbal stems ending in *-ayi-/-eyi-;* suffix *-gir* added to verbal stems ending in *-ii̯-;* the final *yi* and *i̯* of the stem are dropped. Function: to form nouns designating qualities resulting from action.

qabtaγar flat	< *qabtayi-* to become flat
serteger dishevelled	< *serteyi-* to stand on end (of hair)
buǰigir curly	< *buǰii̯-* to curl

151. Suffix *-γasun/-gesün.* Function: to form nouns designating objects undergoing the actions concerned.

qadaγasun nail	< *qada-* to drive in (nails)
nökögesün patch-up	< *nökö-* to mend

152. Suffix *-γu/-gü.* Function: to form nouns designating qualities resulting from the action.

qataγu hard	< *qata-* to dry, to become hard
soγtaγu drunk, intoxicated	< *soγta-* to become drunk
qariγu returning, answer	< *qari-* to return
yadaγu poor	< *yada-* to be unable
ülegü superfluous	< *üle-* to remain

153. Suffix *-γul/-gül.* Function: to form nouns designating names of occupations.

qaraγul watchman, guard	< *qara-* to look at
turšiγul spy	< *turši-* to investigate, to reconnoitre
tangnaγul spy	< *tangna-* to reconnoitre
manaγul watchman	< *mana-* to watch
ǰasaγul commander	< *ǰasa-* to arrange

154. Suffix *-γun/-gün.* Function: to form nouns designating qualities or abstract nouns.

qalaγun hot	< *qala-* to become warm
serigün sober, cool	< *seri-* to wake
medegdegün object of study	< *medegde-* to be known

155. Suffix *-γur/-gür;* added to stems with the consonant *r* in any syllable the suffix is, in consequence of dissimilation, *-γul/-gül.* Function: to form nouns designating names of tools.

qanaγur lancet	< *qana-* to bleed someone
qaduγur sickle	< *qadu-* to mow
ölgügür clothes-peg	< *ölgü-* to hang up
bariγul handle	< *bari-* to take, to keep

156. Suffix *-γuri/-güri;* added to stems with the consonant *r* in any syllable the suffix is, in consequence of dissimilation, *-γuli/-güli.* Function: to form nouns designating the place where an action is performed, sometimes abstract ideas.

angnaɣuri hunting ground	< *angna-* to hunt
ejelegüri dominion	< *ejele-* to dominate, to rule
ǰigšigüri disgust	< *ǰigši-* to loathe
ičegüri shame	< *iče-* to be ashamed
suryaɣuli school	< *surya-* to teach

157. Suffix -*qulang*/-*küleng*. Function: to form nouns designating abstract ideas.

bayasqulang joy	< *bayas-* to be glad
urusqulang current	< *urus-* to flow
ölösküleng hunger	< *ölös-* to starve
čadqulang satiety	< *čad-* to be satisfied

158. Suffix -*ǰa*/-*ǰe*. Function: to form nouns designating results of actions.

olǰa booty, income	< *ol-* to find
oruǰa income	< *or-* to enter
ɣaruǰa expenditure	< *ɣar-* to go out

159. Suffix -*l*. Function: to form nouns designating abstract ideas.

ükül death	< *ükü-* to die
ǰirɣal happiness	< *ǰirɣa-* to be happy
töröl birth	< *törö-* to be born
angqarul attention	< *angqar-* to pay attention, to notice

160. Suffix -*lang*/-*leng*. Function: to form nouns designating abstract ideas, an object undergoing an action.

qadulang hayfield	< *qadu-* to mow
ǰobalang pain, suffering	< *ǰoba-* to suffer
ǰirɣalang happiness	< *ǰirɣa-* to be happy

161. Suffix -*lya*/-*lge*. Function: to form nouns designating process.

barilya building	< *bari-* to build
ungšilya reading	< *ungši-* to read
bodolya opinion	< *bodo-* to think
bosulya uprising	< *bos-* to rise

162. Suffix -*li*. Function: to form deverbal nouns.

sačuli libation	< *saču-* to strew, to spurt
saɣali milking	< *saɣa-* to milk

163. Suffix -*lta*/-*lte*. Function: to form nouns designating process.

qasulta subtraction	< *qasu-* delete
bučalta return	< *buča-* to return
nemelte addition	< *neme-* to add
ergilte turn	< *ergi-* to turn

164. Suffix -*m*. Function: to form deverbal nouns.

toqom saddle cloth	< *toqo-* to saddle
sačum a distance one can throw grains	< *saču-* to strew

qaram avarice   < *qara-* to look at
naɣadum game, play   < *naɣad-* to play

165. Suffix *-ma/-me*. Function: to form nouns designating fitness or possibility of an action.

    ɣayiqama wonderful, astonishing   < *ɣayiqa-* to be astonished
    bayima such (place) where there can   < *bayi-* to be
       be something

166. Suffix *-maɣ/-meg*. Function: to form nouns designating result of actions.

    qaɣurmaɣ fraud   < *qaɣur-* to deceive
    jorimaɣ bravery   < *jori-* to make a decision
    egedemeg leaven   < *egede-* to sour

167. Suffix *-maɣaɨ/-megeɨ* or *-mqaɨ/-mkeɨ*. Function: to form nouns designating inclination or ability to act.

    surumaɣaɨ gifted   < *sur-* to learn
    martamqaɨ oblivious   < *marta-* to forget
    umtamqaɨ sleepy   < *umta-* to sleep
    idemkeɨ voracious   < *ide-* to eat

168. Suffix *-mal/-mel*. Function: to form nouns designating qualities.

    jirumal painted, multicolor   < *jiru-* to paint
    bičimel written   < *biči-* to write
    barlamal xylographed   < *barla-* to print
    darumal printed   < *daru-* to press, to print
    nekemel woven   < *neke-* to weave
    širimel quilted   < *širi-* to quilt

169. Suffix *-mar/-mer*. Function: to form nouns designating suitableness, fitness.

    idemer edible   < *ide-* to eat
    üjemer worth seeing   < *üje-* to see

170. Suffix *-mi*. Function: to form nouns designating names of tools.

    uqumi chisel   < *uqu-* to dig
    boɣomi loop   < *boɣo-* to wind round

171. Suffix *-mji*. Function: to form nouns designating abstract ideas.

    seremji vigilance   < *sere-* to be awake
    ilɣamji difference   < *ilɣa-* to distinguish
    bolɣomji precaution   < *bolɣo-* to be cautious, to
                                       take care
    uqamji understanding   < *uqa-* to understand

172. Suffix *-msar/-mser* with the negative *ügeɨ*. Function: to form nouns designating qualities (= English "-less").

    sanamsar ügeɨ thoughtless   < *sana-* to think
    uqamsar ügeɨ unintelligent   < *uqa-* to understand

173. Suffix *-mšiγ/-mšig* or *-mšiγtaị/-mšigteị*. Function: to form nouns designating ability to evoke someone's action.

> *γayiqamšiγ(taị)* wonderful, amazing   < *γayiqa-* to be astonished
> *ayumšiγ(taị)* dreadful, horrible   < *ayu-* to be frightened

174. Suffix *-mta/-mte*.

> *boγomta* fortification, barricade   < *boγo-* to block
> *barimta* matter of fact, evidence   < *bari-* to seize, to keep

175. Suffix *-n*.

> *šinggen* fluid   < *šingge-* to be absorbed

176. Suffix *-ng*. Function: to form nouns designating result of actions.

> *qaldang* speck, stain   < *qalda-* to adhere to, to infect
> *egedeng* dough, sour paste   < *egede-* to sour

177. Suffix *-ngγuị/-nggüị*. Function: to form nouns designating result of actions.

> *soγtangγuị* drunkenness   < *soγta-* to become drunk
> *quriyangγuị* brief, abbreviated   < *quriya-* to gather
>   version
> *ǰokiyangγuị* deed, composition   < *ǰokiya-* to found, to compile

178. Suffix *-r*.

> *amur* rest, peace   < *amu-* to rest
> *belčir* embouchure, conflux   < *belči-* inundate
> *belčiger* pasturage   < *belčige-* to pasture
> *irüger* > *irügel* prayer, blessing   < *irüge-* to bless

179. Suffix *-ri*. Function: to form nouns designating place or result of an action.

> *saγuri* seat   < *saγu-* to sit
> *baγuri* slope   < *baγu-* to descend
> *nemeri* supplement   < *neme-* to add

180. Suffix *-sun/-sün*. Function: to form nouns designating results of actions.

> *nilbusun* spittle   < *nilbu-* to spit
> *kögesün* foam   < *köge-* to foam, to rise

181. Suffix *-ši*. Function: to form nouns designating result or object of an action.

> *ideši* food   < *ide-* to eat
> *bulaši* grave, excavation   < *bula-* to dig

182. Suffix *-ši* with the negative *ügeị*. Function: to form nouns designating qualities rendering something unfit to act on.

> *dabaši ügeị* unpassable   < *daba-* to pass
> *uγuši ügeị* not potable   < *uγu-* to drink

Nouns Derived from Adverbs

183. Suffix -du/-dü added to adverbs of place. Function: to form locative-adjectives.

dooradu inferior, lower	< *door-a* below
degedü upper	cf. *deger-e* on, above
emünedü being in front	< *emün-e* before, in front of
dotoyadu inner	cf. *dotor-a* in, within
yadayadu outer	cf. *yadan-a* outside
inadu being on this side	cf. *inayši* to this place

184. Suffix -*ki* added to various adverbs. Function: to form adjectives expressing the same general idea as that of the primary adverb.

degereki upper	< *deger-e* on, above
dooraki lower	< *door-a* below, under
edügeki present	< *edüge* now
endeki being here	< *ende* here
tendeki being there	< *tende* there
maryašiki taking place tomorrow	< *maryaši* tomorrow

Pronouns
General Remarks

185. The pronouns consist of personal, possessive, demonstrative, interrogative, reflexive, and indefinite pronouns. The personal and demonstrative pronouns differ, morphologically, from the nouns in the respect that their nominative form and their stems are not identical.

Personal Pronouns

186. The nominatives and the stems of the personal pronouns are shown in the following table.

Person	Nominative	Stems
1st sing.	*bi* I	*min, na, nama*
2nd sing.	*či* thou	*čin, čima*
3rd sing.	**i* he	*in, ima*
1st plur. incl.	*bida* we	*bidan*
1st plur. excl.	*ba* we	*man*
2nd plur.	*ta* you	*tan*
3rd plur.	**a* they	*an*

The first person plural is *bida* and *ba*. The former is an inclusive pronoun "we" (including both the persons speaking and the audience), the latter is an exclusive pronoun "we" (including only the persons speaking and excluding the audience). The nominative *ba* occurs in ancient books. In modern books this is replaced by *bida*, whereas the oblique cases are still used.

187. The nominative **i* "he" and **a* "they" are not attested even in the most ancient books. Of the oblique cases, only the genitive is used in modern books, but some of the remaining oblique cases are attested in books of the pre-classical period.

Possessive Pronouns

188. The possessive pronouns are derived with the suffix *-qaį* from the genitive of the personal pronouns.

minuqaį mine	< *minu*, gen. of *bi*
činuqaį thine	< *činu*, gen. of *či*
bidanuqaį (rare) ours	< *bidan-u*, gen. of *bida*
manuqaį (usual) ours	< *manu*, gen. of *ba*
tanuqaį yours	< *tanu*, gen. of *ta*

Sometimes the back vocalic forms *minuqaį* and *činuqaį* are replaced by front vocalic forms *minükeį* and *činükeį*.

There are no possessive pronouns derived from the personal pronouns of the third person. Instead the forms *tegünükeį* "his" and *tedenükeį* "theirs", which are derived from the demonstrative pronouns, are used.

Demonstrative Pronouns

189. There are the following demonstrative pronouns:

ene this, stem *egün*
ede these, stem *eden*
edeger these, stem *edeger*
ele this (indeclinable)
eyimü such as this, stem *eyimü*
edüį as much as this, stem *edüį*
edün as many as these, stem *edün* (only in ancient language)
tere that, stem *tegün*
tede those, stem *teden*
tedeger those, stem *tedeger*
teyimü like that, stem *teyimü*
tedüį as much as that, stem *tedüį*
tedün as many as those, stem *tedün* (only in ancient language)
mön the same, just this, stem *mön*
möd (in ancient language) these same, just these, stem *möd*
önȫ or *önüge* this (indeclinable)

The pronouns *ene, ede, edeger, tere, tede, tedeger* replace the personal pronouns of the third person.

There are diminutive forms *eneken* "this" and *tereken* "that".

Interrogative Pronouns and Adverbs

190. The nominative forms and the stems of the interrogative pronouns coincide with few exceptions.

> *ken* who (singular)
> *ked* who (plural)
> *kedüį* (singular) how much
> *kedün* (plural) how many
> *ker* (indeclinable) how
> *keli* (indeclinable) when (pre-classical)
> *keǰiy-e* (stem *keǰiyen*) when
> *yaɣun* (as adjective and substantive) what
> *yambar* (indeclinable, only as adjective) what
> *yan* (in pre-classical language) what
> *ali* (stem *alin*) which

In the pre-classical language the interrogative pronouns are used also as relative pronouns.

Reflexive Pronouns

191. There are the following reflexive pronouns:

> *öber-iyen* (stem *öber*) self
> *öbesüd-iyen* or (seldom) *ögesüd-iyen* (stems *öbesüd* and *ögesüd*) selves

Indefinite Pronouns

192. The indefinite pronouns are derived from the interrogative pronouns with the particles *ba*, *ber*, *ču*. The particle *ču* occurs mainly in the modern language whereas the particles *ba* and *ber* are more characteristic of the classical language.

> *ken ba* whoever, somebody, someone, anybody
> *ked ba* (plural)
> *ken ber* whoever, somebody, someone, anybody
> *ked ber* (plural)
> *ken ču* whoever, somebody, someone, anybody
> *ked ču* (plural)
> *kedüį ba* any quantity
> *kedüį ber*
> *kedüį ču*
> *yaɣun ba* or *yaɣuba* whatever
> *yaɣun ber*
> *yaɣun ču*
> *yambar ba* whatever, any
> *yambar ber*
> *yambar ču*
> *aliba* whoever, whatever, anybody
> *ali ber*
> *alin ču*

The pronoun *yaɣuma* or *yaɣum-a* "something", "anything", also "thing" is formed with *-ma*.
The indefinite pronouns occur with the negative *ügeį:*

ken ba ügeį or *ken ber ügeį* or *ken ču ügeį* nobody
yayun ba ügeį or *yayun ber ügeį* or *yayun ču ügeį* nothing

Numerals

General Remarks

193. The numerals are classified as cardinal, ordinal, collective, distributive, multiplicative, and diminutive numerals.
When used as substantives, they are declinable and can form the plural.

Cardinal Numerals

194. The cardinal numerals are the following:

1	*nigen* (ancient pronunciation *niken*)	11	*arban nigen* (ancient pronunciation *arban niken*)
2	*qoyar*	20	*qorin*
3	*yurban*	30	*yučin*
4	*dörben*	40	*döčin*
5	*tabun*	50	*tabin*
6	*jiryuyan*	60	*jiran*
7	*doloyan*	70	*dalan*
8	*naįman*	80	*nayan*
9	*yisün*	90	*yeren*
10	*arban*	100	*jayun*

1000 𑱺 *mïŋɣan*

10 000 𑱺 *tümen*

100 000 𑱺 *bum*

1 000 000 𑱺 *say-a*

The last three numerals (*tümen*, *bum*, and *say-a*) do not have ordinal or any other forms.

The Mongolian figures are written from left to right, as Arabic figures:

1	2	3	4	5	6	7	8	9	0
𝟿	𝟸	𝟹	𝟶	𝟻	𝟼	𝟽	𝟾	𝟿	𝟶

195. In ancient texts there occurs another numeral, *ǰirin* "two", which is used in reference to women: *ǰirin qatud* "two dames".

196. The higher numerals are of Tibetan origin:

100,000 *bum* < Tib. *ḥbum*
1,000,000 *say-a* < Tib. *sa-ya*

10,000,000 𑱺 *bšiba* or 𑱺 *byeba* (pronounced *ǰivā*) < Tib. *bye-ba*

100,000,000 𑱺 *düngšiür* (pronounced *düngšŭr*) < Tib. *duṅ-ḥpʻyur*

In modern books, especially those published in Outer Mongolia, the European word *miliyon* "million" is used.

Ten thousand is either *tümen* or *arban mingɣan*. The former also expresses immense quantities.

The numbers 20,000, 30,000, etc. are composed of 2 or 3 and *tümen* or of 20 or 30 and *mingɣan:*

20,000 *qoyar tümen* or *qorin mingɣan*
30,000 *ɣurban tümen* or *ɣučin mingɣan*

The composite numerals 11 to 19 are composed of *arban* and *nigen*, etc.; 21 to 29 is *qorin nigen* etc.

Ordinal Numerals

197. Suffix *-duɣar/-düger* with the final consonant and the ending *-ɣan* of the cardinal numeral dropped.

first *nigedüger*	sixth *ǰiryuduyar*
second *qoyaduyar*	seventh *doloduyar*
third *yurbaduyar*	eighth *naimaduyar*
fourth *dörbedüger*	ninth *yisüdüger*
fifth *tabuduyar*	tenth *arbaduyar*

In both the pre-classical and classical languages the ordinal numerals "third", "fourth", and "fifth" usually occur in the following forms:

third *yutuyar*, fourth *dötüger*, fifth *tabtayar*

198. Instead of the ordinal numerals *nigedüger* and *qoyaduyar*, in many cases the following words are used:

first *angqaduyar* < *angqan* beginning
first *terigün* head, beginning
first *ekin* beginning, (in pre-classical texts) head
second *nögüge* next, following
second *ded* the following, the succeeding

Although not a numeral, the word *kedüi* or *kedün* "how much, how many" occurs in the ordinal form *kedüdüger* "which number?"

Collective Numerals

199. Suffix *-yula(n)/-güle(n)* with the final consonant and the ending *-yan* of the cardinal numeral dropped. Function: to form numerals with the meaning of "two together", "three together", etc.

qoyayula(n) both, two together
yurbayula(n) all three, three together
dörbegüle(n) all four, four together
tabuyula(n) all five, five together
ǰiryuyula(n) all six, six together
doloyula(n) all seven, seven together
naimayula(n) all eight, eight together
yisügüle(n) all nine, nine together
arbayula(n) all ten, ten together

Although they are not numerals, the words *olan* "many" and *kedün* "how many" sometimes occur in collective forms.

olayula(n) many together, all of them
kedügüle(n) how many together

Distributive Numerals

200. Suffix *-yad/-ged* with the final consonant and ending *-yan* of the cardinal numeral dropped. Function: to form numerals with the meaning of "by twos", "in twos", "by threes", "in threes", and so on. The numerals *nigen* and *qoyar* have irregular forms.

niǰiged one and one	*ǰiryuyad* by sixes
qošiyayad by twos	*doloyad* by sevens

γurbaγad by threes	*naịmaγad* by eights
dörbeged by fours	*yisüged* by nines
tabuγad by fives	*arbaγad* by tens

Multiplicative Numerals

201. Suffix *-ta/-te*. Function: to form numerals meaning "one time", "two times or twice", etc.

nigente once	*γurbanta* three times
qoyarta twice	*dörbente* four times
	tabunta five times

Although *olan* "many" and *kedün* "how many" are not numerals, there exist the forms *olanta* "many times" and *kedünte* "how many times".

202. Another form of the multiplicative numerals is that without the final consonant *n* of the cardinal form.

nige once
qoyar twice
γurba three times

Diminutive Numerals

203. The diminutive or limitative numerals are formed with the diminutive suffix *-qan/-ken* (see § 124). Function: to form numerals meaning "only one", "only two", and so on.

nigeken only one
qoyarqan only two
γurbaqan only three

Numerical Words

204. There are words which, while not being numerals, manifest a certain affinity with numerals. Such words, here called numerical words, express quantities, mainly indefinite quantities.

γayča sole, single, the only	*örügesün* one of a pair
qayas half	*örügele* half

The word *tümen* "immense quantity, ten thousand" is also a numerical word.

All these words have neither ordinal nor other forms.

Adverbs

General Remarks

205. The adverbs are words of nominal origin: nouns, pronouns, or numerals. Therefore, they will now be discussed in connection with nouns.

There are primary and secondary adverbs. The adverbs do not change their forms except for a few fossilized case forms.

The adverbs are classified as local, temporal, and modal adverbs.

They will now be discussed in connection with their suffixes.

Suffix -a/-e

206. This is the old dative suffix. The original nominative of a few derivatives with this suffix no longer exists. Adverbs with this suffix are mainly adverbs of manner.

ilangγuï-a particularly, especially	< **ilangγuï*
mayuï-a badly	< *mayuï* bad
qatayuï-a cruelly	< *qatayuï* cruel

Suffix -čar/-čer

207. This suffix occurs in but a few adverbs of manner (cf. § 113).

busučar otherwise, in another manner < *busu* another

Suffix -da/-de

208. This suffix occurs in local, temporal, and modal adverbs.

a) Local adverbs

ende here, ablative *endeče* from here	
tende there, ablative *tendeče* from there	
qotalada everywhere, throughout	< *qotala* common, general
dergede at, beside, by	< **derge*

b) Temporal adverbs

maryada tomorrow	cf. *maryaši*
urtuda always, for a long time	< *urtu* long
önide long ago	< *öni* ancient
urida formerly	< **uri*
kejiyede always	< *kejiy-e* when
nasuda always	< *nasun* age, lifetime

c) Modal adverbs

batuda firmly	< *batu* firm
nutada firmly	< *nuta* firm
γuu-a-da nicely, beautifully	< *γuu-a* nice, beautiful
mašida very, exceedingly	< *maši* id.

Suffix -γa/-ge

209. This suffix occurs in local and temporal adverbs.

a) Local adverbs

γaday-a out of doors	< **γada*
qamiy-a where	< **qami*

b) Temporal adverbs

edüge now < **edü*, cf. *edüï* as much as this

kejiye < **kedige* when < **kedi*, cf. *kedüï* how much, cf. ancient *keli* when

Suffix -γar/-ger

210. This suffix occurs in local, temporal, and modal adverbs. It is an old variant of the instrumental suffix -*γar ∥ -bar ∥ -iyar < -*iγar.

a) Local adverbs

qotalaγar everywhere   < qotala common, general

b) Temporal adverbs

manaγar tomorrow   < manan mist, fog (primary meaning, probably, "with the morning fog")

c) Modal converbs

γaγčaγar alone   < γaγča sole, single
yosuγar according to   < yosun rule, law
busuγar otherwise, in another   < busu another
   manner

Suffix -γši/-gši

211. This suffix occurs in local adverbs answering the question "whither?"

dotoγši into   < ˇüoto < *dota, cf. dotor-a within
doγoγši down < *doγo, cf. doγodu inferior
inaγši hitherward < *ina, cf. inadu on this side
činaγši thitherward < *čina, cf. činadu on that side
degegši upwards < *dege, cf. deger-e above, on

Suffix -γur/-gür

212. This suffix occurs in local and temporal adverbs only in the modern written language influenced by the spoken dialects.

a) Local adverbs

doγoγur under < *doγo, cf. doγoγši down
qoyiγur along the background, behind < *qoyi, cf. qoyin-a behind
degegür over < *dege, cf. degegši upwards

b) Temporal adverbs

üglügegür early in the morning < üglüge⌢ürlüge morning, ür aurora

Suffix -na/-ne

213. This suffix occurs mainly in local adverbs.

qoyin-a behind < *qoyi, cf. qoyitu behind, northern
γadan-a without (opposite of within) < *γada, cf. γadaγadu outer
dotora within   < *dota, cf. dotor-a within
ečin-e secretly   < *eči
emün-e in front of < *emü

These adverbs form also an ablative:

qoyin-a-ača from behind
emün-e-eče from the front
γadan-a-ača from the outside

Suffix -ra/-re

214. This suffix occurs in local adverbs answering the question "where?" Originally such adverbs must have been dative forms in -a of stems ending in -r (e. g., γadar "outside").

door-a below	< *do, cf. doγoγši down
deger-e on, above	< *dege, cf. degegši upwards
dotor-a within	< *dota, cf. dotoγši into

Suffix -ru/-rü

215. The suffix -ru occurs in adverbs used also as postpositions.

inaru prior, before	< *ina, cf. inaγši hitherward
činaru after	< *čina, cf. činaγši thitherward
tedrü (pre-classical) to the contrary	< *ted
asuru very	< *asu

Suffix -ši

216. The suffix -ši plays a role similar to that of the suffix -γši.

a) Local adverbs

qamiγaši whither	< qamiγ-a where
qoγiši backward, after	< qoγin-a behind
eγiši hitherward	< eγin in this manner, so
teγiši thitherward	< teγin in that manner

b) Temporal adverbs

marγaši tomorrow	< marγada
manaγarši tomorrow	< manaγar

Suffix -ta/-te

217. This suffix occurs in adverbs of manner.

uγuγata completely, cf. uγ origin	
genedte suddenly	< *gened
joriγuta purposely	< joriγu intending

Cf. the multiplicative numerals *nigente, qoγarta* (see § 201).

Adverbs Ending in -b

218. There are modal adverbs with the meaning "completely", derived by reduplication of the first syllable of the word with the inserted consonant -b. If the first syllable of the word concerned is *no*, the adverb is *nob;* if the first syllable is *qa*, the adverb is *qab*, and so on.

qab qar-a completely black
qab qarangγui pitch dark
šib šir-a completely yellow
ub ulaγan completely red
čab čaγan snow-white

> *nob noγuγan* grass green
> *küb küren* completely or dark brown
> *köb köke* completely blue
> *geb genedte* unexpectedly
> *ab ali* anybody, whoever
> *keb keǰiγ-e* always
> *dub duγuį* dead silent

Postpositions
General Remarks

219. The postpositions have a function similar to that of the prepositions in European languages with the difference that they follow the word which they govern.

The postpositions are nouns, adverbs, and even verbs in origin. Most of these words can act as independent words as well as postpositions. A few postpositions are used only as such.

The postpositions will be discussed under syntax. (See § 418.) A few examples, however, will be given here.

Nouns as postpositions:

> *učir-a* because of, a dative of *učir* cause
> *šiltaγa-bar* in consequence of, an instrumental of *šiltaγan* cause, reason

Adverbs as postpositions:

> *deger-e* on, as adverb "above"
> *dotor-a* in, as adverb "within"

Verbal forms as postpositions:

> *kürtele* till, unto, a converb of *kür-* to reach
> *boltala* till, a converb of *bol-* to become

Postpositions which are only postpositions:

> *tula* or *tulada* for

Verbs
General Remarks

220. The secondary verbs are derived from verbs, nouns, pronouns, adverbs, and interjections.

Deverbal Verbs

221. There are two groups of deverbal verbs. To the first group belong those which can be derived from all verbs. Such secondary verbs are nothing but voices or *genera verbi* like the active or passive of the European verbs. To the other group belong secondary verbs which can be derived from a limited group of verbs.

First Group (Genera)

222. To this group belong the factitive, passive, reciprocal, co-operative, and plural verbs.

Factitive and Transitive Verbs

223. In general, these verbs express the idea of causing (letting, ordering, permitting) someone to perform the action expressed by the primary verb.

224. Suffix -γa-/-ge- (the vowel of the suffix is pronounced long) on intransitive stems ending in vowels. Function: to make transitive verbs.

qataγa- to dry something	< *qata-* to become dry
jobaγa- to torment someone	< *joba-* to suffer
unaγa- to overthrow	< *una-* to fall
untaraγa- to extinguish	< *untara-* to go out (of fire)
bütüge- to fulfill, to accomplish	< *bütü-* to be fulfilled
üledege- to leave (something behind)	< *ülede-* to remain

225. Suffix -γa-/-ge- (the vowel of the suffix is short) on both the transitive and intransitive verbs ending in the consonant *l* or *r;* suffix -qa-/-ke- on both the transitive and intransitive verbs ending in *b*, *d*, or *s*. Function: to make primary intransitive verbs transitive, primary transitive verbs factitive verbs ("to cause to do something").

surγa- to teach	< *sur-* to learn
kürge- to deliver	< *kür-* to arrive
γarγa- to take out, to let out	< *γar-* to go out
bolγa- to make	< *bol-* to become
ködelge- to move (someone)	< *ködel-* to move
kötelge- to cause to lead, to cause to direct	< *kötel-* to lead, to direct
getülge- to cause to cross a river, to rescue	< *getül-* to cross a river
bosqa- to erect	< *bos-* to rise
öske- to breed, to raise (cattle)	< *ös-* to become numerous
usadqa- to liquidate	< *usad-* to vanish
čadqa- to satiate	< *čad-* to be satisfied

226. Suffix -γul-/-gül- added to transitive and intransitive verbal stems ending in vowels. Function: to make intransitive verbs transitive, transitive primary verbs factitive.

oroγul- to let in	< *oro-* to go in
üjegül- to show	< *üje-* to see
idegül- to feed	< *ide-* to eat
ükügül- to cause to die	< *ükü-* to die
γarγaγul- to cause to take out	< *γarγa-* to take out
bayiγul- to found	< *bayi-* to be

227. Suffix -l- added to primary stems ending in a syllable consisting of γ (or g) + vowel. This suffix occurs only in the pre-classical language and its equivalent is now -lγa- (see next section).

sayul- to set	< *sayu-* to sit down
uγul- to give a drink	< *uγu-* to drink

228. Suffix *-lγa-/-lge-* added to intransitive and transitive primary stems ending in the syllable mentioned in § 227 and diphthongs and also to monosyllabic stems. Function: to make intransitive verbs transitive, transitive primary stems factitive.

saγulγa- to set	< *saγu-* to sit down
šitaγalγa- to make let burn	< *šitaγa-* to let burn
negülge- to let migrate, to move someone to another place	< *negü-* to migrate, to nomadize
baγulγa- to lower, to let down	< *baγu-* to descend
kilge- to cause to do, to let do	< *ki-* to do
qaraγilγa- to let jump	< *qaraγi-* to jump
baγilγa- to let be	< *baγi-* to be

Passive Verbs

229. Passive verbs can be formed from both transitive and intransitive verbs. If the primary verb is transitive, its passive form has the same function as the passive voice of an English verb, e. g., "to be killed". If the primary verb is an intransitive verb, e. g., "to go", such a form cannot be translated into English literally and an approximate translation would be "to be the object of someone's going". Yet often such passive intransitive verbs also have another function: to express the idea of the necessity of an action, e. g., not "to be the object of someone's going" but "to be obliged to go".

230. Suffix *-γda-/-gde-* added to stems ending in vowels and sometimes in the consonant *l*. In the latter case the connective vowel *u/ü* is inserted.

alaγda- to be killed	< *ala-* to kill
bariγda- to be seized	< *bari-* to seize
üjegde- to be seen	< *üje-* to see
yabuγda- to be the object of someone's going	< *yabu-* to go
tayiluγda- to be explained	< *tayil-* to explain

231. Suffix *-da-/-de-* added to verbs ending in *l*; suffix *-ta-/-te-* added to stems ending in *b, s, d, g, r*.

olda- to be found	< *ol-* to find
bolda- to be obliged to be	< *bol-* to be
abta- to be taken	< *ab-* to take
ögte- to be given	< *ög-* to give
γarta- to be surpassed	< *γar-* to surpass

Reciprocal Verbs

232. Suffix *-ldu-/-ldü-*. Function: to express mutual interaction, e. g., to kill each other.

alaldu- to kill each other	< *ala-* to kill
qarbuldu- to shoot at each other	< *qarbu-* to shoot
baγildu- to fight	< *baγi-* to stand, to be

Co-operative Verbs

233. Suffix *-lča-/-lče-*. Function: to express co-operation with others, taking part in joint action.

ungšilča- to read together	< *ungši-* to read
sayulča- to be present at the meet- ing of others	< *sayu-* to sit down
idelče- to take part in eating	< *ide-* to eat
surulča- to learn together with others	< *sur-* to learn

Plural Verbs

234. Suffix *-čaya-/-čege-*. Function: to express actions performed by many actors.

ungšičaya- to read (of many people)	< *ungši-* to read
yabučaya- to go (of many people)	< *yabu-* to go

Series of Suffixes

235. A verbal stem can carry more than one suffix at the same time, e. g., on a factitive stem there can be a passive suffix or on a reciprocal stem there can be a factitive suffix. Sometimes even three suffixes can be attached to a primary stem.

a) Factitive on factitive:

bosqayul- to cause to erect < *bosqa-* to erect < *bos-* to rise

čadqayul- to cause to satiate < *čadqa-* to satiate < *čad-* to be satisfied

bayiyulya- to make found < *bayiyul-* to found < *bayi-* to be

b) Passive on factitive:

bayiyuluyda- to be founded < *bayiyul-* to found < *bayi-* to be

bolyayda- to be made < *bolya-* to make < *bol-* to become

c) Factitive on passive:

alaydayul- to cause one to be killed < *alayda-* to be killed < *ala-* to kill

üjegdegül- to cause one to be seen < *üjegde-* to be seen < *üje-* to see

d) Factitive on reciprocal:

barilduyul- to let wrestle < *barildu-* to wrestle < *bari-* to seize, to keep

bayilduyul- to let fight < *bayildu-* to fight < *bayi-* to stand

e) Factitive on co-operative:

idelčegül- to cause to participate in eating < *idelče-* to participate in eating < *ide-* to eat

sayulčayul- to cause to be present < *sayulča-* to be present < *sayu-* to sit down

Second Group

Iterative Verbs

236. Suffix *-l-*. Function: to express repeated actions.

čokil- to hit, to knock incessantly < *čoki-* to beat
čakil- to lighten, to flash < *čaki-* to strike fire
dusul- to drip < *dusu-* to fall (of drops)

Middle Verbs (Verba media)

237. Suffix *-ra-/-re-*. Function: to express an action by the subject in relation to himself or the undergoing of an action not caused by anyone other than the subject, e. g., "to betake oneself", "to go to pieces".

asqara- to be spilled	< *asqa-* to spill
ebdere- to go to pieces	< *ebde-* to break

Durative Verbs

238. Suffix *-balǯa-* or *-ɣalǯa-*. Function: to express lasting actions.

sanaɣalǯa- to reflect on	< *sana-* to think
anibalǯa- to twinkle	< *ani-* to shut his eyes

239. Suffix *-lǯa-/-lǯe-* on stems expressing motions. Function: to express rhythmic motions.

nayiɣulǯa- to bob up and down	< *nayiɣu-* to swing
ɣangqulǯa- to rock	< *ɣangqu-* to swing

Denominal Verbs

240. Suffix *-čila-/-čile-*. Function: to indicate that the object is rendered into, made into, or made like the thing or quality designated by the primary word.

boɣolčila- to enslave	< *boɣol* slave
köbegünčile- to take someone as his son	< *köbegün* son
tarbaɣačila- to hunt marmots	< *tarbaɣan* marmot

241. Suffix *-d-*. Function: to express the acquirement of the quality designated by the primary word (intransitive verbs).

urtud- to become long	< *urtu* long
sulad- to weaken	< *sula* weak
boɣonid- to become short	< *boɣoni* short
örged- to become large	< *örgen* large, broad

242. Suffix *-da-/-de-*. Function: to express the use of the object designated by the primary word (mostly transitive verbs).

daɣuda- to call	< *daɣun* voice
buuda- to shoot	< *buu* rifle
degermede- to rob	< *degerme* robbery
arɣada- to outwit	< *arɣa* trick

243. Suffix *-ǰi-*. Function: to express the acquirement of whatever is designated by the primary word. (See § 244 below.)

bayaǰi- to become rich	< *bayan* rich
üreǰi- to increase	< *üre* descendant
amurǰi- to be peaceful, to enjoy peace	< *amur* rest, peace

244. Suffix *-ǰira-/-ǰire-*. Function: the same as that in § 243.

sayiǰira- to improve	< *sayin* good
anggiǰira- to separate	< *anggi* separate
mayuǰira- to deteriorate	< *mayu* bad

245. Suffix *-la-/-le-* or *-na-/-ne-* when added to stems ending in the nasal sounds *ng* and *m*.

emegelle- to saddle	< *emegel* saddle
gerle- to marry (to found a house of his own)	< *ger* house
usula- to water	< *usun* water
altala- to gild	< *altan* gold
šibayula- to hunt birds	< *šibayun* bird
qurdula- to rush, to be quick	< *qurdun* quick
angna- to hunt	< *ang* game
emne- to cure	< *em* medicine

246. Suffix *-ra-/-re-* or *-la-/-le-* (dissimilation) when added to stems containing the consonant *r*. Function: to denote acquirement of a quality.

kökere- to become blue	< *köke* blue
kögšire- to become old	< *kögšin* old
ügeyire- to become poor	< *ügei̯* poor
širala- to become yellow	< *šir-a* yellow

247. Suffix *-rqa-/-rke-* with the final consonant of the primary word dropped. Function: to denote possession of something in abundance.

bayarqa- to be proud of one's richness	< *bayan* rich
omorqa- to be proud	< *omoy* pride
čilegerke- to be ill	< *čilegen* illness, ailment
eǰerke- to impose one's rule upon someone	< *eǰen* master

248. Suffix *-ši-*. Function: to express attainment of a quality or condition.

aldarši- to become glorious	< *aldar* glory
nutuyši- to get settled	< *nutuy* country
sayuriši- to lead a sedentary life	< *sayuri* seat

249. Suffix *-šiya-/-šiye-*. Function: to express acknowledgment of qualities expressed by the primary noun.

sayišiya- to approve	< *sayin* good
ǰöbšiye- to agree	< *ǰöb* right

5 Poppe, Mongolian Grammar

aldaršiya- to praise	< *aldar* glory, fame
mayušiya- to blame, to slander	< *mayu* bad

250. Suffix *-ta-/-te-* or *-tu-/-tü-*. Function: to express acquirement of the condition expressed by the primary noun.

gemte- to be damaged	< *gem* damage, harm
kirte- to become dirty	< *kir* dirt
oyiratu- to approach	< *oyir-a* near

Verbs of Pronominal Origin

Demonstrative verbs

251. The following demonstrative verbs are derived from roots of demonstrative pronouns.

> *eyi-* to act in this manner, cf. *eyimü* such as this
> *teyi-* to act in that manner, cf. *teyimü* such as that
> *čingge-* to act in that manner < colloquial language

Interrogative verbs

252. The following interrogative verbs are derived from roots of the interrogative pronouns.

> *yayaki-* to do what, cf. *yayun* what?
> *yeyi-* to do what
> *yeki-* to do what

Verbs of Adverbial Origin

253. Suffix *-či-*. Function: to express actions performed energetically or with strength (transitive verbs).

suyuči- to pull out	< *suyu* off
tasuči- to tear to pieces	< *tasu* asunder
kemkeči- to break in pieces	< *kemke* in pieces

254. Suffix *-l-*. Function: to form transitive verbs expressing destructive actions.

suyul- to pull out	< *suyu* out, off
quyul- to break asunder	< *quyu* asunder
tasul- to tear to pieces	< *tasu* asunder

255. Suffix *-ra-/-re-*. Function: to form intransitive (middle) verbs (*verba media*).

suyura- to fall out	< *suyu* out, off
tasura- to be pulled off	< *tasu* asunder
qayara- to burst	< *qaya* asunder

Verbs Derived from Interjections

256. Suffix *-čigina-/-čigine-*. Function: to form onomatopoetic verbs expressing various sounds. (See §§ 257 and 258 below.)

| *tarčigina-* to rattle, to crackle | < *tar* |
| *šarčigina-* to rush, to rustle | < *šar* |

257. Suffix *-gi-*. Function: the same.

| *čuugi-* to make noise | < *čuu* |
| *šagi-* to rustle | < *ša* |

258. Suffix *-gina-/-gine-*. Function: the same.

| *qanggina-* to make a noise | < *qang* |
| *ginggine-* to whimper | < *ging* |

259. Suffix *-kira-/-kire-*. Function: to form verbs expressing shouting, bellowing, etc.

| *qaskira-* to shout | < *qas* |
| *barkira-* to roar, to bellow, to cry | < *bar* |

V. Accidence

Noun

Plural

260. Only words acting as substantives have a plural form, but words expressing qualities and numerals used as substantives can form a plural. The plural stem is, at the same time, the nominative plural. Suffixes of oblique cases follow the plural suffix.

The plural presents a varied picture. There are several plural suffixes, but their use often depends neither upon the final sound of the stem nor upon the function of the respective word. There are words having more than one form and their different plural forms have different functions. Certain suffixes even alter the meaning of the word and transform the latter into another word with the function of a singular, even though it is formally a plural.

261. The suffix *-nar/-ner* may be added to a limited number of stems ending in vowels and diphthongs with *i̯* and denoting human beings (mainly relatives and respected people) and deities. This suffix is written separately from the stem.

aq-a-nar elder brothers	< *aq-a* elder brother
degüü-ner younger brothers	< *degüü* younger brother
egeči-ner elder sisters	< *egeči* elder sister
ači-nar grandsons	< *ači* son of the brother, grandson
ǰiči-ner great-grandsons	< *ǰiči* great-grandson
γuči-nar the children of *ǰiči*	< *γuči* the son of *ǰiči*
döči-ner the children of *γuči*	< *döči* the son of *γuči*
ǰige-ner sons of the daughter	< *ǰige* son of the daughter
böle-ner children of sisters	< *böle* child of the sister
abaγ-a-nar uncles, brothers of the father	< *abaγ-a* uncle
naγaču-nar maternal uncles	< *naγaču* the brother of the mother
abuγai̯-nar gentlemen	< *abuγai̯* gentleman
bayši-nar teachers	< *bayši* teacher
šabi-nar pupils	< *šabi* pupil
blam-a-nar lamas	< *blam-a* lama
bandi-nar novices	< *bandi* novice
bandita-nar pundits	< *bandita* pundit
gabǰu-nar the *gabǰus*	< *gabǰu* a learned degree of Buddhist monks, Tibetan *dkaḥ-bču*
kiy-a-nar pages, bodyguards	< *kiy-a* page, bodyguard
loǰava-nar learned translators	< *loǰava* learned translator of Buddhist literature
böge-ner shamans	< *böge* shaman

tngri-ner gods	< *tngri* god, deity
asuri-nar Asuri-ghosts	< *asuri* Asuri ghost

The word *eke-ner* "woman" is formally a plural of *eke* "mother", but it
is used as singular, never expressing the idea "mothers". The plural of
eke "mother" is *ekes* "mothers".

262. The suffix *-nad/-ned* occurs only in the language of the *Secret
History of the Mongols*, which is not Written Mongolian, although it
may also occur in some ancient Written Mongolian texts as yet undis-
covered. It is used instead of the suffix *-nar/-ner*.

aq-a-nad elder brothers	< *aq-a*
degüü-ned younger brothers	< *degüü*

263. The suffix *-mad/-med* (cf. § 129a) occurs on a few stems ending in
vowels and denoting people. Originally this was a suffix of collective
nouns, but it is becoming fossilized and can be found in few words no
longer having the plural meaning. Sometimes it acts, however, as a
plural suffix.

  aqamad seniors, headmen, authorities < *aq-a* elder brother

264. The suffix *-s* occurs on stems ending in vowels or in the diphthong
ai, replacing *i*. The use of this suffix is independent of the meaning of
the nouns concerned.

emes women	< *em-e* woman
ekes mothers	< *eke* mother
eres men	< *er-e* man
nilqas infants	< *nilqa* infant
aqas older people	< *aq-a* elder brother
üges words	< *üge* word
üres fruit, berries	< *ür-e* fruit, berry
aγulas mountains	< *aγula* mountain
baqas toads	< *baq-a* toad
noqas dogs	< *noqai* dog
γaqas pigs	< *γaqai* pig

Of words ending in the consonant *n* only *kümün* "man" has a plural in
-s: kümün-nügüd or *kümüs* "people."

265. Suffix *-d*. This suffix may be added to stems ending in various
sounds. Words ending in the consonant *n*, as a rule, form the plural
with this suffix. The final *n* of the stem is dropped.

noyad princes, nobles	< *noyan* prince, nobleman
qaγad khaghans	< *qaγan* khaghan
qatud wives of khans, queens	< *qatun* the wife of a khan, queen
burqad Buddhas	< *burqan* Buddha
ebüged old men	< *ebügen* old man
šibaγud birds	< *šibaγun* bird
morid horses	< *morin* horse
usud waters	< *usun* water
modud trees	< *modun* tree

In pre-classical texts the plural of *modun* "tree" is *mod* "trees." The plural of *keüken* "child, girl" is *keüked* "children" or "*boy*" (the latter is a singular).

The word *sayid* "minister" is, formally, a plural of *sayin* "good" but in function it is a singular.

Some names of tribes are plural forms in *-d*.

dörbed Dörbet   < *dörben* four
bayad Bayat   < *bayan* rich

266. The suffix *-d* occurs on dissyllabic words ending in *r* with the latter dropped.

γaǰad countries   < *γaǰar* country
nököd friends   < *nökör* friend
šiküd umbrellas   < *šikür* umbrella
šingqud falcons   < *šingqur* falcon

In pre-classical language monosyllabic words ending in *r* also take the suffix *-d*.

möd ways   < *mör* way

267. In the pre-classical language words ending in *l* sometimes also take the suffix *-d*. The final *l* is dropped.

turšiγud spies   < *turšiγul* spy
turγaγud the name of Chinggis Khan's daytime bodyguard < *turγaγul* standing
kebtegüd the name of Chinggis Khan's nighttime bodyguard < *kebtegül* lying

In the modern language only the word *tüšimel* "official" takes the suffix *-d: tüšimed* "officials." The latter form is used as *pluralis majestatis* and means "official" (singular). As plural only the form *tüšimel-nügüd* is used.

In the classical language words ending in the syllable *-sun* form their plural by dropping the syllable *-sun* and adding the suffix *-d* to the stem.

nuγud ducks   < *nuγusun* duck
qubčad clothes, dresses   < *qubčasun* cloth, dress

268. A few words ending in vowels take the suffix *-d*.

busud the others   < *busu* another
berid sisters-in-law   < *beri* sister-in-law

269. All nouns ending in *-či*, *-γači/-geči*, and *-γči/-gči* form the plural with the suffix *-d*.

elčid ambassadors, messengers < *elči* ambassador, messenger
aduγučid horse grooms   < *aduγuči* horse groom
emčid physicians   < *emči* physician
bičigečid scribes, clerks   < *bičigeči* clerk
suruγčid pupils   < *suruγči* pupil

270. The suffix *-n* is added to words ending in *-či*, *-γači/-geči*, and *-γči/-gči* in both ancient and modern texts.

elčin ambassadors	< *elči* ambassador
aduγučin horse grooms	< *aduγuči* horse groom
ködelmüričin workers	< *ködelmüriči* worker
bičigečin clerks	< *bičigeči* clerk
küsegčin those who wish	< *küsegči* wishing

271. The suffix *-n* is also added to words ending in *-taï/-teï* in both ancient and modern texts. The final *ï* of the ending *-taï/-teï* is dropped (cf. § 139).

moritan horsemen	< *moritaï* horseman
erdemten learned people	< *erdemteï* scholar

272. The suffix *-n* occurs, in ancient books, on all stems ending in the vowel *i* or in the diphthong *aï/eï* or *uï/üï* with the final *ï* dropped.

čerbin cherbies	< *čerbi* cherby (a title in the thirteenth century)
γaqan pigs	< *γaqaï* pig
qulaγan thieves	< *qulaγaï* thief
maγun villains	< *maγuï* villain
yabuqun those going	< *yabuquï* one going

273. Suffix *-ud/-üd* added to stems ending in consonants other than *n*.

tölüb-üd forms, patterns	< *tölüb* form, pattern
bičig-üd letters	< *bičig* letter
bulaγ-ud springs, wells	< *bulaγ* spring, well
ulus-ud peoples	< *ulus* people
nom-ud books	< *nom* book
debter-üd copy books	< *debter* copy book

274. In books of the seventeenth century (and earlier) the suffix *-γud/-güd* is added to stems ending in vowels and *n*.

čaγaγčiγud white mares	< *čaγaγčin* white mare
tayiǰiγud Taijigud (name of a tribe)	< *tayiǰi* son of a prince
alaγčiγud motley bows	< *alaγči* motley bow

275. The suffix *-nuγud/-nügüd* occurs on any stems regardless of their final sounds.

dalaï-nuγud seas	< *dalaï* sea
noqaï-nuγud dogs	< *noqaï* dog
bičig-nügüd letters	< *bičig* letter
naγur-nuγud lakes	< *naγur* lake
kümün-nügüd people	< *kümün* man
üker-nügüd oxen	< *üker* ox

276. The suffix *-čud/-čüd* occurs on stems ending in vowels, in *n* or *l*, or the syllable *-güï*, and denoting human beings.

ǰalaγučud young people, youth	< *ǰalaγu* young
bayačud children	< *bay-a* little

bayačud rich people	< *bayan* rich
mongyolčud Mongols	< *mongyol* Mongol
büsügüyičüd women	< *büsügüi̯* woman

277. A word can have several plural forms, as said above, but sometimes with semantic differentiation.

> *aq-a* elder brother — *aq-a-nar* elder brothers
>   *aqas* older people
>   *aqamad* seniors, authorities

On the other hand, a word can take more than one plural suffix at the same time.

> *blam-a-nar-ud* lamas
> *qayad-ud* khaghans
> *eres-üd* men

Declension

General Remarks

278. There are the following cases: nominative, genitive, dative-locative, accusative, ablative, instrumental, and comitative.

The case suffixes are the same in the singular and plural. They are written separately from the stem, which coincides with the nominative.

Stems ending in *n* may lose the latter in certain cases or they may also retain it in all cases.

There are two principal kinds of declension: the simple declension and a declension with the reflexive-possessive suffix indicating the possessor of the object concerned.

Besides, certain case forms may take an additional suffix of another case. Such combined forms are called double cases.

The Simple Declension of Nouns

279. The simple declension is the same as the declension in Indo-European languages. This is a system of forms expressing various relations of the object in question to other objects or actions.

Nominative

280. The nominative ("who?," "what?") has no suffix and coincides with the stem. Under the influence of the colloquial language stems ending in *n* may drop the final *n*.

The nominative of the plural ends in one of the plural suffixes.

kümün man	*ger* house
morin or *mori* horse	*ulus* state
dalai̯ sea	*ayula* mountain

Genitive

281. The genitive ("whose?") has several suffixes. Their use depends upon the final sound of the stem.

Stems ending in vowels or diphthongs take the suffix *-yin*.

    aq-a-yin of the elder brother   *aɣula-yin* of the mountain
    er-e-yin of the man   *dalaị-yin* of the sea
          činu-a-yin of the wolf

282. Stems ending in the consonant *n* take the suffix *-u/-ü*.

    noyan-u of the prince   *keüken-ü* of the child
    morin-u of the horse   *sün-ü* of the milk

283. Stems ending in the remaining consonants take the suffix *-un/-ün*.

    ulus-un of the people, of the state
    ɣajar-un of the country
    ɣal-un of the fire
    bičig-ün of the letter
    jobalang-un of the sufferance
    em-ün of the medicine

284. In the non-classical language, especially in the language influenced by dialects, there occur other genitive suffixes.
The suffixes *-yin*, *-u*, and *-un* are used at random:

    surɣaɣuli-u of the school   *ɣajar-yin* of the country

Instead of the suffix *-u* the colloquial suffix *-i* is used:

    qaɣan-i of the khaghan   *morin-i* of the horse

Instead of the suffix *-u* another colloquial suffix *-aị/-eị* is sometimes used:

    qaɣanaị of the khaghan   *usunaị* of the water

Stems ending in diphthongs or long vowels sometimes take the colloquial suffix *-giyin* instead of the classical suffix *-yin:*

    buluu-giyin of the club

Dative-Locative

285. The dative-locative ("to whom?," "where?") is formed with the suffixes *-dur/-dür*, *-tur/-tür*, and *-a/-e*.
Stems ending in vowels, in all sorts of diphthongs, and in the consonants *n, ng, l,* and *m* take the suffix *-dur/-dür*. Stems ending in any of the remaining consonants, i. e., *ɣ, b, s, d, g,* and *r* take the suffix *-tur/-tür*.
The suffix *-dur* is written with the medial character for *d*, the suffix *-tur* is written with the initial character for *t*.

    dalaị-dur to the sea, in the sea
    aq-a-dur to the elder brother
    em-e-dür to the woman
    tüšimel-dür to the official
    qadum-dur to the father-in-law
    qaɣan-dur to the khaghan
    jirɣalang-dur to the happiness
    aday-tur in the end
    tölöb-tür to the pattern
    ulus-tur to the people

nököd-tür to the friends
bičig-tür in the letter
nökör-tür to the friend

286. In the non-classical language the suffixes *-du/-dü* and *-tu/-tü* or *-da/-de* and *-ta/-te* are used.

morin-du or *morin-da* to the horse
γajar-tu or *γajar-ta* in the country

287. Another dative-locative suffix is *-a/-e*. In the modern language this is less used than in the classical and especially in the pre-classical language, where it was widely used. There is no difference between the function of this suffix and that of the suffixes discussed in the previous sections.
The suffix *-a/-e* occurs with stems ending in consonants and in diphthongs with final *i̯*.

γajar-a to or in the country   *yabuqui̯-a* in order to go
edür-e to the day   *taulai̯-a* to the hare
qaγan-a to the khaghan   *dalai̯-a* to the sea

Accusative

288. The accusative ("whom?," "what?") is formed with the suffix *-yi* which is added to stems ending in vowels and diphthongs or with the suffix *-i* which is added to stems ending in consonants. The final *n* of the stem may be dropped and in this case the suffix is *-yi*.

aq-a-yi the elder brother   *modun-i* or *modu-yi* the tree
noqai̯-yi the dog   *nökör-i* the friend
morin-i or *mori-yi* the horse   *ulus-i* the people

289. In the non-classical language the suffixes *-yi* and *-i* are sometimes used indifferently. Words ending in long vowels or diphthongs may take the colloquial suffix *-gi* or *-yigi*.

γajar-i or *γajar-yi* the country
noqai̯-gi or *noqai̯-yigi* the dog

Ablative

290. The ablative ("from whom?," "whence?") has the suffix *-ača/-eče* written with the medial letter for *a/e*.

aq-a-ača from the elder brother   *dalai̯-ača* from the sea
em-e-eče from the woman   *qaγan-ača* from the khaghan
        ger-eče from the house

291. In the pre-classical language the suffix is often *-ča/-če*. The suffix *-ača/-eče* is a compound ending consisting of the ancient dative-locative suffix *-a/-e* and the primary ablative suffix *-ča/-če*.

morin-ča from the horse   *ger-če* from the house

292. In modern popular books the colloquial suffix *-asa/-ese* sometimes occurs.

        usunasa from the water

Instrumental

293. The instrumental ("with whom?," "by whom?," "through what?," "by means of what?") is formed with the suffixes *-bar/-ber* or *-iyar/-iyer.* Stems ending in vowels or diphthongs take the suffix *-bar/-ber.*

> *kituya-bar* with the knife
> *dalai̯-bar* by sea
> *kele-ber* by means of the tongue

294. Stems ending in consonants take the suffix *-iyar/-iyer.* If the final *n* of the stem is dropped, the suffix is *-bar/-ber.* If the final *n* is retained, the suffix is *-iyar/-iyer.*

> *γar-iyar* with the hand
> *köl-iyer* with the foot
> *morin-iyar* or *mori-bar* by horse

Comitative

295. The comitative ("with whom?," "together with whom?") has the suffix *-luγ-a/-lüge.*

> *aq-a-luγ-a* with the elder brother
> *qaγan-luγ-a* with the khaghan
> *keüken-lüge* with the child
> *eme-lüge* with the woman

In modern popular books and manuscripts by semi-literate people, the colloquial suffix *-la/-le* occurs.

> *keükenle* with the child

296. In modern books influenced by the colloquial language, the colloquial suffix *-tai̯/-tei̯,* with the final *n* of the stem dropped, is used (cf. § 138).

> *aq-a-tai̯* with the elder brother
> *ekener-tei̯* with the woman
> *mori-tai̯* with the horse

Examples of Declension

297. The following words will be declined here: *aq-a* "elder brother," *eke* "mother," *noqai̯* "dog," *morin* or *mori* "horse," *jobalang* "suffering," *γajar* "country," *ulus* "people," and *bulaγ* "spring, well."

Nominative	*aq-a*	*eke*	*noqai̯*	*morin* or *mori*
Genitive	*aq-a-yin*	*eke-yin*	*noqai̯-yin*	*morin-u*
Dative-	*aq-a-dur* or	*eke-dür* or	*noqai̯-dur* or	*morin-dur* or
Locative	*aq-a-du*	*eke-dü*	*noqai̯-du*	*morin-du*
Accusative	*aq-a-yi*	*eke-yi*	*noqai̯-yi*	*morin-i* or
				mori-yi
Ablative	*aq-a-ača*	*eke-eče*	*noqai̯-ača*	*morin-ača*
Instrumental	*aq-a-bar*	*eke-ber*	*noqai̯-bar*	*morin-iyar*
				or *mori-bar*
Comitative	*aq-a-luγ-a*	*eke-lüge*	*noqai̯-luγ-a*	*morin-luγ-a*

Nominative	jobalang	γajar	ulus	bulaγ
Genitive	jobalang-un	γajar-un	ulus-un	bulaγ-un
Dative-	jobalang-dur	γajar-tur	ulus-tur	bulaγ-tur
Locative or	jobalang-du	γajar-tu	ulus-tu	bulaγ-tu
or	jobalang-a	γajar-a	ulus-a	bulaγ-a
Accusative	jobalang-i	γajar-i	ulus-i	bulaγ-i
Ablative	jobalang-ača	γajar-ača	ulus-ača	bulaγ-ača
Instrumental	jobalang-iyar	γajar-iyar	ulus-iyar	bulaγ-iyar
Comitative	jobalang-luγa	γajar-luγ-a	ulus-luγ-a	bulaγ-luγ-a

The same examples in Mongolian script

The Double Declension

298. To certain case forms suffixes of other cases can be added. Thus double case forms arise. Such double cases are the following: 1) the genitive-dative (-locative), 2) the dative- (locative-) ablative, 3) the comitative-instrumental, and 4) almost all cases of the comitative in -taï/-teï.

Genitive-Dative-Locative

299. The genitive-dative-locative ("to whom?," "at whose?," e. g., English "at father's"), which is rarely used, is an influence of the colloquial language where such forms are usual. Only the genitive in -*yin* or -*ai̯* can take a dative-locative suffix. The combined genitive-dative-locative suffix is -*yin-du(r)* or -*ai̯-du(r)*.

> *bayši-yin-dur* to the teacher's, at the teacher's
> *eke-yin-dür* to mother's, at mother's
> *noyan-ai̯-dur* to the prince's, at the prince's

Dative-Locative-Ablative

300. The usual ablative suffix -*ača/-eče* is, as indicated in § 291 above, a combination of the original dative-locative suffix -*a/-e* and the ancient ablative suffix -*ča/-če*. Now, there is another combination of the pre-classical dative-locative suffix and the ablative suffix -*ča/-če*. This is the combined suffix -*dača/-deče*, -*tača/-teče* which sometimes occurs in the pre-classical language. Very few words, however, are now used in this form.

> *ger-teče* from the house
> *morin-dača* from the horse (pre-classical)
> *usun-dača* from the water

Comitative-Instrumental

301. The comitative-instrumental has the same function as the simple comitative.

> *noyan-luy-a-bar* together with the prince
> *bayši-luy-a-bar* together with the teacher

302. In the non-classical language the double comitative-instrumental suffix is -*lar/-ler*.

> *qatun-lar* together with the queen

Further Declension of the Comitative

303. The colloquial comitative with the suffix -*tai̯/-tei̯*, which was originally a denominal noun with the meaning "possessing something" (see § 138), can take almost all case suffixes.

Comitative	-*tai̯/-tei̯* with someone, he and another person
Comitative-Genitive	-*tai̯-yin* someone's and another person's
Comitative-Dative-Locative	-*tai̯-dur* to someone and another person
Comitative-Accusative	-*tai̯-yi* someone with another person
Comitative-Ablative	-*tai̯-ača* from someone and another person
Comitative-Instrumental	-*tai̯-bar* or -*tayiyar* with someone

The Reflexive-Possessive Declension

General Remarks

304. The reflexive-possessive declension is a system of case forms not only indicating the relations of the object concerned to other objects (or actions) but also indicating that the object belongs to the person acting. While *aq-a-dur* merely means "to the elder brother," not indicating to whose brother, the corresponding reflexive-possessive form signifies "to his own (i. e., the subject's) elder brother." The cases of this declension differ from the cases of the plain declension in having an additional suffix which expresses the idea "his" (Latin *suus*). This "his" refers to the subject. For instance in the sentence "He took his book," "his" refers to "he." In English there is no special reflexive possessive pronoun. Therefore "his" can express in English two different ideas "his," i. e., "the subject's" and "another person's."

The reflexive-possessive declension does not have a nominative.

Genitive

305. All nouns, regardless of the final sound of the stem, can take the suffix *-yuγan/-yügen*.

> *γar-yuγan* of his own hand
> *nayaču-yuγan* of his own (maternal) uncle
> *ger-yügen* of his own house

306. Nouns ending in consonants can take the suffix *-iyan/-iyen;* those ending in vowels take the suffix *-ban/-ben*.

> *nayaču-ban* of his own uncle
> *γar-iyan* of his own hand
> *ger-iyen* of his own house

307. A third possible form includes the usual genitive suffixes and *-iyan/-iyen* or *-ban/-ben*. If the genitive suffix ends in *n* (*-un* or *-yin*) the reflexive-possessive suffix is *-iyan;* if the genitive suffix ends in a vowel (suffix *-u*) the possessive suffix *-ban/-ben* is added. Thus there are the following combinations: *-un-iyan/-ün-iyen*, *-yin-iyan/-yin-iyen*, and *-u-ban/-ü-ben*.

> *nayaču-yin-iyan* of his own uncle
> *ger-ün-iyen* of his own house
> *morin-u-ban* of his own horse

Dative-Locative

308. The usual dative-locative with the suffix *-dur/-dür* (and *-tur/-tür*) takes the reflexive-possessive suffix *-iyan/-iyen*. The non-classical form in *-du/-dü* or *-tu/-tü* takes the other suffix, *-ban/-ben*.

The dative-locative in *-a/-e* does not occur in this declension.

> *nayaču-dur-iyan* to his own (maternal) uncle
> *γar-tur-iyan* in his own hand
> *nayaču-du-ban* to his own (maternal) uncle
> *γar-tu-ban* in his own hand

309. The usual dative-locative suffix is *-daγan/-degen, -taγan/-tegen*. (The latter occurs on stems ending in *γ, b, s, d, g*, and *r*.)

This suffix is a combined ending consisting of the pre-classical dative-locative suffix *-da/-de* and the reflexive-possessive suffix (*-*γan*).

> *nayaču-daγan* to his own uncle
> *γar-taγan* in his own hand
> *eke-degen* to his own mother
> *ger-tegen* in his own house

Accusative

310. The accusative ending in *-i* or *-yi* takes the possessive suffix *-ban/-ben.*

γar-*i-ban* his own hand

naγaču-yi-ban his own uncle

311. Another possible form is that coinciding with the genitive: the suffix is either *-yuyan/-yügen* or *-iyan/-iyen* and *-ban/-ben* according to the rules given in reference to the genitive.

naγaču-yuyan or *naγaču-ban* his own (maternal) uncle

γar-*yuyan* or γar-*iyan* his own hand

ger-yügen or *ger-iyen* his own house

em-e-yügen or *em-e-ben* his own wife

Ablative

312. The usual ablative suffix takes the possessive suffix *-ban/-ben.*

naγaču-ača-ban from his own uncle

ger-eče-ben from his own house

313. Another possible form includes the combined suffix *-ačayan/-ečegen.*

naγaču-ačayan from his own uncle

ger-ečegen from his own house

Instrumental

314. To the usual instrumental forms, the possessive suffix *-iyan/-iyen* is added.

ǰida-bar-iyan with his own spear

köl-iyer-iyen with his own foot

Comitative

315. The comitative ending in *-luγ-a/-lüge* takes the possessive suffix *-ban/-ben.*

naγaču-luγ-a-ban together with his own (maternal) uncle

em-e-lüge-ben together with his own wife

316. The colloquial comitative ending in *-la/-le* takes the suffix *-γan/-gen.*

bayši-layan together with his own teacher

em-e-legen together with his own wife

317. The other colloquial comitative ending in *-taǐ/-teǐ* takes either the suffix *-ban/-ben* or *-γan/-gen.* In the latter case the combined suffix is *-tayiyan/-teyigen.*

bayšitayiyan or *bayši-taǐ-ban* together with his own teacher

emeteyigen or *em-e-teǐ-ben* together with his own wife

Examples of the Reflexive-Possessive Declension

318. The following words will be declined here: *aq-a* "the elder brother," *eke* "mother," *noqaǐ* "dog," *morin* "horse," *ǰobalang* "suffering," γ*aǰar* "country," *ulus* "people," and *bulaγ* "well, spring."

Genitive			
	aq-a-yin-iyan	*eke-yin-iyen*	*noqaǐ-yin-iyan*
	aq-a-ban	*eke-ben*	*noqaǐ-ban*
	aq-a-yuyan	*eke-yügen*	*noqaǐ-yuyan*

Dative-	aq-a-dur-iyan	eke-dür-iyen	noqaɨ-dur-iyan
Locative	aq-a-du-ban	eke-dü-ben	noqaɨ-du-ban
	aq-a-dayan	eke-degen	noqaɨ-dayan
Accusative	aq-a-yi-ban	eke-yi-ben	noqaɨ-yi-ban
	aq-a-ban	eke-ben	noqaɨ-ban
	aq-a-yuyan	eke-yügen	noqaɨ-yuyan
Ablative	aq-a-ača-ban	eke-eče-ben	noqaɨ-ača-ban
	aq-a-ačayan	eke-ečegen	noqaɨ-ačayan
Instrumental	aq-a-bar-iyan	eke-ber-iyen	noqaɨ-bar-iyan
Comitative	aq-a-luy-a-ban	eke-lüge-ben	noqaɨ-luy-a-ban
	aq-a-taɨ-ban	eke-teɨ-ben	noqaɨ-taɨ-ban
	aq-a-tayiyan	eke-teyigen	noqaɨ-tayiyan

Genitive	morin-u-ban	jobalang-un-iyan	yajar-un-iyan
	morin-iyan	jobalang-iyan	yajar-iyan
	morin-yuyan	jobalang-yuyan	yajar-yuyan
Dative-	morin-dur-iyan	jobalang-dur-iyan	yajar-tur-iyan
Locative	morin-du-ban	jobalang-du-ban	yajar-tu-ban
	morin-dayan	jobalang-dayan	yajar-tayan
Accusative	morin-i-ban	jobalang-i-ban	yajar-i-ban
	mori-yi-ban	jobalang-iyan	yajar-iyan
	mori-ban		
	mori-yuyan	jobalang-yuyan	yajar-yuyan
Ablative	morin-ača-ban	jobalang-ača-ban	yajar-ača-ban
	morin-ačayan	jobalang-ačayan	yajar-ačayan
Instrumental	morin-iyar-iyan	jobalang-iyar-iyan	yajar-iyar-iyan
	mori-bar-iyan		
Comitative	morin-luy-a-ban	jobalang-luy-a-ban	yajar-luy-a-ban
	moritaɨ-ban	jobalang-taɨ-ban	yajar-taɨ-ban
	moritayiyan	jobalangtayiyan	yajartayiyan

Genitive	ulus-un-iyan	bulay-un-iyan
	ulus-iyan	bulay-iyan
	ulus-yuyan	bulay-yuyan
Dative-	ulus-tur-iyan	bulay-tur-iyan
Locative	ulus-tu-ban	bulay-tu-ban
	ulus-tayan	bulay-tayan
Accusative	ulus-i-ban	bulay-i-ban
	ulus-iyan	bulay-iyan
	ulus-yuyan	bulay-yuyan
Ablative	ulus-ača-ban	bulay-ača-ban
	ulus-ačayan	bulay-ačayan
Instrumental	ulus-iyar-iyan	bulay-iyar-iyan
Comitative	ulus-luy-a-ban	bulay-luy-a-ban
	ulus-taɨ-ban	bulay-taɨ-ban
	ulus-tayiyan	bulay-tayiyan

The Same Examples in Mongolian Script

Genitive

Dative-Locative

Accusative

Ablative

Instrumental

Comitative

Genitive									

Genitive

Dative-Locative

Accusative

Ablative

Instrumental

Comitative

6*

Genitive					

Dative-Locative					

Accusative					

Ablative				

Instrumental		

Comitative					

The Simple Declension of Pronouns

General Remarks

319. The case suffixes in the declension of pronouns are the same as in the declension of nouns, but the stems of the personal and demonstrative pronouns vary in different cases. There is, in Mongolian, the factor of suppletion. The pronouns have two declensions: a simple declension and a declension with the possessive suffix.

Personal Pronouns

320. The personal pronouns are as follows: *bi* "I," *či* "thou," **i* "he," *ba* "we" (exclusive), *bida* "we" (inclusive), *ta* "you," and **a* "they."

Nominative	*bi*	*či*	**i*	*bida*
Genitive	*minu*	*činu*	*inu*	*bidan-u*
Dative-				
Locative	*nadur*	*čimadur*	*imadur*	*bidan-dur*
				bidan-a
Accusative	*namayi*	*čimayi*	*imayi*	*bidan-i*
Ablative	*nama-ača*	*čima-ača*	*ima-ača*	*bidan-ača*
	nada-ača			
Instrumental	*nama-bar*	*čima-bar*	*ima-bar*	*bidan-iyar*
	nada-bar			
Comitative	*nama-luγ-a*	*čima-luγ-a*	*ima-luγ-a*	*bidan-luγ-a* or
				biden-lüge

Nominative	*ba*	*ta*	**a*
Genitive	*manu*	*tanu*	*anu*
Dative-	*man-dur*	*tan-dur*	**andur*
Locative	*man-a*	*tan-a*	**ana*
Accusative	*man-i*	*tan-i*	**ani*
Ablative	*man-ača*	*tan-ača*	**anača*
Instrumental	*man-iyar*	*tan-iyar*	**an-iyar*
Comitative	*man-luγ-a*	*tan-luγ-a*	**an-luγ-a*

Forms marked with an asterisk are reconstructed forms not attested in texts. Except for the genitive, no forms of the third person of the singular are used in the modern or classical language, though they occur in manuscripts of the pre-classical period.

The genitive of the third person singular is *inu*. In the non-classical language this is sometimes *ni*, when used in postnominal position.

321. Besides *bida* and *ta* there are, in the modern language, the forms *bida-nar* "we" (a pleonastic form of the plural) and *tanar* "you" (also with the plural suffix *-nar*). In the modern language *ta* "you" is used in addressing one person and *tanar* is "you" when addressing many people. The declension of both *bida-nar* and *tanar* is normal.

322. The pronouns of the first and second person are given here in Mongolian script.

Nominative

Genitive

Dative-Locative

Accusative

Ablative

Instrumental

Comitative

Demonstrative Pronouns

323. The demonstrative pronouns are as follows: *ene* "this," *ede* or *edeger* "these," *tere* "that," *tede* or *tedeger* "those," *eyimü* "such as this," and *teyimü* "such as that."

Nominative	*ene*	*tere*	*ede*	*edeger*	*eyimü*
Genitive	*egün-ü*	*tegün-ü*	*eden-ü*	*edeger-ün*	*eyimü-yin*
Dative-	*egün-dür*	*tegün-dür*	*eden-dür*	*edeger-tür*	*eyimü-dür*
Locative	*egün-e*	*tegün-e*	*eden-e*		
Accusative	*egün-i*	*tegün-i*	*eden-i*	*edeger-i*	*eyimü-yi*
Ablative	*egün-eče*	*tegün-eče*	*eden-eče*	*edeger-eče*	*eyimü-eče*
	egünče	*tegünče*			
Instrumental	*egün-iyer*	*tegün-iyer*	*eden-iyer*	*edeger-iyer*	*eyimü-ber*
	egüber	*tegüber*			
Comitative	*egün-lüge*	*tegün-lüge*	*eden-lüge*	*edeger-lüge*	*eyimü-lüge*

The pronouns *tede*, *tedeger*, and *teyimü* are declined in the same manner as *ede*, *edeger*, and *eyimü*. The remaining demonstrative pronouns are declined according to the general rules.

324. The same demonstrative pronouns are given here in Mongolian script.

Nominative					
Genitive					
Dative-Locative					
Accusative					
Ablative					
Instrumental					
Comitative					

Interrogative Pronouns

325. The declension of the interrogative pronouns *ken* "who," *yayun* "what," and *ali* (stem *alin*) "which" is carried on according to the general rules.

Indefinite Pronouns

326. The indefinite pronouns are derived from the interrogative pronouns with the particles *ba, ber* or *ču*. In the declension the case suffixes occupy the place between the pronoun and the particle.

Nominative	ken ču	yayun ču	alin ču
Genitive	ken-ü ču	yayun-u ču	alin-u ču
Dative-	ken-dür ču	yayun-dur ču	alin-dur ču
Locative	ken-e ču	yayun-a ču	alin-a ču

Accusative	*ken-i ču*	*yaɣun-i ču*	*alin-i ču*
Ablative	*ken-eče ču*	*yaɣun-ača ču*	*alin-ača ču*
Instrumental	*ken-iyer ču*	*yaɣun-iyar ču*	*alin-iyar ču*
		yaɣu-bar ču	
Comitative	*ken-lüge ču*	*yaɣun-luɣ-a ču*	*alin-luɣ-a ču*

As the particle *ču* is the one most used in the modern language, the
words with which it is used have been chosen as examples. The remaining
particles *ba* and *ber* occupy the same place as the particle *ču*.

The Reflexive-Possessive Declension of Pronouns

General Remarks

327. The pronouns also occur in this declension. The meaning of such
forms is similar to that of the English "to his own," "from his own,"
and so on.
All pronouns occur in this declension.

Personal Pronouns

328. Only the declension of the pronouns *bi* "I," *či* "thou," and *ta* "you"
will be given here.

Genitive	*minu-ban*	*činu-ban*	*tanu-ban*
	minu-yuɣan	*činu-yuɣan*	*tanu-yuɣan*
Dative-	*nadur-iyan*	*čimadur-iyan*	*tan-duriyan*
Locative	*namadayan*	*čimadayan*	*tan-dayan*
Accusative	*nama-yuɣan*	*čima-yuɣan*	*tan-yuɣan*
Ablative	*nama-ačayan*	*čima-ačayan*	*tan-ačayan*
Instrumental	*nama-bar-iyan*	*čima-bar-iyan*	*tan-iyar-iyan*
Comitative	*nama-luɣ-a-ban*	*čima-luɣ-a-ban*	*tan-luɣ-a-ban*

Demonstrative Pronouns

329. The pronouns declined here are: *ene* "this," *tere* "that," *ede* "these,"
and *tede* "those."

Genitive	*egün-yügen*	*tegün-yügen*	*eden-yügen*	*teden-yügen*
Dative-	*egün-degen*	*tegün-degen*	*eden-degen*	*teden-degen*
Locative	*egün-dür-iyen*	*tegün-dür-iyen*	*eden-dür-iyen*	*teden-dür-iyen*
Accusative	*egün-yügen*	*tegün-yügen*	*eden-yügen*	*teden-yügen*
	egün-i-ben	*tegün-i-ben*	*eden-i-ben*	*teden-i-ben*
Ablative	*egün-ečegen*	*tegün-ečegen*	*eden-ečegen*	*teden-ečegen*
	egün-eče-ben	*tegün-eče-ben*	*eden-eče-ben*	*teden-eče-ben*
Instru-	*egün-iyer-iyen*	*tegün-iyer-iyen*	*eden-iyer-iyen*	*teden-iyer-iyen*
mental	*egüber-iyen*	*tegüber-iyen*		
Comitative	*egün-lüge-ben*	*tegün-lüge-ben*	*eden-lüge-ben*	*teden-lüge-ben*

Reflexive Pronouns

330. The reflexive pronouns *öber-iyen* "himself" and *öbesüd-iyen* (*ögesüd-
iyen*) "themselves" do not occur in the simple declension. They have
only this reflexive-possessive declension, with the exception of the
genitive, which is a simple one.

Nominative	*öber-iyen*	*öbesüd-iyen*
Genitive	*öber-ün*	*öbesüd-ün*
Dative-Locative	*öber-tegen*	*öbesüd-tegen*
Accusative	*öber-iyen*	*öbesüd-iyen*
Ablative	*öber-ečegen*	*öbesüd-ečegen*
Instrumental	*öber-iyer-iyen*	*öbesüd-iyer-iyen*
Comitative	*öber-lüge-ben*	*öbesüd-lüge-ben*

Conjugation of the Verb

General Remarks

331. The verbal forms are classified as (a) those serving as the predicate of a completed sentence (finite verbs), (b) those serving as subject, object, attribute or predicate of a sentence, and (c) those serving as attribute to verbs or logical (not grammatical) predicates of incomplete sentences.

To the first group belong the imperative and optative forms and all indicative forms. To the second group belong the verbal nouns. To the third group belong the converbs.

The imperative and optative forms express orders and wishes. These are as follows: the imperative, prescriptive, voluntative, optative, and dubitative.

The verbal nouns are more or less the same as the participles of the Indo-European languages.

The converbs do not serve as predicates of completed sentences.

Imperative and Optative Forms

The Imperative

332. The imperative of the second person expresses a strict order addressed to one person (thou) or to several persons (you). This form has no suffix and coincides with the stem of the verb.

yabu go!   *ungši* read!
kele say!   *ire* come!

333. The imperative of the second person of the plural, or the so-called benedictive, expresses a polite entreaty addressed to one person or to several persons.

The suffix is *-γtun/-gtün*, a plural in *-n* of *-γtuį/-gtüį* (see § 335). Verbs ending in consonants take a union vowel *-u-/-ü-*.

yabuγtun Please go!
kelegtün Please say!
yabuγuluγtun (*yabuγul-*) Please send!
öggügtün (*ög-*) Please give!

334. In the pre-classical language the suffix is usually *-dqun/-dkün*, which is added to stems ending in consonants with the union vowel *-u-/-ü-*.

yabudqun Please go!
keledkün Please say!

335. The suffix *-γtuį/-gtüį* occurs mainly in Buriat manuscripts. Originally this was an imperative of the singular (the plural was *-γtun/-gtün*, see § 333) but in the modern language it is used instead of the form in *-γtun/-gtün*.

> *yabuγtuį* Please go!
> *kelegtüį* Please say!

The Prescriptive

336. The prescriptive occurs only in the language influenced by the dialects. This form expresses a commission or a wish addressed to a second person. The action which the person concerned is ordered to perform may be done later on, if not immediately.

The suffix is *-γaraį/-gereį*, after a final consonant *-uγaraį/-ügereį*.

> *yabuγaraį* go!
> *kelegereį* say!
> *yabuγuluγaraį* (*yabuγul-*) send!

The Imperative of the Third Person

337. This form expresses an order to be executed by a third person ("let him do!," "he must do!").

The suffix is *-tuγaį/-tügeį*.

> *yabutuγaį* He must go!
> *keletügeį* Let him say! He must say!
> *yabuγultuγaį* Let him send! He must send!

The Voluntative

338. The voluntative expresses a wish to perform an action ("let me do!," "let us do!").

The voluntative suffix of the singular is *-suγaį/-sügeį*, in the pre-classical language *-su/-sü*.

> *yabusuγaį* Let me go!
> *kelesügeį* Let me say!
> *yabuγulsuγaį* Let me send!

339. In modern books the suffixes *-suγaį/-sügeį* and *-tuγaį/-tügeį* (see § 337) are sometimes confused and used indiscriminately in reference to both the first and third person.

340. The voluntative of the first person of the plural is formed with the suffix *-y-a/-y-e*, which is added to stems ending in consonants with the union vowel *-u-/-ü-*.

In modern books and newspapers this form is often used in reference to both the singular and plural.

> *yabuy-a* Let us go!
> *keley-e* Let us say!
> *yabuγuluy-a* (*yabuγul-*) Let us send!

The Optative

341. The optative occurs only in popular books. It expresses a wish, usually impossible of attainment, and refers to all persons ("Ah, if he did!").

The suffix is *-yasaị/-geseị*, which is added to stems ending in consonants, with the union vowel *-u-/-ü-*.

> *yabuyasaị* Ah, if he went!
> *kelegeseị* Ah, if he said!
> *yabuyuluyasaị* Ah, if he sent!

The Dubitative

342. The dubitative expresses the fear that someone might perform an action, which is considered undesirable ("But what if he, nevertheless, does?").

The suffix is *-yuǰaị/-güǰeị* with this union vowel *-u-/-ü-* on stems ending in consonants.

> *yabuyuǰaị* What if he comes?
> *kelegüǰeị* What if he says?
> *yabuyuluyuǰaị* (*yabuyul-*) What if he sends?

Indicative Forms

General Remarks

343. The indicative forms express present, future, or past actions. They are equivalent to the present, future, or past tenses of the English verb.

Each form may refer to any of the persons, singular or plural.

There are the following indicative forms: (a) three different forms of the present tense and (b) three forms of the past tense.

The Present Tense

344. There are two narrative present forms and a deductive form. The narrative present forms express actions which take place either at the time of speaking (present tense) or will take place in the future. In other words this is a *praesens* and *futurum*.

345. The first narrative present takes the suffix *-muị/-müị*, with the union vowel *-u-/-ü-*, which is added to stems ending in consonants.

This form also occurs with the interrogative particle *uu/üü*, in which case the suffix and the particle fuse into *-muu/-müü*.

> *yabumuị* He goes, or He will go.
> *kelemüị* He says, or He will say.
> *yabuyulumuị* (*yabuyul-*) He sends, or He will send.
> *yabumuị-uu* or *yabumuu* Does he go? or Will he go?

346. In the pre-classical period the ending was *-m* or *-mu/-mü*.

> *yabum* He goes, or He will go.
> *yabumu* He goes, or He will go.

347. Another suffix of the narrative present, less usual in the classical language, is -*nam*/-*nem* with the union vowel -*u*-/-*ü*-.
The function of this form is that of the present tense.

>*yabunam* He goes.
>*kelenem* He says.

348. In popular books, instead of the suffix -*nam*/-*nem*, the suffix -*naį*/-*neį* is used.
With the interrogative particle this is -*nuu*/-*nüü*.

>*yabunaį* He goes, or He will go.
>*keleneį* He says, or He will say.
>*yabunuu* Does he go?, or Will he go?

349. The deductive present expresses actions considered a logical result of previous actions or antitheses to the latter ("Consequently he does," or "Consequently he will do," "Hence he does").
The suffix is -*yu*/-*yü*; with the union vowel -*u*-/-*ü*-, it is added to stems ending in consonants.

>*yabuyu* Consequently he goes, or Consequently he will go. In accordance with the previous actions he goes.
>*medeyü* Hence he knows.
>*yabuyuluyu* (*yabuyul-*) Hence he sends.

The Past Tense

350. There are three forms of the past. Of these the primary form of the past tense is a perfect referring to the recent past.
The suffix is -*ba*/-*be* or -*baį*/-*beį*. Only verbs ending in *b* or *r* take a union vowel -*u*-/-*ü*-.
With the interrogative particle *uu* the suffix is -*ba-uu* or -*buu*/-*büü*.

>*yabuba* or *yabubaį* He has gone.
>*irebe* or *irebeį* He has come.
>*ögbe* or *ögbeį* He has given.
>*asayba* or *asaybaį* He has asked.
>*bosba* or *bosbaį* He has risen.
>*odba* or *odbaį* He has gone, He has departed.
>*abuba* or *abubaį* (*ab-*) He has taken.
>*yaruba* or *yarubaį* (*yar-*) He has gone out.
>*yabuba-uu* or *yabubuu* Has he gone?

351. Another past form expresses actions which, without any doubt, have taken (or will take) place. The action is supposed to have been witnessed by the person speaking; at any rate, the latter owes his knowledge of the action to a reliable source.
The suffix is -*luya*/-*lüge* in the classical language, with the union vowel -*u*-/-*ü*-, added to stems ending in consonants.
In the pre-classical language the suffix is -*luyaį*/-*lügeį* or sometimes -*laya*/-*lege*.
In modern popular books the suffix is often -*la*/-*le* or -*laį*/-*leį*. With the interrogative particle it is -*la-uu*/-*le-uu* or -*luu*/-*lüü*.

yabuluya He has gone.
ükülügei̦ He has died.
medelüü Did he know?

352. The third past tense form expresses actions which took place before other actions. In certain cases this is a pluperfect. The speaker claims to have witnessed the action and to have been surprised when making the discovery of the action as a *fait accompli*. This past tense is usually used with reference to the second and third persons.
The suffix is -*ĭuqui̦*/-*ĭüküi̦*; when added to stems ending in γ, *b*, *s*, *d*, *g*, and *r* it is -*čuqui̦*/-*čüküi̦*.

yabuĭuqui̦ He was found to have gone.
üküĭüküi̦ It was unexpectedly discovered that he had died.
γarčuqui̦ He was found to have gone out.

353. In the pre-classical language the suffix is either -*ĭuyu*/-*ĭügü* or -*ĭuyui̦*/-*ĭügüi̦* (-*čuyu*/-*čügü* or -*čuyui̦*/-*čügüi̦*). In the modern and classical language only the verb *a-* "to be" occurs with the suffix -*ĭuyu*. Another ancient ending is -*ĭiyai̦*/-*ĭigei̦*.

yabuĭuyu or *yabuĭuyui̦* He was found to have gone.
aĭuyu He had been.
yabuĭiyai̦ He was found to have gone.

354. In modern popular books the suffix is often -*ĭi*/-*či*.

yabuĭi He was found to have gone.
γarči He was found to have gone out.

Verbal Nouns

General Remarks

355. The verbal nouns are declinable and possess all characteristics of nouns. On the other hand, they are verbal forms and can serve as predicates. Verbal nouns, although to some extent comparable, differ from the participles of the European languages in that the area of their syntactical use is larger.

Nomen Actoris

356. The *nomen actoris* designates the person acting and sometimes the process of an action. It is used as subject, object, attribute, and, with a copula, as predicate.
The suffix is -*γči*/-*gči*, with a union vowel, added to stems ending in consonants. The plural form is either -*γčin*/-*gčin* or -*γčid*/-*gčid*.

yabuγči going, goer, one who goes, process of going
kelegči saying, one who says, process of saying
kelegčid or *kelegčin* those who say

Nomen Praesentis

357. The *nomen praesentis* is a sort of present participle. In the classical and modern language it occurs very seldom and only a few verbs occur in this form. This is used as attribute, object, and predicate.

The suffix is -*ị* after a final vowel of the stem, e. g., *kemegdeị* "is said," but with a connective vowel -*u*- after a final consonant:

> *ayisuị* (*ayis-*) approaching
> *oduị* (*od-*) going, departing
> *boluị* (*bol-*) becoming
> *γaruị* (*γar-*) exceeding

Nomen Usus

358. The *nomen usus* expresses a customary, habitual, or usual action, e. g., "someone who usually comes," "the usual visitor." This form is used as subject, object, attribute, and, with a copula, as predicate.
The suffix is -*day*/-*deg*, with the union vowel -*u*-/-*ü*- when the stem ends in a consonant.

> *yabuday* someone who usually goes, the usual goer, the usual act of going, he usually goes
> *keledeg* someone who usually says, the act of usually saying, he usually says

Nomen Futuri

359. The *nomen futuri* expresses an action which will take place in the future or an action of any time other than future. This form is used as subject, object, attribute, and predicate (with a copula). It is frequently referred to as the infinitive of the verb, a profound error.
The suffix is -*qu*/-*kü* without the union vowel.

> *yabuqu* one who will go, going in the future, he will go
> *kelekü* one who will say, saying in the future, he will say

360. Another suffix is -*quị*/-*küị*. In the pre-classical language -*qu* and -*quị* were used indiscriminately, but in the modern and classical language forms in -*quị* are used only as substantive nouns, i. e., they serve as subject and object but not as attribute or predicate.

> *yabuquị* the process of going
> *keleküị* the process of saying

361. The plural of the form in -*quị*/-*küị* is -*qun*/-*kün* in the pre-classical language.

> *yabuqun* those who will go
> *kelekün* those who will say

Nomen Imperfecti

362. The *nomen imperfecti* with the suffix -*γa*/-*ge* expresses an unfinished action which started in the past and continues into the present, e. g., "someone who has sat down and is still sitting." This form is used as any part of sentence, although mainly as attribute and predicate.

> *yabuγa* someone who started going and is still going
> *kelege ügeị* someone who has not yet said

363. In the pre-classical language the suffix is sometimes -*γaị*/-*geị*.

> *yabuγaị* someone who has gone and is still going

Nomen Perfecti

364. The *nomen perfecti* expresses a completed past action, e. g., "someone who has died" or "is dead." This form is used as subject, object, attribute, and predicate.

The suffix is *-ysan/-gsen* with the union vowel *-u-/-ü-* when the stem ends in a consonant.

> *yabuysan* one who has gone (and is no longer here)
> *kelegsen* one who has said (and is no longer speaking)

Converbs

General Remarks

365. The converbs do not serve as predicates of complete sentences, but only as attributes of verbs, indicating the manner in which the action is being performed, or as logical (not grammatical) predicates of word groups rendered in European languages as subordinate clauses.

The converbs are classified into two groups: the genuine and the pseudo-converbs. The former are fossilized oblique case forms of verbal nouns; the latter are, from the historical viewpoint, purely verbal forms.

The genuine and pseudo-converbs manifest a syntactical difference: while the actor is always designated by the nominative case in constructions with pseudo-converbs he can, under certain circumstances, be designated by the genitive (or accusative) in constructions with genuine converbs.

The genuine converbs are the following: *converbum terminale, converbum abtemporale, converbum contemporale, converbum successivum, converbum finale*, and *converbum praeparativum*. The pseudo-converbs are: *converbum conditionale, converbum concessivum, converbum imperfecti, converbum modale*, and *converbum perfecti*.

Pseudo-Converbs

Converbum Conditionale

366. The *converbum conditionale* expresses an action indicating the condition under which the main action is performed.

If the main action is a *praesens* or *futurum* the conditional converb expresses a condition, e. g., "if he does."

If the main action is a *praeteritum* (past tense form) the conditional converb indicates the time at which the main action takes place: "when he did."

The suffix is *-basu/-besü* with the union vowel *-u-/-ü-* if the stem ends in *b* or *r*.

> *yabubasu* if he goes, when he went
> *yarubasu* (*yar-*) if he goes out, when he went out
> *abubasu* (*ab-*) if he takes, when he took
> *bosbasu* if he rises, when he rose
> *ögbesü* if he gives, when he gave

367. In writings of the pre-classical and, sometimes, of the classical period this converb occurs with the particle *ber*. The latter does not change the meaning. But in the modern language this converb with the particle *ber* and a negative is a concessive converb (see § 370): "although he does not," "although he did not."

> *yabubasu ber* "if he goes" or "when he went" (in pre-classical language), "although he goes" or "although he went, nevertheless . . ." (in classical and modern language).

368. In the language of popular writings the suffix is -*bala*/-*bele*, with the union vowel -*u*-/-*ü*- when the stem ends in *b* or *r*.

> *yabubala* if he goes (or) when he went
> *abubala* (*ab*-) if he takes (or) when he took
> *ögbele* if he gives (or) when he gave

369. In the language of popular writings the suffix is sometimes -*yasu*/ -*gesü* with the union vowel -*u*-/-*ü*- when the stem ends in a consonant. In the classical language only the verb *bü*- "to be" takes this suffix.

> *yabuyasu* if he goes (or) when he went
> *bügesü* if he is (or) when he was

Converbum Concessivum

370. The concessive converb expresses an action, which, although performed, does not yield the expected result, e. g., "although he promised to come, he has not."

The suffix is -*baču*/-*bečü*, with the union vowel -*u*-/-*ü*- when the stem ends in *b* or *r*.

> *yabubaču* although he goes
> *kelebečü* although he says

371. In the language of popular books the suffix is often -*bači*/-*beči*. As to the suffix -*baču*/-*bečü*, the particle *ču* may precede the converb.

> *yabubači* although he goes
> *tere ču kelebe* although he says

Converbum Imperfecti

372. The *converbum imperfecti* expresses an action performed simultaneously with the main action.

The suffix is -*ju*/-*jü* when the stem ends in a vowel, diphthong, or the consonant *l*; -*ču*/-*čü* when it ends in *γ*, *b*, *s*, *d*, *g*, and *r*.

In non-classical language the suffix is sometimes -*ji*/-*či*.

> *abču* taking　　　　　*olju* finding
> *bosču* rising　　　　　*ögčü* giving
> *kelejü* saying　　　　 *yabuju* going
> *bosči* (under colloquial influence) rising
> *yabuji* (under colloquial influence) going

Converbum Modale

373. The modal converb expresses an action indicating the manner in which the main action is performed. The action of the converb and that of the main verb are closely related or fuse into one, e. g., "to arrive riding horseback."

The suffix is *-n* with the union vowel *-u-/-ü-* if the stem ends in a consonant.

nisün (*nis-*) flying in *nisün irebe* He came flying.
güyin running in *güyin yaruba* He came out running, or He ran out.

373 a. The *converbum modale* is by origin a verbal noun. Its plural (with the suffix *-d* replacing the final *n* of this converbal form) acted in Preclassical Mongolian as a form of the present tense (vide § 413).

Converbum Perfecti

374. The *converbum perfecti* expresses an action completed before the main action starts, e. g., "he did and . . . ," "after doing . . ."
The suffix is *-γad/-ged* with a union vowel on stems ending in consonants.

yabuγad after having gone
keleged he said and . . . , after saying . . .

Genuine Converbs
Converbum Terminale

375. This converb expresses an action which marks the time limit of the main action. In certain combinations this form can also express an action which is being performed simultaneously with the main action. Thus it means "until he does" or "while he is doing."
The suffix is *-tala/-tele*.

yabutala until he goes
keletele while he was talking

Converbum Abtemporale

376. This converb expresses an action of which the inception marks the point of time at which the main action takes place, e. g., "since he died . . ." The action of this converb can be of long duration and in this case such a form means: "since the beginning and during the action," e. g., "while he was sitting."
The suffix is *-γsayar/-gseger* with the union vowel *-u-/-ü-*.

yabuγsayar while he was going
törögseger (*törö-*) since he was born

Converbum Contemporale

377. This converb expresses an action of which the inception is immediately followed by the main action, or simultaneously contemporal with that of the main action, e. g., "scarcely had he done something, when . . ."
The suffix is *-mayča/-megče* in the classical language, and *-mači/-meči* in the language influenced by colloquial dialects, with the union vowel *-u-/-ü-*, when the stem ends in a consonant.

γarumayča (*γar-*) he had scarcely gone out, when . . .
iremegče he had scarcely come, when . . .
oromayča he had scarcely entered, when . . .
barimači he had scarcely seized, when . . .

Converbum Successivum

378. The successive converb expresses an action of which the performance is immediately followed by that of the main action, e. g., "as soon as he did . . ." Sometimes this form replaces the conditional converb ("when he did . . .").

This converb does not occur in the classical language, as it is a typical colloquial form.

The suffix is *-qula/-küle*.

> *yabuqula* as soon as he started going
> *ireküle* as soon as he came, simultaneously with the arrival

Converbum Finale

379. The final converb expresses the purpose of an action and corresponds to the Latin *supinum* ("in order to . . .").

The suffix is *-r-a/-r-e* with the union vowel *-u-/-ü-*, when the stem ends in a consonant.

> *yabur-a* in order to go
> *üjer-e* in order to see

Converbum Praeparativum

380. The preparative converb expresses an action which is preparatory to and induces the main action: "in consequence of doing . . .," "as he did . . .," "because he did . . ."

This form is little used both in the classical and modern language and only a few verbs occur in this form. These are: *ügüle-* "to say, to speak," *keme-* or *geme-* "to say" (seldom), *bol-* "to become" (only in the expression *jarliy bol-* "to order"), *bü-* "to be," and *üje-* "to see." But in the pre-classical language this was a very common form.

The suffix is *-r-un/-r-ün*.

> *eyin kemen ügüler-ün* as he said in this manner
> *qayan jarliy bolur-un* as the khaghan ordered
> *barir-un* in consequence of taking
> *jobayulur-un* in consequence of causing sufferings
> *bolyar-un* in consequence of doing

Examples of Conjugation

381. The verbs *oro-* "to enter," *ire-* "to come," *od-* "to go out," and *ög-* "to give."

Imperative and Optative Forms

Imperative of the 2nd pers.:	*oro*	*ire*	*od*	*ög*
Benedictive:	*oroytun*	*iregtün*	*oduytun*	*öggügtün*
Voluntative of the 1st pers. sing.:	*orosuyaị*	*iresügeị*	*odsuyaị*	*ögsügeị*
Voluntative of the 1st pers. plur.:	*oroy-a*	*irey-e*	*oduy-a*	*öggüy-e*
Imperative of the 3rd pers.:	*orotuyaị*	*iretügeị*	*odtuyaị*	*ögtügeị*
Optative:	*oroyasaị*	*iregeseị*	*oduyasaị*	*öggügeseị*
Dubitative:	*oroyujaị*	*iregüjeị*	*oduyujaị*	*öggügüjeị*

The same examples in Mongolian script:

Imperative of the 2nd pers.:	Imperative of the 3rd pers.:
Benedictive:	
	Optative
Voluntative of the 1st pers. sing.:	Dubitative:
Voluntative of the 1st pers. plur.:	

Indicative Forms

First narrative present:	*oromuỉ*	*iremüỉ*	*odumuỉ*	*öggümüỉ*
Second narrative present:	*oronam*	*irenem*	*odunam*	*öggünem*
Deductive present:	*oroyu*	*ireyü*	*oduyu*	*öggüyü*
First past:	*oroba*	*irebe*	*odba*	*ögbe*
	orobaỉ	*irebeỉ*	*odbaỉ*	*ögbeỉ*
Second past:	*oroluγ-a*	*irelüge*	*oduluγ-a*	*öggülüge*
Third past:	*oroǰuquỉ*	*ireǰüküỉ*	*odčuquỉ*	*ögčüküỉ*

The same examples in Mongolian script:

Narrative present:

Deductive present:

First past:

Second past:

Third past:

Verbal Nouns

Nomen actoris:	*oroγči*	*iregči*	*oduγči*	*öggügči*
Nomen usus:	*orodaγ*	*iredeg*	*oduday*	*öggüdeg*
Nomen futuri:	*oroqu*	*irekü*	*odqu*	*ögkü*
	oroquį	*ireküį*	*odquį*	*ögküį*
Nomen imperfecti:	*oroγ-a*	*irege*	*oduγ-a*	*öggüge*
Nomen perfecti:	*oroγsan*	*iregsen*	*oduγsan*	*öggügsen*

The same examples in Mongolian script:

Nomen actoris:

Nomen usus:

Nomen futuri:

Nomen imperfecti:

Nomen perfecti:

Converbs

Converbum conditionale:	*orobasu*	*irebesü*	*odbasu*	*ögbesü*
	orobala	*irebele*	*odbala*	*ögbele*
Converbum concessivum:	*orobaču*	*irebečü*	*odbaču*	*ögbečü*
Converbum imperfecti:	*oroǰu*	*ireǰü*	*odču*	*ögčü*
Converbum modale:	*oron*	*iren*	*odun*	*öggün*
Converbum perfecti:	*oroγad*	*ireged*	*oduγad*	*öggüged*
Converbum terminale:	*orotala*	*iretele*	*odtala*	*ögtele*
Converbum abtemporale:	*oroγsaγar*	*iregseger*	*oduγsaγar*	*öggügseger*
Converbum contemporale:	*oromaγča*	*iremegče*	*odumaγča*	*öggümegče*
Converbum successivum:	*oroqula*	*ireküle*	*odqula*	*ögküle*
Converbum finale:	*oror-a*	*irer-e*	*odur-a*	*öggür-e*

The same examples in Mongolian script:

Converbum conditionale:				
Converbum conditionale:				
Converbum concessivum:				
Converbum imperfecti:				
Converbum modale:				
Converbum perfecti:				
Converbum terminale:				
Converbum abtemporale:				
Converbum contemporale:				
Converbum successivum:				
Converbum finale:				

Auxiliary Verbs

382. The auxiliary verbs *a-* "to be," *bü-* "to be", and *bol-* "to become" have either irregular or defective conjugations.

The Verb a-

383. Not all forms of the verb a- "to be" occur. A few forms differ from the respective forms of other verbs.

The conjugation of the verb a- "to be" is as follows:

Imperative of the 2nd pers. sing.:	does not exist
Imperative of the 2nd pers. plur.:	aytun or adqun (only pre-classical)
Voluntative of the 1st pers. sing.:	asuyai̯
Voluntative of the 1st pers. plur.:	ay-a (only pre-classical)
Imperative of the 3rd pers.:	atuγai̯
Optative:	ayasai̯ (seldom)
Narrative present:	amui̯
Deductive present:	ayu (only pre-classical)
First past:	aba or abai̯
Second past:	aluγ-a (only pre-classical)
Third past:	aǰuγu and (only pre-classical) aǰuγui̯
Nomen actoris:	ayči
Nomen usus:	does not exist
Nomen futuri:	aqu and aqui̯, plur. (only pre-classical) aqun
Nomen imperfecti:	aγ-a (only pre-classical)
Nomen perfecti:	aysan
Converbum conditionale:	abasu
Converbum successivum:	aqula (used as conditional)
Converbum concessivum:	abaču
Converbum imperfecti:	aǰu, in popular books aǰi
Converbum modale:	does not exist
Converbum perfecti:	aγad
Converbum terminale:	atala
Converbum abtemporale:	aysaγar
Converbum contemporale:	does not exist
Converbum finale:	does not exist
Converbum praeparativum:	ar-un (only pre-classical)

The current forms (voluntative, imperative of the third person, narrative present, deductive present, first past, third past, *nomen actoris, nomen futuri, nomen perfecti, converbum conditionale, successivum, concessivum, imperfecti, perfecti, terminale,* and *abtemporale*) are given in Mongolian script:

The Verb bü-

384. Only a few forms of the verb bü- "to be" have been preserved, hence its conjugation is much more defective than that of the verb a-.

Second past:	*bülüge*, in popular books *bile* (pronounced *bile*)
Third past:	*büjügü* or *büjükü̧* (only pre-classical and very rare)
Nomen perfecti:	*bügsen* (only pre-classical and very rare)
Nomen futuri:	*bükü* and *bükü̧*, plural (only pre-classical) *bükün*
Converbum conditionale:	*bügesü*
Converbum perfecti:	*büged*
Converbum terminale:	*bügetele*
Converbum praeparativum:	*bür-ün* (pre-classical and classical)

The current forms are given in Mongolian script:

The Verb bol-

385. The verb *bol-* "to become" has a regular and complete conjugation with one exception: in the pre-classical language it had the *nomen praesentis* in -*u̧*, which is a rare form. The *nomen praesentis* of this verb is *bolu̧*. It is used only as predicate and means "he is."

Another exceptional form is *bolai* "he is." No other verb has such a form.

In all other respects the conjugation of this verb is regular.

The Verb bu̧

386. This verb has but this one form, *bu̧*, which is used as noun and verb. It serves as subject ("existence" or "the existing"), as object, as attribute ("existing"), and as predicate ("exists," "is").

The deductive present and the interrogative form is *buyu* "is."

Under the influence of the colloquial language, this verb occurs sometimes in the form *bi* or *bei̧∽bai̧*.

VI. Syntax

Syntactical Peculiarities of Some Forms and Constructions

Substantives and Adjectives

387. There are no morphological differences between the simple forms of substantives and of adjectives. Therefore, the substantives and adjectives are treated as one part of speech—nouns.

Almost all nouns can serve as attributes—that is, they can function attributively as the adjectives in the European languages, e. g., *modun* "tree" means "wooden" as an attribute. But as subject or object of a sentence *modun* serves as a substantive and means "tree." On the other hand, words expressing qualities can also serve as syntactical subject or object and, in such cases, they function as the substantives in European languages, e. g., *sayin* "good" as attribute or predicate and "goodness" as syntactical subject or object.

> *öndür modun* a high tree
> *modun bayišing* a wooden building
> *sayin nökör* a good friend
> *tegün-ü sayin-i inu šinjilesügei* I shall examine his goodness.

As a substantive, a noun is characterized by the following features:

a) It is declinable.
b) It has a singular and a plural.

As an adjective, a noun is indeclinable and has a plural only in the pre-classical language.

> *mayus aran* bad people
> *busud buyan-nuyud* other benefits
> *bilig ügegün qulayas* thieves having no intellect

388. As shown above, a substantive may serve as subject, predicate, object, or attribute. It is obvious that a noun expressing a quality can serve as attribute, because words expressing such ideas as "good" or "bad" are attributive words *par excellence*. But on the other hand, they can also serve as subject or object:

> *urtu inu tabun alda amui* Its length (*urtu* "long") is five fathoms.
> *bi urtu-yi inu ese medemüi* I do not know its length.

389. Nouns indicating anything animate or inanimate can also express qualities, without undergoing any change in their grammatical form:

> *modun bayišing* a wooden building (*modun* tree, wood)
> *kümün görügesün* monkey (a man animal, *kümün* man, *görügesün* animal)

Only nouns suitable from the point of view of their meaning can serve as attributes, e. g., *surtal* "doctrine" cannot serve as an attribute unless it changes its grammatical form.

390. Nouns serving as attributes may be modified by adverbs. Of course, not all nouns may be modified by adverbs, but only those which express ideas of qualities which can be quantified, e. g., *sayin* "good" may be modified by the adverb *maši* "very," but *temür* "iron" cannot be modified by an adverb, as it is impossible to say "a very iron tool" as an antithesis to a tool which is not "very iron."

> *maši türgen* very fast, very quick
> *čab čayan* completely white

391. Many words expressing qualities can serve as adverbs.

> *yeke mayu* very bad (*yeke* great, big)
> *türgen yabuqu* to go quickly (*türgen* quick, fast)
> *sayin ungšiqu* to read well (*sayin* good)

Grammatical Number

392. Mongolian has a grammatical singular and plural. The latter is not so usual as in many other languages.

Singular

The singular is used in the following cases:

a) When speaking of a single object:

> *manu bayši irebe* Our teacher has come.
> *qayan ǰarliy bolur-un* The khaghan said (lit., "ordered").

b) When speaking of things in general or of a multitude of indeterminate size or of things of which the number is supposed to be unimportant:

> *tere yaǰar-a kümün sayuǰu ülü bolumui* In that country people (man) cannot live.
> *šine nom maryaši iremüi* New books (book) will come tomorrow.
> *ebügen qoni qariyulumui* The old man pastures sheep.
> *šibayu bariyči ebügen* an old man catching birds (bird).

c) Words qualified by numerals or words expressing a multitude are usually used in the singular form. But the plural was used in the pre-classical language in such cases (see § 393 b):

> *doloyan ebügen* Ursa Major (astron., lit., "the seven old men")
> *mingyan ǰil* a thousand years
> *qoyar kümün* two people
> *olan kümün* many people
> *kümün-ü čiyulyan* a gathering of people

d) Certain words always express a multitude and, therefore, have no plural:

> *aduyun* horses
> *mal* cattle
> *aran* people (in the pre-classical language. In modern Mongolian it is replaced by a plural form *arad* which means "ordinary man." Its plural is now *arad-ud* "working people.")

e) Words designating objects existing normally only in pairs, not as single units (ears, hands), are never used in the plural. An exception may be a case in which it is necessary to state that somewhere the ground was littered with heads and arms of injured and slain people (e. g., a battle field). On the other hand, if it is necessary to say that someone has but one eye, the word *örügesün* "single" (never *nigen* "one") is used:

örügesün nidün a single eye

örügesün köl-tei̯ kümün a one-legged man

f) Neither the nominal predicate nor the attribute agrees in number with the word qualified and in the classical language the attribute and the nominal predicate are always singular (as in English). In the pre-classical language they often agree.

sayin morid good horses

mergen lam-a-nar wise lamas

enelkün amitan suffering creatures (pre-classical)

bilig-ten burqad the wise Buddhas (pre-classical)

Plural

393. The plural is used in the following cases:

a) Mainly in reference to animate things, especially people and deities:

bodisadv-nar-un yabudal-nuyud the deeds of the Bodhisattvas

merged bayši-nar the wise teachers

luus-un qayad the kings of the dragons (*Nāgas*)

b) Words designating animate things are often used in the plural, even if they are qualified by numerals or other numerical words:

doloyan ebüged Ursa Major (lit., "seven old men")

mingyan burqad thousand Buddhas

yučin yurban tngri-ner thirty-three deities

olan čerig-üd many soldiers

c) Certain words are grammatically plural forms, but they denote single beings. If it is necessary to indicate the notion of multitude, these words take a plural suffix. Thus they will have two plural suffixes:

ekener woman∽*ekener-üd* women

sayid minister∽*sayid-ud* ministers

d) The plural of proper names indicates the person in question and all the people accompanying him:

sayid dorǰi-nar Minister Dorǰi and his retinue

e) The *pluralis majestatis* is used in reference to honorable people:

tüšimed official, sing. *tüšimel*

f) There are two pronouns of the second person of the plural: *ta* "you" and *tanar* "you." The former is used when addressing a person who may not be addressed with the familiar second singular form. The latter (*tanar*) is used in reference to a multitude (German *Ihr*).

g) There are two pronouns of the first person of the plural: *ba* "we" (exclusive) and *bida* "we" (inclusive).

The pronoun of the first person in the expression "you and I" is either *bi* "I" or *bida* "we":

> *bi či qoyar* I and you or
> *či bida qoyar* you and I (lit., "thou and we two") (See § 399.)

h) In the pre-classical language the attribute often agrees in number with the qualified word, but in the classical and modern language only a few words so agree:

> *ene kümüs* or *ede kümüs* these people
> *tede bayši-nar* those teachers
> *tede nököčeldügčid* those causes
> *busud buyan-nuɣud* other virtues
> *kilinglegsed čidküd* angry devils

i) If the predicate is a plural verb (see § 234), the subject can be either a plural or a singular, as the verb indicates that a multitude is meant:

> *čerig yabučayaǰuquị* The soldiers had gone.

The Reflexive-Possessive Suffix

394. The reflexive-possessive suffix refers to the person acting and functions in the same manner as the Latin pronoun *suus:*

> *šabi nom-iyan ungšimuị* The pupil reads his book.
> *egüde-ben tayiluǰu ög* Open your door!

395. Even adverbs of place can take this suffix. In which case they indicate the place where the actor is or whither he is moving:

> *bi tende-ben sayumuị* I am living there—at my (place).
> *čerig činayši-ban mordoba* The army rushed farther in its direction.

396. If the object concerned does not belong to the person acting or has nothing to do with the latter, the possessive suffix can not be used and the possessor of the object concerned must be indicated by the genitive either of a noun or of a personal pronoun:

> *či minu nom buu ab* Do not take my book!
> *šabi tegün-ü nom ungšimuị* The pupil reads his (not his own but someone else's) book.
> *bayši ger-tür inu sayuǰu amuị* The teacher is living in his (not his own but someone else's) house.

In such cases, the genitive of the personal pronoun of the third person *inu* (singular) or *anu* (plural) is used with the adverbs of place. This indicates the place of something which is not being identified with the person acting:

> *činayši inu talbiba* He put it farther (not farther from him but from its former place).

Numerals

General Remarks

397. In general, the use of numerals does not differ from English usage, but there are two special uses of Mongolian numerals which should be discussed here. These are: a) numerals in dates and b) numerals as conjunctions.

Dates

398. Instead of ordinal numerals in dates only cardinal numerals are used:

a) Instead of Tibetan names of days new expressions consisting of the word *gray* "planet" and a cardinal number before it, in the same way as in modern Chinese, are used:

Sunday:	*sayin edür*	Good Day
Monday:	*nige gray*	First Planet
Tuesday:	*qoyar gray*	Second Planet
Wednesday:	*yurban gray*	Third Planet
Thursday:	*dörben gray*	Fourth Planet
Friday:	*tabun gray*	Fifth Planet
Saturday:	*jiryuyan gray*	Sixth Planet

b) The months, too, are designated by cardinal numerals.

January:	*nige sar-a*	First Month
February:	*qoyar sar-a*	Second Month
March:	*yurban sar-a*	Third Month
April:	*dörben sar-a*	Fourth Month
May:	*tabun sar-a*	Fifth Month
June:	*jiryuyan sar-a*	Sixth Month
July:	*doloyan sar-a*	Seventh Month
August:	*naiman sar-a*	Eighth Month
September:	*yisün sar-a*	Ninth Month
October:	*arban sar-a*	Tenth Month
November:	*arban nige sar-a*	Eleventh Month
December:	*arban qoyar sar-a*	Twelfth Month

c) The dates of the month are also designated by cardinal numerals:

doloyan sar-a-yin qorin doloyan edür	the 27th of July
dörben sar-a-yin arban yisün edür	the 19th of April
naiman sar-a-yin qorin tabun edür	the 25th of August
arban nige sar-a-yin dörben edür	the 4th of November

d) According to an ancient tradition, months are divided into three decades: the first decade is called *šin-e* "new" (this is the new moon), the second decade is *tergel sar-a* (this is the full moon), and the last decade is *qayučin* "old" (this is the old moon).

According to this system, the second day of the first decade, i. e., the second of the month concerned, is *šin-e-yin qoyar edür* "the second day

of the new." The third day of the last decade is *qayučin-u yurban edür*
"the third day of the old."

> *arban nige sar-a-yin šin-e-yin dörben edür* the fourth day of the
> new (moon) of the eleventh month, i. e., the fourth of November
> *tabun sar-a-yin qayučin-u yurban edür* the third day of the old
> (moon) of the fifth month, i. e., the twenty-third of May.

The word *edür* "day" may be omitted:

> *tabun sar-a-yin yurban-a* on the third of the fifth month

e) The years are always designated by ordinal numbers. There are two
words for "year" in Mongolian: *on* and *jil*. The latter is used only with
the names of the twelve-year animal cycle or to express the idea of the
year as a space of time (365 days). Therefore this is used only in such
expressions as:

> *ene jil* this year
> *önggeregsen jil* last year
> *qoyitu jil* next year
> *qorin jil-ün urida* twenty years ago
> *olan jil boluysan-u qoyin-a* after many years
> *tabun jil* five years

The names of the years of the twelve-year cycle are the following:

> 1. *quluyan-a jil* mouse year
> 2. *üker jil* ox year
> 3. *bars jil* tiger year
> 4. *taulai jil* hare year
> 5. *luu jil* dragon year
> 6. *moyai jil* serpent year
> 7. *morin jil* horse year
> 8. *qonin jil* sheep year
> 9. *bečin jil* ape year
> 10. *takiy-a jil* hen year
> 11. *noqai jil* dog year
> 12. *yaqai jil* hog year

f) The other word for "year" is *on*. This expresses the idea of a year
of a period or era. Therefore, this is used with numerals to denote a
year of a period. Only ordinal numerals are used.

> *engke amuyulang-un arban qoyaduyar on* the twelfth year of K'ang-
> hsi, i. e., 1673
> *olan-a ergügdegsen-ü tabuduyar on* the fifth year of the "Pro-
> claimed-by-Many" (the title of the first and last emperor of
> Outer Mongolia who died in 1924), i. e., 1915
> *mongyol ulus-un qoriduyar on* the twentieth year of the Mongolian
> State, i. e., 1930
> *nige mingy-a yisün jayun döčin yisüdüger on* the year 1949

Numerals as Conjunctions

399. Two or more words acting as equal members of a sentence can be connected by a numeral denoting the total of the persons or objects in question. The numeral follows the words to which it refers. The numeral is *qoyar* "two," if the total of the persons in question is two; it is *ɣurban* "three," if the total is three, and so on. The numeral takes all the grammatical endings, and the nouns to which it refers have no case suffixes.

It is not exact to speak of numerals as conjunctions. It would be more nearly correct to call them aggregating terms denoting the total of the objects concerned. But this definition is too long and, therefore, with the above reservations, the numerals are here called "numerals as conjunctions."

> *bi či qoyar* I and you
> *či bida qoyar* you and I (lit., "thou and we two")
> *aq-a degüü qoyar-i* the elder and the younger brothers (accusative)
> *morin üker temegen ɣurban-dur* to the horse, ox, and camel (dative-locative)
> *qaɣan qatun qoyar-ača* from the khaghan and the queen (ablative)

Duplication

400. The duplication of a word expresses what in English can be expressed by the words "each" and "every."

A doubled subject means that each of the persons mentioned is acting. A doubled object refers to the action of each person acting.

> *tede bügüdeger ǰüg ǰüg-tür-iyen odbaị* They all started off, each in his direction. (Lit., "They all went in their direction-direction.")
> *ɣar ɣar-iyan barilčaɣabaị* They shook hands. (Lit., "They took their hands-hands.")
> *kümün kümün-dür nigen ǰoyos ögbe* He gave a coin to each man. (Lit., "He gave one coin to man-man.")

401. The idea "each other" is expressed by the duplicated word *bey-e* "body" or *nigen* "one" in the appropriate case form. The former is always used with the reflexive-possessive suffix, but in the case of *nigen* the use of the suffix is optional.

> *tede kümüs bey-e bey-e-ben üǰen yadamuị* Those people hate each other. (Lit., "Those people hate their body-body.")
> *bey-e bey-e-ben taɣalaqu* to caress each other
> *tedeger inu bey-e bey-e-degen beleg ergümüị* They present each other gifts.
> *nigen nigen-i ese üǰebe* They did not see each other.
> *nigen nigen-degen tusalamǰi üǰegülümüị* They help each other. (Lit., "One shows assistance to his one.")

402. Distributive numerals are often replaced by duplicated cardinal numbers.

tede kümüs-tür qoyar qoyar tögörig ögbei He gave each of those
people two *tögrig*. (Lit., "He gave those people two-two *tögrig*."
Tögrig is an Outer Mongolian coin.)

403. Certain converbs, too, can be doubled. In such a case they express
the gradual intensification of the action.

güičen güičen aldajuqui He almost overtook him. (Lit., "In over-
taking he failed.")

Verbal Nouns

404. The verbal nouns are participles but their functions are more varied
than those of the participles of most European languages. They are
used to designate:

a) the actor (English substantive: reader, author, speaker, and so on)
b) the process of an action (English gerund: the reading, writing, speaking, and so on
c) the idea of an action as someone's characteristic (English participle:
the reading pupil, the writing girl, and so on)
d) the idea of an action = *verbum finitum* (English indicative forms:
he reads, he wrote, and so on)

405. There are the following verbal nouns:

    a) *Nomen actoris*   d) *Nomen futuri*
    b) *Nomen praesentis*   e) *Nomen imperfecti*
    c) *Nomen usus*   f) *Nomen perfecti*

As to the functions of these verbal nouns, it must be emphasized that
they do not express any absolute time of action, but only the relative
time. For example, the *nomen futuri* does not express any action taking
place in the absolute future, but an action taking place in the future
seen from the point of view of the absolute time of the predicate: if the
latter is a present or a future tense, the *nomen futuri* is a future, but if
the predicate is a past tense, the *nomen futuri* is a future in reference to
the past. Verbal nouns express an absolute time only when they act as
predicates.

bi qayan-i jalaysan I invited the khaghan (absolute past).
jalaydaysan kümün irebe The invited man came (past in past).
The man who had been invited came.
jalaydaysan kümün iremüi The invited man will come. (Past in
reference to the future: The man who has or will have been
invited will come.)
sayin köbegün törökü em-e-yi abqu bui He will take a wife who
will bring forth a good boy (future).
sayin köbegün törökü em-e-yi abuba He took a wife who would bring
forth a good boy (future in reference to the past).

406. In the case of a predicate which is a present or future the nomen
futuri *irekü* designates:

a) one who will come (comer in the future)
b) coming (as a process) in the future (future arrival)
c) coming in the future as someone's characteristic (The man who will come)

As a predicate the *nomen futuri* is always a future tense; e. g., He will come.

On the other hand, if the predicate of the sentence concerned is in a past tense, the same *nomen futuri* designates:

a) one who had not come at that time but would come
b) coming as a process which at that time was being planned
c) coming as someone's characteristic which at that time was a future characteristic ("the man who would come")

Similarly the *nomen perfecti* does not express merely any action which took place in the absolute past, but an action which had been or has been or will have been completed, depending upon the absolute time of the finite verb.

Thus the nomen perfecti *iregsen* designates:

a) one who had come (if the predicate is a past tense)
   one who has come (if the predicate is a present tense)
   one who will have come (if the predicate is a future)
b) someone's coming which had taken place (if the predicate is a past tense)
   someone's coming which has taken place and can be now stated as an accomplished fact (if the predicate is a present tense)
   someone's coming which would have taken place in the future (if the predicate is a future tense)
c) coming as a characteristic which had been acquired in the past (if the predicate is a past tense)
   coming as a characteristic which has been acquired (if the predicate is a present tense)
   coming as a characteristic which in the future will have been considered as having been acquired in the past (the person concerned will be one who has come, if the predicate is a future)

As a predicate *iregsen* is a perfect: He has come.

407. Verbal nouns may either designate the actor or express the process of an action. Consequently, they can serve as subjects and objects:

> *suruyči nom ungšimui* The pupil (the learner) reads a book.
> *ašida sayuqu-yi buu sedki* Do not imagine that you will live forever. (Lit., "Do not imagine living forever.")
> *ene yirtinčü-yin čay samuyu boluysan-i daruyalan čidaqu qan törökü buyu* Will there be born any king able to suppress the upheaval of the time of this world?
> *aqai minu ene činu-a yabuqu-yi medebüü či* Dad, do you realize that a wolf is running there? (Lit., "Dad, do you know the going of this wolf?")

8 Poppe, Mongolian Grammar

408. The verbal nouns express actions as someone's characteristic and, therefore, they serve as attributes:

> *ükügsen kümün* the dead man (lit., "a man who has died")
>
> *irekü jil* next year (lit., "the coming year" or "the year which will come")
>
> *qoyin-a irekün jobalang-ud* the sufferings which will come later on
>
> *burtay-tu šinuqayiraqui sedkil* the thought burning with passion for sin (lit., "the thought burning with passion for uncleanness")
>
> *quričayči aran* people burning with passion
>
> *busud-i jiryayulqui küsel* the wish to give happiness to others
>
> *naran-u gerel-iyer delgeregülügsen jalayu linqus* young lotus-flowers unfolded by the rays of the sun

409. Verbal nouns express actions and, therefore, they can serve as finite verbs, i. e., as predicates of completed sentences:

> *manu bayši irege ügei* Our teacher has not come as yet.
>
> *kümün-ü bey-e-yi ber qamiy-a olqu* But where will the human body be acquired?
>
> *nadur jobalang-un qoor-a inu daki yayun j-a bolqu* What does the harm brought by these sufferings matter to me?
>
> *kerkin mayad tonilqu bi* How will I really be saved?
>
> *qamuy amitan nigen bolur-a odqu* All living beings will become the same.

410. The verbal nouns are used with converbs:

> *abču iregsen kümün* a man who has brought (lit., "a man who has come taking")
>
> *egürčü yabuysan kümün* a man who was carrying on his shoulders (lit., "a man who went carrying on his shoulders")
>
> *činu noqai-yi qarbuju alaqu bi* I shall shoot your dog. (Lit., "I shall kill shooting your dog.")
>
> *naran sar-a qoyar-i qamtu-bar jergečegülün oruyulun kigsen manglai čayan duyuly-a-ban ača* give your high white helmet made in such a manner that sun and moon were put in one beside the other!

Therefore, members of sentences can consist of a verbal noun preceded by one or more converbs. This makes the verbal nouns entirely different from deverbal nouns, i. e., nouns derived from verbs, as the latter are true nouns which can not be qualified by adverbs, whereas the verbal nouns possess all characteristics of both the nouns and verbs.

411. An important trait of the verbal nouns is that all of them, even verbal nouns of active verbs, function actively and passively.

> *yabuysan kümün* the man who has gone
>
> *yabuysan jam* the way someone has gone (lit., "the way gone")
>
> *miqa idegsen noqai* the dog which has eaten the meat
>
> *noqai-yin idegsen miqan* the meat eaten by the dog (lit., "the dog's eaten meat")

namayi üǰegsen kümün the man who saw me
minu üǰegsen kümün the man seen by me (lit., "my seen man")

Nomina verbalia of passive verbs occur often in the classical, but primarily in the pre-classical language.

> *tačiyangγuį-a endegüregüldegsen mungqay-ud* the fools misled by passion
>
> *nisvanis-ta abtaysan amitan* the living beings obsessed by vanity
>
> *küčütü-de daruydaysan-u tulada* because of being suppressed by a strong sensation

Converbs

412. The converbs do not express any absolute time of action but only the circumstances under which the main action takes place. Therefore, there is no converb expressing present or past actions. The converbs cannot act as predicates of completed sentences, but they act as a part of the predicate and, used with verbal nouns, they act as components on any part of speech.

As to the time of the action of a converb, it depends upon the time of the finite verb. This means that the time of a converb is, when considered absolutely, the past, if the finite verb is in a past tense, or it is the present, if the finite verb is in the present tense.

The converbs express actions taking place either synchronically with the action of the finite verb or before the latter, actions regarded as a consequence of the action of the finite verb, actions supposed to be the aim of the action of the finite verb, and so on. An action synchronous with the action of the finite verb in the present tense is also a present, but an action synchronous with the action of the finite verb in a past tense refers, of course, to past time, if taken absolutely.

413. Certain converbs—the *converba imperfecti, perfecti,* and *modalia*—can act as predicates of a completed sentence if there is a copula:

> *dani-yin kümüs tariyalang-un aǰil-i kiǰü buį* The people of Denmark do agricultural work (lit., "are doing").
>
> *tere kümün bidan-i qayurču amuį* That man deceives us.
>
> *bi tani mongyol kümün bolbauu geǰü sanaǰu bülüge* I thought you were a Mongol.
>
> *nökör suryayuli-dur oroyad buį* The friend has already entered a school.
>
> *čerig ǰiysayad bayimuį* The soldiers have formed into ranks.

The same converbs without a copula serve as predicates of incomplete, juxtaposed sentences within larger sentences.

> *yurban köbegün inu malaya-ban abču sögüdčü mörgübeį* His three sons took off their caps, knelt down, and bowed.
>
> *senglün ebügen mal-iyan tuyuǰu arban oyoton-a egürčü nigen yartayan yisün salay-a-tu temür uruya čirčü irebe* Old man Senglun came, driving his cattle and carrying on his back ten oghotona

(a rodent of the Lagomys family) and dragging with one hand an iron hook with nine prongs.

er-e kümün ger-tür törön keger-e ükükü A man is born at home and dies in the steppe.

The *converbum modale* was once a verbal noun and was also used as an indicative form.

Its plural form has the ending *-d* which replaces the *-n* of the singular. Forms in *-d* occur in old documents of the pre-classical language. They were usually followed by the particle *ǰe*, e. g., *uqad ǰe* "will understand."

414. The remaining converbs express the circumstances under which the action of the finite verb takes place.

a) The *converbum conditionale* expresses, if the finite verb is in a past tense, the circumstances under which the main action takes place: "when . . ."; if the main action is a present or a future, this converb · expresses actions conditioning the main action: "if . . ."

b) The *converbum concessivum* expresses an action, which, although performed, does not have the desired result: "although . . ."

c) The *converbum terminale* expresses an action regarded as a temporal limit or result of the main action: "till . . .," "unto . . .," "so that..."

d) The *converbum abtemporale* expresses an action since the inception of which that of the finite verb takes place: "since . . ."

e) The *converbum contemporale* expresses an action which is immediately followed by the main action: "scarcely had he done that, when . . ."

415. The *converba imperfecti, modale,* and *perfecti* can be used with verbal nouns. The latter can serve as any part of speech and, therefore, those converbs can act as components of compound parts of sentences: as a component of a subject, object, attribute, predicate. Thus *nisčü yabuqu:*

> as a subject: flying, flight (Lit., "the going in flying")
> as an object: *id.*
> as an attribute: flying
> as a predicate: He will fly. (Lit., "He will go in flying.")

416. Since certain converbs, as remarked above, express the circumstances under which the action of the predicate takes place, some of them have lost their original meanings and are now used as postpositions corresponding to the English prepositions:

> *boltala* until (lit., "until he becomes," *bol-* to become)
> *kürtele* till (lit., "until he reaches," *kür-* to reach)

Other converbs have become conjunctions:

> *bolun* and (lit., "becoming," *bol-* to become)
> *büged* and (lit., "having been," *bü-* to be)
> *kiged* and (lit., "having done," *ki-* to do)

The *converbum modale* of the verb *geme-* or *keme-* "to say," *gemen* or *kemen* "saying," is used as the conjunction "that": *iremüi gemen ügülebei*

"He said that he would come." (Lit., "He spoke, saying: 'I shall come.'")

The converbs of the pronominal verb *yayaki-* "to do what?" and the fossilized converbs *eyin* "doing in this manner," *teyin* "doing in that manner" are used as adverbs "how," "why," "so."

> *či yayakin irebeį* Why did you come? (Lit., "What doing didst thou come?")

> *eyin ügülebeį* He said so. (Lit., "He said doing in this manner.")

Postpositions

417. The postpositions function in the same manner as prepositions in European languages. They follow the word they govern. Most of them are of nominal origin.

The postpositions govern various cases, but primarily the genitive case. Some of them govern the simple stem of the noun, e. g., *yajar door-a* "under the earth." The postpositions will be discussed in connection with the use of the case forms. (See §§ 503, 510, 530.) Here only one particular characteristic of the postpositions will be discussed.

Many postpositions can be accompanied by a personal pronoun in the genitive. This indicates the possessor of the object designated by the word governed by the postposition:

> *ger dergede inu* by his house

Sometimes the genitive forms *inu* and *anu* are only pleonastic elements:

> *tegün-ü ger dergede inu* by his house (lit., "by his house his")

The same postpositions can also take the reflexive-possessive suffix. In this case the latter indicates that the object designated by the word governed by the postposition belongs to the person acting:

> *toluyaį deger-e-ben talbiba* He put (it) on his (own) head.

418. The postpositions governing various oblique cases will be given in the respective sections where the cases are discussed. Only such postpositions as govern the simple stem will be mentioned here.

Postpositions governing the simple stem are the following:

deger-e on:	*ayula deger-e* on the mountain
	nama deger-e on me
	tegün deger-e on him
door-a under:	*yajar door-a* under the earth
dotor-a in:	*ger dotor-a* in the house
yaruį exceeding, more than:	*arba yaruį* more than ten

Juxtaposed Nominal Groups

General Remarks

419. There are two categories of groups of juxtaposed nouns:

a) juxtaposed nouns constituting a compound word serving as a single part of sentence

b) juxtaposed nouns mutually independent and serving as two or more equal parts of sentence.

The difference between these two categories can be easily discovered by eliminating one of the two nouns from such groups: while the elimination of a noun from a group of the former category results in another word, the elimination of a member from a group of the latter category merely transforms a sentence with two equal members into a sentence with one member: e. g., instead of two direct objects there will be but one. This can be illustrated by the following examples: *γaǰar usun* "territory" consists of two words: *γaǰar* "earth" and *usun* "water"; the sentence *γaǰar usun-i anu buliyaǰu abuba* means "He took their territory." If we eliminate the word *γaǰar* "earth" the sentence *usun-i anu buliyaǰu abuba* means "He took their water." On the other hand, *ger mal-i inu buliyaǰu abuba* means "He took his house and cattle." If we eliminate the word *ger* "house" the sentence *mal-i inu buliyaǰu abuba* means "He took his cattle." The examples given above show that a compound word like *γaǰar usun* "territory" becomes something quite different, if one of the elements is eliminated, while, on the other hand, the sentence only loses one of its two objects if *ger* is eliminated from the compound *ger mal*.

Both categories possess the common trait that only the last noun of a group takes the requisite case ending. Thus, if there are two or more nouns standing in a dative-locative relation to the governing word, only the last of them takes the dative-locative suffix. The same is true of all oblique cases. Thus, in Mongolian, a case suffix can refer to a whole group of words. This resembles, to some degree, such algebraic expressions as $n(a+b)$ instead of $an+bn$. For example, *tegün-ü ger mal keüked ekener-i abuba* "He took his house, cattle, children, and wife." Here the accusative suffix refers to a whole group: *tegün-ü* $+$ *(ger mal keüked ekener)-i* $+$ *abuba*, i. e., to all words put in parentheses.

Compound Nouns

Numerals

420. In compound numbers the higher numbers are followed by the lower ones as in English: *qorin tabun* "twenty-five." The number of hundreds, thousands, ten thousands, hundred thousands, and millions is expressed by numerals placed before the numerals *ǰaγun* "hundred," *mingγan* "thousand," *tümen* "ten thousand," *bum* "hundred thousand," and so on.

All numerals ending in the consonant *n* keep it, when followed by other numerals.

> *arban nigen* eleven
> *qorin tabun* twenty-five

In the modern language the numerals *nigen* "one" and *mingγan* "thousand" often drop their final *n* when followed by other numerals.

nige mingγan one thousand
mingγa tabun ǰaγun thousand five hundred

The numeral *nigen* "one" can be omitted in such expressions as:

100 *ǰaγun* instead of *nige ǰaγun*
1,000 *mingγan* instead of *nige mingγan*
100,000 *bum* instead of *nige bum*

421. The numerals 11—19 are composed of *arban* "ten" and the respective units.

11 *arban nigen*	14 *arban dörben*	17 *arban doloγan*
12 *arban qoyar*	15 *arban tabun*	18 *arban naiman*
13 *arban γurban*	16 *arban ǰirγuγan*	19 *arban yisün*

The numerals 21—29, 31—39, 41—49, and so on consist of the numerals *qorin* "twenty," *γučin* "thirty," *döčin* "forty," and so on and the respective units.

21 *qorin nigen*	28 *qorin naiman*	84 *nayan dörben*
22 *qorin qoyar*	29 *qorin yisün*	85 *nayan tabun*
23 *qorin γurban*	31 *γučin nigen*	86 *nayan ǰirγuγan*
24 *qorin dörben*	45 *döčin tabun*	87 *nayan doloγan*
25 *qorin tabun*	51 *tabin nigen*	88 *nayan naiman*
26 *qorin ǰirγuγan*	62 *ǰiran qoyar*	89 *nayan yisün*
27 *qorin doloγan*	73 *dalan γurban*	91 *yiren nigen*
		99 *yiren yisün*

422. The numerals 200, 300, 400, 500, 2,000, 3,000, 4,000, 5,000, and so on are composed of the respective units and the words *ǰaγun* "hundred" and *mingγan* "thousand."

100 *ǰaγun* or *nige ǰaγun*	1000 *mingγan* or *nige mingγan*
200 *qoyar ǰaγun*	2000 *qoyar mingγan*
300 *γurban ǰaγun*	3000 *γurban mingγan*
400 *dörben ǰaγun*	4000 *dörben mingγan*
500 *tabun ǰaγun*	5000 *tabun mingγan*
600 *ǰirγuγan ǰaγun*	6000 *ǰirγuγan mingγan*
700 *doloγan ǰaγun*	7000 *doloγan mingγan*
800 *naiman ǰaγun*	8000 *naiman mingγan*
900 *yisün ǰaγun*	9000 *yisün mingγan*

423. The word expressing the concept of "ten thousand" is *tümen*. Combined with the numerals *nigen, qoyar, γurban*, and so on, this expresses the concepts of "ten thousand," "twenty thousand," "thirty thousand," and so on. But the same concepts can be also expressed by the numerals *arban, qorin, γučin*, and so on, and *mingγan* "thousand." Thus there are two systems: either two ten-thousand (*tümen*) or twenty thousand (*mingγan*).

10,000 *tümen* or *nige tümen* or *arban mingγan*
20,000 *qoyar tümen* or *qorin mingγan*
30,000 *γurban tümen* or *γučin mingγan*
40,000 *dörben tümen* or *döčin mingγan*

50,000 *tabun tümen* or *tabin mingyan*
60,000 *ǰiryuyan tümen* or *ǰiran mingyan*
70,000 *doloyan tümen* or *dalan mingyan*
80,000 *naiman tümen* or *nayan mingyan*
90,000 *yisün tümen* or *yiren mingyan*

Numbers such as 12,000, 15,000, and so on are expressed by the word *tümen* "ten thousand" and the respective thousand or by the numerals twelve, fifteen, and so on, and *mingyan* "thousand."

11,000 *nige tümen nige mingyan* or *arban nige mingyan*
12,000 *nige tümen qoyar mingyan* or *arban qoyar mingyan*
13,000 *nige tümen yurban mingyan* or *arban yurban mingyan*
14,000 *nige tümen dörben mingyan* or *arban dörben mingyan*
15,000 *nige tümen tabun mingyan* or *arban tabun mingyan*

In the same manner, numbers such as 24,000, 36,000, and so on, can be expressed either by *tümen* or *mingyan* with the respective numerals:

25,000 *qoyar tümen tabun mingyan* or *qorin tabun mingyan*
32,000 *yurban tümen qoyar mingyan* or *yučin qoyar mingyan*

424. The hundred thousands can be expressed in two different manners: with the numerals 200, 300, etc. and *mingyan* "thousand" or with the numerals two, three, and so on, and the Tibetan word *bum* <*ḥbum* "hundred thousand."

200,000 *qoyar ǰayun mingyan* or *qoyar bum*
300,000 *yurban ǰayun mingyan* or *yurban bum*
500,000 *tabun ǰayun mingyan* or *tabun bum*

425. Only the last word of such groups takes the necessary grammatical ending:

arban doloduyar the seventeenth
arban yisüdüger the nineteenth
qorin tabuduyar the twenty-fifth
mingyan tabun ǰayun tabin yurbaduyar the one thousand five
    hundred and fifty-third
arban tabun-ača from fifteen
qorin-tabun-u of twenty-five

Compound Nouns

426. Compound nouns are pairs of words. The meaning of any given pair is not a mechanical total of the meaning of each element taken separately. Thus *oron toy-a* ("place-number") is "office staff" or "personnel," not "number of places." Such pairs are sometimes called binoms.
There are binoms consisting of two synonymous nouns but, on the other hand, there are also binoms of which the component parts have opposite meanings. Binoms are very numerous and dictionaries contain many of them. Only a few examples will be given here.

emegel qaǰayar (saddle-bridle) harness
öngge düri (color-shape) appearance

ǰer ǰebseg (top of a lance-weapon) arms
buǰar bulai̯ (dirt-vice) immorality
ači tusa (merit-usefulness) benefit
erke čilüge (right-freedom) liberty
γaǰar usun (earth-water) territory
küi̯ten qalaγun (cold-hot) temperature
oroly-a ǰaruly-a (income-expenditure) budget
urtu boγoni (long-short) length
γal usun in: *γal usun-u aγul* (fire-water) fatal emergency
čaγ uliral (time-vicissitude) climate
erdem soyul (science-civilization) culture
kög daγun (tune-song) music

427. Only the second component of a binom takes the requisite case suffix.

čaγ uliral-un of the climate (genitive)
ači tusa-bar through the benefit (instrumental)
küi̯ten qalaγun-i the temperature (accusative)

Juxtaposed Equal Parts of Sentence

428. Juxtaposed equal parts of a sentence can be connected by means of conjunctions, but the latter are not indispensable and such groups of words may be used without them.

The simplest case of juxtaposition is a group of two nouns not connected by anything.

idegen umdaγan-u amtan-i kelen medekü The tongue knows the taste of food (and) drink.

ečige eke-degen ači qariγulqu to return the benefits to one's own father (and) mother

tedeger inu tala aγulas-iγar negüdellemüi̯ They transhume along the plains (and) mountains.

429. The most usual conjunction is a numeral indicating the total of the objects concerned and occupying the place after the last word of such a group. The numeral can take any grammatical ending.

bi či qoγar-i me and you (accusative; lit., "me thee two")

baγši šabi qoγar-tur to the teacher and the pupil (lit., "to the teacher, the pupil, two")

qaγan qatun tayiǰi γurban-dur to the khaghan, the queen, and the prince (lit., "to the khaghan, the queen, the prince, three")

tere ebügen emegen qoγar yeke bayan aγsan aǰuγu That old man and the old woman were very rich.

köbegün tayaγ süke qoγar-iγan abuγad eke-degen kürčü iremüi̯ The boy has taken his stick and axe and comes to his mother.

buruγu ǰöb qoγar-i ilγaqu to distinguish between good and bad.

430. There are several conjunctions. One of them is *ba* "and." In the classical and modern language this occupies the place before the last word of a group (as the English "and").

Only the last word (noun) of a group takes the requisite case suffix, but plural suffixes are taken by all words, if it is necessary to point out that each of them expresses a multitude.

> *omoγ kiged ülü süsülküį ba tusalan ülü keregleküį kiged γadaγadu-da alγasquį ba sedkil-iyen quričaquį kiged uyidquį-bar sonosquį anu kkir-tü bolaį* Pride and lack of faith, not taking care to be useful, passion for external things, passion in thoughts, and hearing with boredom are unclean.
>
> *qaγan ba albatan* the khaghan and the subjects
> *ene ba tere γaǰar-a* in this and in that country
> *ene ba qoyitu nasun-dur* in this and in the future life
> *tngri-ner asuri-nar ba olan amitan-nuγud-tur* to the gods, the Asura-deities, and to all the living beings
> *ene nom-un gün ba gün busu-yin kedüį bükü kiri-yi üǰesü* I shall see what the degree of the profoundness and ("or" is better here) the shallowness of this doctrine is.

431. In the pre-classical language the conjunction *ba* may be repeated after each word of a group. Here, too, only the last word takes the requisite case suffix.

> *surtaban ba sakardagam ba anagam ba arqad ba bratikabud ba dörben ǰüg-ün ayaγ-qa tegimlig-ün quvaraγ-ud-tur* to the Çrōta-āpanna and Sakṛidāgāmī, Anāgāmī, and Arkhat, and Pratyēka-Buddhas, and the monkhood of the four quarters

432. Instead of *ba* another conjunction, *kiged*, is used often. The latter is the *converbum perfecti* of the verb *ki-* "to do" and its literal translation is "having done" or "he did and ..."

In the classical and modern language *kiged* is placed before the last word of a group, but in the pre-classical language and even in the early stage of the classical period *kiged* was placed after the last word of a group and took the requisite case suffix.

> *qaγan kiged qatun* the khaghan and the queen
> *eldeb erdenis ünürten küǰis kiged-i ergümüį* I offer various jewels and incense.

433. The conjunctions *bolun* and *büged* are converbs of the verbs *bol-* "to become" and *bü-* "to be." They are used as conjunctions connecting nouns in the same manner as the above-mentioned conjunctions with the difference that they cannot be put at the end of a group.

> *bayši büged šabi* the teacher and the pupil
> *eldeb erdenis bolun küǰis-i ergümüį* I offer various jewels and incense.

434. As stated above, only the last word of a group takes the case suffix. Yet, if there are more than three equal parts of speech, each pair of words may take a common case suffix; compound words always take them.

> *ekener keüked-iyen aduγu mal-iyan abču* taking his wife and children, his horses and cattle

tegün-ü küiten qalayun-i könggen kündü-yi ülü medemüi One does
not know its temperature or weight.

435. If each of the equal parts of sentence has an attribute qualifying
only it, each word of a group obtains the requisite case suffix.

bi kögšin eke-lüge-ben bay-a degüü-lüge-ben qamtu sayuju amui I am
living together with my old mother and my little brother.

436. In the modern language, verbal noun forms cannot be connected
with conjunctions nor are there any groups of verbal forms as there are
in English, e. g., "He saw and recognized him." In one sentence there
can be only one finite verb and all the remaining verbs must be converbs.
Only verbal nouns can constitute groups of equal parts of sentence.
They can be used together without conjunctions or they can be connected
by the conjunction *büged* or (rarely) *kiged*.

tegün-i medegsen büged darui kemjiy-e-nügüd-i abuysan amui He
learned it and immediately took measures.

437. In the pre-classical language there occurred groups of indicative
forms connected by the conjunction *kiged*.

sečeg-üd-iyer takimui kiged . . . terigüten čimeg-üd-iyer takimui I
sacrifice with flowers and I sacrifice with . . . and other jewels
(lit., "adornments").

The Sentence
The Members of a Sentence

438. The main members of a sentence are the subject, predicate, object,
and attribute. A sentence may consist of only a subject and predicate
without an object or attribute. The subject, too, may be omitted, if it
is understood.

The Subject

439. The subject is always the nominative case of a declinable part of
speech: a noun, a pronoun, a numeral, or a verbal noun.
The subject usually occupies the place before the predicate, but in the
pre-classical language and, under the influence of the colloquial language,
in modern popular books it sometimes occupies the place after the
predicate.

a) Noun as subject:

bayši irebe The teacher came.

mungqay ese medemüi The fool does not know.

qan köbegün yeke bolba The prince (lit., "the khan's son") became
big (i. e., an adult).

jiryuyan üsüg orčilang-ača getülgekü ongyoča sal mön The six
letters (i. e., the syllables *om ma ni pad me hum*) are the ship
rescuing from the rebirths.

ebügen nočoba juru-yi The old man struggled with Juru.

irebe geser Geser came.

b) Pronoun as subject:

bi ese üjebe I have not seen.

bi nigen čay-tu nökör-lüge-ben aryamji-bar usun-ača morin-i yaryabaị Once, together with my friend, I pulled a horse from the water with a rope.

bi nige šibayu alabaị I killed a bird.

ken iregsen buị Who has come?

ene yayun buị What is this?

či qamiy-a odumuị Where will you go?

c) Numeral as subject:

qoyar anu daqutaị qoyar anu daqu ügeị Two of them have put on fur coats, two of them have no fur coats. (Lit., "Their two with fur coats, their two without fur coats.")

tede yurban ali buị kemebesü if one asks what those three are, . . .

d) Verbal noun as subject:

suruyči ungšimuị The pupil (lit., "the learning") reads.

suruysan dalaị, suruy-a ügeị balaị One who has learnt is an ocean (of wisdom); one who has not learnt is blind.

yabuysan inu yasu möljikü, kebtegsen inu kegeli-ben aldaqu One who has gone will gnaw at a bone; one who has lain down will lose his belly (i. e., will starve). This is a proverb meaning that one who works will have food and one who is idle will die of starvation.

e) Verbal-nominal construction (see sections 642—643) as subject:

manu bayši-yin bičigsen inu čöm ünen buị Everything our teacher has written is true.

ene čay samayu boluysan inu er-e em-e qoyar-ača bolba The fact that the present times are troubled comes from the man and (his) wife.

jegün nidü-ben qaraysan minu ene jayayan tere jayayan qoyar-i tegši qaraysan minu buyu That I looked (into the distance) with my left eye means that I considered this life and that (i. e., the future) life equal.

440. It has been stated that the subject is usually placed before the predicate.

In the pre-classical language, personal and demonstrative pronouns are often placed after the finite verb. Sometimes a personal pronoun is placed, as usual, before the predicate, but is repeated after the latter.

tere metü jalbarin ügülemüị bi I am praying in that manner.

qamuy teden-ü ilede anu nasuda sayuju amu bi I shall live always, evident to all of them.

yar köl terigüten-iyen tebčiküị-e ayumu bi I fear I shall lose my hands, feet, and so on.

ükül-ün ejen-ü aman-dur oduysan-iyan ejiyede ese kü medebe či You never knew that you had gone into the mouth of the Master of the Death.

yekin ene metü nuta amuḭ či Why are you so calm?
inegeldüküḭ-yi yekin tayalamu či Why do you like laughter?
öd ügeḭ orčin tögerin yabumu tede They go around aimlessly.
čimayi bi ene edür minu dergede sayu gejü ese kelebeüü bi Did I
    not tell you to sit by me today?

This repetition of the pronoun after a verb has produced personal endings
on verbal forms in certain colloquial languages, e. g., in Buriat, Kalmuck,
and others, e. g., Buriat *bi abanab* I take, *ši abanaš* you take, etc.

441. As said above, the subject is a nominative. Not infrequently the
subject is emphasized by special words: *inu* or *anu, bolbasu, bügesü, ber*.
The latter are the so-called subject designators. They will be discussed
in the sections dealing with the nominative (§§ 495—499).

The Predicate

442. The predicate is a verb, a noun, a pronoun, or a numeral. The predicate is placed after the subject, although, as remarked above (§ 440),
the subject is sometimes placed after the predicate.
The predicate is the most important member of the sentence and is
omitted only in some inscriptions or signboards, e. g., *utasun medegen-ü
qoriy-a* "telegraph." But old book titles are always complete sentences
with a predicate, e. g., *altan gerel kemekü yeke kölgen sudur orošibaḭ* "The
Mahāyāna Sūtra called the Golden Ray (i. e., *Suvarṇaprabhāsa*) has
begun."

443. A verbal predicate is either an imperative, optative, or indicative
form. Such a predicate does not need a copula.
All other sorts of predicate have a copula. The latter is a finite verb of
an auxiliary verb.
A predicate in the form of a converb always has a copula, as, without
the latter, the sentence could not be complete. If the predicate is a noun,
pronoun, numeral, or verbal noun, the copula can be omitted. A predicate expressed with one of the latter parts of speech is a nominal predicate.

Verbal Predicate

Imperative or optative as predicate:
    ta čaḭ uyuytun You, drink tea!
    bi tegün-i üjesügeḭ Let me see it!

Indicative forms as predicates:
    šabi ungšimuḭ The pupil reads.
    bayši irebeḭ The teacher has come.

Converbal Predicate

Converbum imperfecti as predicate:
    bi ende sayuju amuḭ I am living here.
    šabi ungšiju amuḭ The pupil is reading.

Converbum modale as predicate:

> *šibayun nisüin irebe* The bird flew in. (Lit., "came flying.")
> *ebügen güįn yaruba* The old man ran out. (Lit., "Went out running.")

Nominal Predicate

Noun as predicate:

> *tanu köbegün bayši bolba* Your son became a teacher.
> *tegün-ü üge qudal amuį* His speech is a lie.
> *ene morin sayin buį* This horse is good.

Pronoun as predicate:

> *tere yurba ali buį* What are those three?
> *ene kümün ken buį* Who is this person?

Numeral as predicate:

> *kümün-ü erdem yurban buį* Man's virtues are three.

Verbal noun as predicate:

> *tere kümün ükügsen ajuyu* That man had been dead.
> *či qamiy-a odqu buį* Where will you go?

As said above, the copula can be omitted:

> *suruysan dalaį, suruy-a ügeį balaį* One who has learnt is an ocean (of wisdom), one who has not learnt is blind.
> *ene yayun* What is this?
> *qoyar anu daqutaį, qoyar anu daqu ügeį* Two of them are with fur coats, two of them are without fur coats.
> *nasun inu tabun* His age is five.
> *tere kümün ükügsen* That man is dead.

444. There is no agreement in number of person between the predicate and subject. As all indicative forms refer to all persons of both singular and plural, there cannot be any such agreement.

In the pre-classical language there seemed to be agreement in gender between the predicate and subject (sometimes also object) as there were several verbal forms used only in reference to female beings. These were the past tense in -*ba*/-*bi* referring to male and female beings, respectively, the past tense in -*juyu*/-*jiyaį* (-*jiyi*) referring to male and female respectively, but in the classical and modern language there is no such agreement.

The imperative and certain optative forms refer to definite persons, although in popular books even these forms are not always used in reference to the same persons.

The nominal predicate does not agree with the subject in number today, but in the pre-classical language there was agreement in number between the verbal noun and the subject.

> *bi (či, bayši, bida, ta, bayši-nar) iremüį* I (thou, the teacher, we you, the teachers) will come.
> *bi iresügeį* Let me come!

či buu ire Do not come!

šabi iretügei̯ Let the pupil come!

bida maryaši irey-e We shall come to-morrow.

ta iregtün You, come please!

bi (či, bayši, bida, ta, bayši-nar) iregesei̯ If only I (thou, the teacher, we, you, the teachers) came!

manu bayši sayin Our teacher is good.

manu bayši-nar sayin Our teachers are good.

The following sentences taken from a pre-classical work (*Bodhicaryāva-tāra*) are examples of agreement in number between the predicate and subject:

> *qamuy tngri-ner asuri-nar ker ber minu dayisun bolbasu ber tede ber ayus tamu-yin yal-un dotor-a uduridču oroyulun ülü čidaqun* Even if all deities and Asura became my enemies, they could not lead me into the fire of the horrible hell.

> *meses-iyer ǰočilalduqun ber . . . sečeg-üd uyurulčaqun boltuqai̯* Let those stabbing with knives begin strewing flowers!

> *minu buyan-u küčün-dür tngri-ner-ün bey-e olǰu bürün tngri-ner-ün ökid-lüge nigen-e . . . nayur-tur aqun boltuyai̯* Let them be together with the daughters of the deities in the lake, because they have obtained divine bodies by virtue of my *puṇya*.

Sometimes the predicate is a plural of a verbal noun while the subject is formally a singular:

> *kölösün ögküi̯ talbiysan-u šiltaya-bar ene ba qoyiči ber töröl-ün tusa inu ebderekün* Because of suspension of payment of wages, the profit of this rebirth and the future one will break down.

445. The nominal predicate is a nominative or an oblique case.

minu aq-a blam-a bui̯ My elder brother is a lama.

ene nom minu bui̯ This book is mine.

mori unuqui̯ dur-a-bar, ekener abqui̯ ǰayaya-bar Riding horseback is something depending upon one's desire; marrying is something depending upon destiny. (A proverb; lit. "Riding horseback—through desire, marrying—through destiny.")

The Object

446. The object is a word governed by either a verb or a noun. There are two main types of object: an object governed directly by a verb or a noun, and an object governed by a postposition.

Any declinable part of speech can serve as an object which is always an oblique case. Of the cases the only one which is not directly governed by a verb is the genitive, but it can depend upon a verb, if there is a postposition.

The object usually immediately precedes the governing word, but, if the latter is a verb, the object sometimes follows the verb, especially in poetical works of the pre-classical period, but also in popular books of recent periods.

Object governed by a noun:

> *mal-iyar bayan* rich in cattle

Object governed by a verb:

> *bi tegün-i ese medemüi* I do not know it.

Object with a postposition:

> *amitan-u tula buyan üiledkü* to practise virtue for the sake of living beings

447. Just as in other languages, there is a direct and an indirect object. The direct object takes an accusative suffix or no suffix whatever. Only transitive verbs govern a direct object. In many cases the equivalent of an English transitive verb is an intransitive one in Mongolian and *vice versa*.

Verbs which are transitive in both Mongolian and English:

ala- to kill	*ol-* to find
ab- to take	*yabuyul-* to send
ög- to give	*usadqa-* to liquidate

Verbs which are intransitive in both Mongolian and English:

ükü- to die	*sayu-* to sit down
umta- to sleep	*ire-* to come
kebte- to lie down	*nis-* to fly

Verbs which are intransitive in Mongolian but transitive in English:

asayu- to ask	*ayu-* to fear

448. As remarked above, the object precedes the predicate. As for the subject, it precedes the object. The usual word order in a sentence is Subject — Object—Predicate.

> *šabi nom ungšimui* The pupil reads a book.
> *bi tegün-i ese medemüi* I do not know it.

In popular books and in the pre-classical language, especially in poetry, the object may follow the predicate.

> *erten-ü burqad ker dügüregsen bolqu öglige baramid* How could the Buddhas of the former (time) complete the *Pāramitā* of alms?
> *uran ber busu bi nayirayulun jokiyaqui-a* I am not skilful in writing poetry.
> *minu kücü-ber abtaqui tegün-i* It is necessary to take him by my strength.
> *jobalang-ud qotala bolbai öber-iyen jiryaqui küseküi-eče* The sufferings became enormous as a consequence of the desire to be happy himself.
> *čiyulyabasu tere bodičid sedkil-i qoyar jüil kemen uqaydaqui* If one summarizes that holy idea (the accusative follows here *čiyulyabasu*), it must be understood that it consists of two categories.

449. When there are several objects depending upon the same word, the object which bears the logical stress is placed immediately before the governing word.

bi čimadur qoyar bičig ilegebe I sent you *two letters.*
bi qoyar bičig čimadur ilegebe I sent two letters *to you.*

450. Only the last of a group of equal objects takes the requisite case suffix. When equal objects are followed by a numeral serving as a conjunction (or by the conjunction *kiged* in the pre-classical language, see § 399, 432) the grammatical ending is taken by the latter.

qayan inu qatun tüšimed kiy-a-nar-iyan dayudabaị The khaghan called his wife, officers, and adjutants.

negüdelčin arad-ud anu ger mal ekener keüked-iyen dayayulun negüdellemüị The nomads transhume carrying with them (lit., "letting follow") their tents, cattle, wives, and children.

köbegün tayay süke qoyar-iyan abuyad eke-degen kürčü iremüị The boy has taken his stick and axe and comes to his mother.

bi čečeg küjis sayin ünürten kiged-i takin ergümüị I offer flowers, sticks of incense, and perfume.

451. An active verb with a direct object can be converted into a passive one. In such a case, the direct object (an accusative or a suffixless form) becomes the grammatical subject and the subject becomes an object. The logical agent is expressed by a dative-locative (*dativus actoris*).

qonin činu-a-dur bariydaba The sheep was caught by the wolf.

ken-dür ču ülü dabaydaqu ayula a mountain impossible to scale by anybody

ada-dur bariydaysan kümün a person possessed by the devil

jobalang-a daruydaysan kümün a man overwhelmed by sufferings

tačiyangyuị-a abtaysan amitan the living beings possessed by vanity

Verbal nouns serving as attributes are rarely used in the passive in the classical and modern language. Even to express passive actions (to be taken, to be eaten, etc.) active verbal nouns are used more frequently. The logical agent is in such cases a genitive (*genitivus actoris*).

noqaị-yin idegsen miqan the meat eaten by the dog

minu bičigsen bičig a letter written by me

burqan-u nomlaysan nom the law preached by Buddha

The literal translation of such a group of words is "the dog's eaten meat." This does not mean "dog's meat which has been eaten (by someone)" but "meat which was eaten by the dog." As for "meat of a dog which has been eaten," this would be *idegsen noqaị-yin miqan* where, as we see, the order of words is different, so that there cannot be any misunderstanding.

The Attribute

General Remarks

452. Any declinable part of speech can be qualified by a word particularizing the idea expressed by the former. Such a word qualifying another serves as an attribute.

A noun with an attribute:
>
> *sayin nökör* the good friend

A pronoun with an attribute:
>
> *üčügüken bi* little I

A substantivated numeral as an attribute:
>
> *baraγun dörben* the right hand (i. e., the Western)
>
> Four (a Mongol group)

A verbal noun with an attribute:
>
> *sayin suruγči* the good pupil (lit., "learning")

The attribute can be a noun, a pronoun, a numeral, or a verbal noun.

Noun as an attribute:
>
> *modun bayišing* a wooden building
>
> *sayin nökör* a good friend

Pronoun as an attribute:
>
> *ene kümün* this person
>
> *yambar nom* what book

Numeral as an attribute:
>
> *γurban erdeni* the Three Jewels (i. e., Buddha, his teachings, and the Buddhist clergy)
>
> *γutuγar bölög* third chapter

Verbal noun as an attribute:
>
> *irekü ǰil* next year (lit., "the year to come")
>
> *ükügsen kümün* the dead person

Verbal nouns may be linked with converbs. Thus a converb can be a component element of an attribute:

> *nisčü iregsen šibaγun* a bird which came flying
>
> *nom ungšiǰu saγuγsan kümün* a person who was sitting and reading

453. The attribute is always placed before the word to which it refers. An exception is the genitive of the personal pronoun serving as an attribute, which is placed after the word to which it refers. The genitive of the pronouns of the third person *inu* "his" and *anu* "their" is always placed after the word concerned and never before the latter, although in the most ancient texts (in the language of the *Secret History* which is not Written Mongolian) it may be placed either before or after.

> *minu aq-a* or *aq-a minu* my elder brother
>
> *manu bayši* or *bayši manu* our teacher
>
> *nom inu* his book

As these cases are the only exceptions, it may be better not to regard them as cases of an attribute. In such cases, the personal pronoun has almost become a possessive suffix. Such suffixes exist in Colloquial Mongolian (e. g., Khalkha *dūmin* "my younger brother", *dūtšin* "your younger brother", Buriat *axam* "my elder brother", *axašni* "your elder brother", and so on). It is also important to point out that such pronouns in postnominal position become enclitics, lose their stress, and change in form to *mini, čini, mani, tani*:

aq-a mini my elder brother
aq-a čini your elder brother

454. The attribute does not agree in case with the qualified word. In the classical and modern language it does not agree in number either, but in the pre-classical language there was agreement in number. In the classical language only the demonstrative pronouns agree.

ene kümün this person
ede nököd these friends
qoyin-a irekün jobalang-ud the sufferings which will come afterward
eldeb yirtinčü-dür bükün qoor-nuγud various sufferings existing in the world
enelkün amitan suffering living beings
jobalang-a tenčirdegsed amitan living beings overwhelmed by sufferings
yeke bilig-ten burqad the Buddhas possessing great wisdom
sansar-un gindan-dur enelkün amitan living beings suffering in the prison of the material existence
mayus aran bad people
busud buyan-nuγud other virtues
bilig ügegün qulayas thieves not having any intellect

455. As remarked above, the attribute does not agree in case with the word qualified. Regardless of the case of the word qualified, the attribute is a nominative, just as in English.

Nominative	*sayin morin* the good horse
Genitive	*sayin morin-u* of the good horse
Dative-Locative	*sayin morin-dur* to the good horse
Accusative	*sayin morin-i* the good horse
Ablative	*sayin morin-ača* from the good horse
Instrumental	*sayin mori-bar* with the good horse
Comitative	*sayin morin-luγ-a* together with the good horse

Thus the attribute is always a nominative. Another kind of attribute is the genitive attribute, showing to whom the object concerned belongs, e. g., *aq-a-yin nom* "the book of the elder brother."

The Nominative as Attribute

The Noun as Attribute

456. Nouns expressing qualities and serving as adjectives in European languages are always nominative, regardless of the case of the word they modify.

ulayan čilayun the red stone
sayin nom the good book
jegerde morin a chestnut horse
türgen γool a fast river (i. e., a torrent)
öndür ayula a high mountain
möngke tngri the eternal heaven

9*

    γuu-a ökin a beautiful girl
    kögšin em-e an old woman
    bay-a keüken a little child

457. Although there is no grammatical gender, words expressing the age and the coat of animals have double forms: a masculine and a feminine one.

    γunan buqa a three-year-old bull
    γunaǰin üniy-e a three-year-old cow
    dönen buqa a four-year-old bull
    döneǰin üniy-e a four-year-old cow
    ulaγan buqa a red bull
    ulaγayčin üniy-e a red cow
    šir-a γaqai̯ a yellow boar
    širayčin γaqai̯ a yellow sow

The last two examples show that names of animals referring both to the male and the female may be qualified by an attribute in a masculine form, when the animal concerned is a male, and in a feminine form, when the animal concerned is a female. Here are some additional examples:

    čaγan takiy-a a white cock
    čaγayčin takiy-a a white hen
    boro qarčaγai̯ a grey hawk
    boroγčin qarčaγai̯ a grey female hawk

458. Nouns designating material and corresponding to European substantives are also in the nominative case.

    modun bayišing a wooden building (lit., "wood building")
    altan bilečüg a golden ring (lit., "gold ring")
    mönggün kituγ-a a silver knife
    temür ǰida an iron spear
    čilaγun süm-e a stone temple

459. Nouns designating living beings may also serve as attributes in the nominative.

    eme takiy-a hen (lit., "a female cock" or even "a woman cock")
    ebügen kümün an old man (lit., "oldster person")
    kümün görügesün ape (lit., "a man animal")
    lama šibaγun a yellow duck (lit., "a lama bird", so called because of its reddish-yellow color resembling a coat of a lama. Its Latin name is *anas nigra L.*)
    tarbaγan kümün dwarf (lit., "a marmot man")
    morin qaračaγai̯ wagtail (lit., "a horse-swallow")
    morin ǰil the horse year (the seventh year of the duodenary cycle)
    üker quluγan-a rat (lit., "an ox mouse")
    üker buu cannon (lit., "an ox gun")
    qan širegen throne (lit., "a khan seat")
    qaγan köbegün prince (lit., "a khaghan's son")

The Pronoun as Attribute

460. All pronouns, except the personal and reflexive pronouns, can serve as attributes in the nominative.

ene kümün this person
aliba kümün whatever person
ken kümün what man (lit., "who man")
yambar ču kümün whatever person, any person
ele kereg this business

461. The demonstrative pronouns agree in number with the word qualified. This is usual in the classical language and at times also occurs in modern books.

ene kümün this person
ede (or edeger) kümün-nügüd these people
tere kümün that person
tede (or tedeger) kümüs those people

The Numeral as Attribute

462. All numerals, except the collective and multiplicative numerals, serve as attributes.

qoyar qani two friends
tabuduyar boti the fifth volume
arbayad kümün about ten people

The Verbal Noun as Attribute

463. All verbal nouns serve as attribute in the nominative case. In the pre-classical language they agreed in number with the word to which they referred.

irekü jil next year (lit., "the year which will come")
ungšiyči šabi the reading pupil
ükügsen kümün a dead person
aburayči yurban erdeni the saving Three jewels (i. e., Buddha, his
    teachings, and the Buddhist clergy)
enelkün amitan the suffering creatures (pre-classical)
jobaysad amitan the suffering creatures (pre-classical)

The Compound Nominal Attribute

464. Compound nouns serve as attributes. A compound nominal attribute may consist of two words, jointly expressing one idea. A very usual compound nominal attribute is a group of words denoting a color. In this manner the idea of various shades of colors can be expressed.

küren ulayan debel a dark red coat
šir-a ulayan čiraį a yellow-red face
qurča ulayan öngge glaring red color
qar-a eriyen bars a black-dappled tiger

465. A compound attribute often consists of a noun expressing a color preceded by another word designating something of which the main characteristic is the color in question, e. g., "snow-white."

čisun ulaɣan tuɣ a blood-red flag
ɣal ulaɣan öngge fire-red color
altan šir-a naran gold-yellow sun
časun čaɣan čaɣasun snow-white paper
dung čaɣan šidün shell-white teeth
ünegen ulaɣan üsün fox-red hair

466. Another kind of compound attribute is a group of words of which
one designates an object and the other a quality. Such groups correspond
to the English "barefooted," "pink-faced," etc., with the difference that
in Mongolian the order of the words is reversed: not "barefooted" but
"foot-bare."

köl ničügen kümün a barefooted person (lit., "a foot-naked person")
am-a čaɣan quluɣan-a a mouse with a white mouth (lit., "a mouth-
white mouse")

Diminutives as Attributes

467. The diminutive suffix *-qan/-ken* (cf. § 124) of a noun serving as an
attribute often transforms the word qualified into a diminutive without
affecting the meaning of the stem to which it refers. In other words, the
diminutive suffix, although belonging to one word, changes the meaning
of the following word.

ulaɣaqan (diminutive) *čečeg* a nice little red flower or a red floweret
baɣaqan (diminutive) *morin* a nice little horse

In the above examples the words *čečeg* "flower" and *morin* "horse" are
not diminutives, but their attributes are diminutives. Nevertheless, we
translate them as "floweret" and "nice horse," because the diminutive
suffixes on their attributes refer to them and not to the attributes.

468. In the same manner, the feminine forms of words expressing the
ages or colors of animals not having different names for males and
females indicate that the animal in question is a female (see § 457).

qar-a šibaɣun a black male bird
qaraɣčin šibaɣun a black female bird
dönen ǰaɣan a four-year-old male elephant
döneǰin ǰaɣan a four-year-old female elephant

Apposition

469. There is but one type of apposition in Mongolian: that of a noun
serving as the proper name given to a person or an object.
Proper names, names of persons, cities, rivers, mountains, countries, and
so on, are usually followed by an appellative. This means that the proper
name is placed first and only the appellative takes the grammatical ter-
mination. As for the proper name, it is always a nominative regardless
of the case of the appellative.

činggis qan Chingis Khan
činggis qan-dur to Chingis Khan
kentei̯ aɣula the Kentei mountain range

ulaɣan baɣatur qota the city of Ulan Bator
ulaɣan baɣatur qotan-a in the city of Ulan Bator

470. In cases of less common proper names, the proper name is linked to the appellative noun by the converb *kemen* and the word *nere-tü* "bearing the name."

ranǰaɣray kemen nere-tü balɣasun the city by the name of *Rājagṛha*
iravadi kemen nere-tü mören or *iravadi nere-tü mören* the river
  Irrawaddy

471. In modern language the appellative noun sometimes precedes the proper name, a fact which must be attributed to foreign influence.

sayid amur Minister Amur
nökör gendüng Comrade Gendung

Permanent Attribute

472. In many cases the attribute expresses, together with the word to which it refers, a single idea. Such constructions can be regarded, from the point of view of their meanings, as one word.

šir-a šibaɣun horned owl (lit., "the yellow bird")
čaɣan buday-a rice (lit., "white millet")
qar-a modun larch tree (lit., "black tree")
qar-a görügesün bear (lit., "black animal")
čaɣan šibaɣun swan (lit., "white bird")

473. To this category also special idiomatic expressions belong.

čaɣan toluɣai primer (lit., "the white head")
qar-a kümün ordinary man, layman (lit., "black person")
šir-a šaǰin Buddhism of the Tsonkapa sect, lamaism (lit., "the Yellow Religion")
šir-a tosun butter (lit., "yellow fat")
ömükei tosun naphtha, rock oil (lit., "the stinking oil")
qalaɣun ger bath (lit., "hot house")
boro ger kitchen (lit., "grey house")
qar-a ger jail (lit., "black house")
muqur tergen motor car (lit., "a carriage without horns")
altan ɣadasun day star (lit., "the Golden Peg")

Interrogative Pronouns as Part of an Attribute

474. The Mongolian language has almost no relative subordinate clauses. Their function is performed by special constructions with interrogative pronouns serving as attributes referring to the word following the interrogative pronoun. Such constructions can be called relative attributive constructions.

These constructions with an interrogative pronoun can serve as subject, attribute, or object of any long sentence.

ken deyilügsen inu abumui He who has vanquished will take.
ali üǰegsen kümün-eče asaɣubai He asked people who had seen.
  (Lit., "He asked what having seen people.")

ali dur-a-taį kümün bügesü tegün-i abču bolumuį Anyone willing
 may take it. (Lit., "If there is what willing person may take it.")
*ene yeke kölgen sudur-i ken ungšiqu kümün inu bodi qutuy-i olqu
 boltuyaį* May the people who read this *Mahāyāna sūtra* obtain
 holiness! (Lit., "This *Mahāyāna sūtra* who reading people may
 obtain holiness!")

Genitive as Attribute

475. The genitive of any declinable part of speech may serve as attribute.
Usually such a genitive indicates the possessor of the object concerned
and answers the question "whose?," though a genitive attribute may
also have other meanings.

All particulars concerning the genitive will be found in the sections
dealing with the genitive (see §§ 500ff.); only a few remarks will be
made here.

476. A word modified by a genitive attribute indicating the possessor
can be followed by the genitive of the personal pronouns *inu* "his" and
anu "their," which connect the attribute and the modified word more
closely.

qayan-u čerig inu khaghan's army (lit., "khaghan's army his")
bayatud-un morid anu the heroes' horses (lit., "the heroes' horses
 theirs")
tegün-ü nom inu his book (lit., "his book his")
teden-ü nom-nuyud anu their books (lit., "their books theirs")

Several Attributes of the Same Word

477. A word can have several attributes. In such cases, all attributes
precede the word modified. An attribute indicating the most important
quality or characteristic of an object is always placed as near as possible
to the word modified. One attribute qualifying another must immediately
precede it. Otherwise both would be attributes of the same word. This
is the case with the genitive attributes, the attributes of which always
precede and cannot be placed between the genitive and the word
modified.

478. Words indicating coats of animals or other living beings as invariable, permanent characteristics are placed as near as possible to the
word to be modified. They usually are placed immediately before the
latter.

qurdun qar-a morin a quick black horse
sayin jegerde morin a good chestnut-colored horse
kögšin jegerde morin an old chestnut-colored horse

479. Words denoting the material of which an object consists are placed
as closely to it as possible.

öndür modun bayišing a high wooden building
ulayan čilayun kerem a red stone castle
urtu temür jida a long iron spear

480. Demonstrative and interrogative pronouns immediately precede other attributes in the nominative case.

> *tere čayan ayula* that white mountain
> *yambar kögšin kümün* what old man?

481. A genitive attribute is placed before the nominative attribute. Otherwise the latter would be its attribute.

> *bayši-yin šin-e nom* the teacher's new book
> *qayan-u yeke bayatur* the khaghan's great knight

482. Numerals precede nominative attributes and follow genitive attributes.

> *dörben qar-a morin* four black horses
> *tabun šin-e nom* five new books

In cases when it is necessary to stress the number of the objects concerned the numeral may be placed immediately before the word to be modified.

> *qar-a dörben morin jegerde tabun morin* black horses four, chestnut-colored horses five

483. Verbal nouns with or without converbs are placed before a nominative attribute, but after numerals.

> *iregsen kögšin kümün* an old man who has come
> *qoyar ükügsen kümün* two dead persons

484. Of two attributes, that ending in *-tai/-tei* (see § 138) or *-tu/-tü* (see § 140) occupies the first place.

> *moritai qar-a kümün* a mounted layman (if *qar-a* were placed first, such a construction would mean "a person with a black horse")

485. As remarked above, an attribute which qualifies another attribute immediately precedes it.

> *šin-e bayši-yin nom* the book of the new teacher
> *olan maltai kümün* a person possessing many cattle

486. A special case is that of nouns ending in *-tai/-tei* (see § 138) and serving as attributes. When there is an attribute of such a word ending in *-tai/-tei*, e. g. *sayin moritai kümün* "a person possessing good horses," the order of the attributes can be reversed. In this event, the word *sayin* "good" (which is an attribute of "horse") takes the suffix *-tai* and the word *moritai* "possessing horses" loses its suffix. The result is *morin sayitai kümün* "a person possessing good horses" (lit., "possessing something good in the way of horses").

> *sayin keletei* or *sayin amatai kümün* a man having a good tongue (or mouth), i. e., a man talking pleasantly
> *kele sayitai* or *am-a sayitai* id.
> *yeke usutai yajar* or *usu yeketei yajar* "a country abundant in water

Adverbs

487. Both nominal and verbal forms may be qualified by adverbs. The latter immediately precede the word they modify.

Many nouns and even numerals may serve as adverbs without changing their form.

Nouns expressing qualities may be qualified by adverbs (*adverbia modi*).

> *maši sayin* very good
> *yeke mayu* very bad
> *ülemǰi sayin* exceedingly good
> *ilangyuį-a čiqula* extremely important
> *tong buruyu* completely wrong
> *qab qar-a* completely black

488. Adverbs may be qualified by other adverbs (*adverbia modi*).

> *maši sayin ungšiday šabi* a pupil who reads very well
> *tong buruyu kelebeį* He spoke completely in error.
> *maši qol-a odba* He went very far.

489. Adverbs (*adverbia loci, temporis, modi*) may refer to verbs.

> *či qamiy-a odumuį* Where are you going?
> *činayši yabuba* He went further.
> *bi maryaši iremüį* I shall come tomorrow.
> *sayin ungšimuį* He reads well.
> *yurbanta dayudabaį* He called three times.
> *qoyar asayuba* He asked twice.
> *genedte irebeį* He came suddenly.

490. Many nouns in various oblique cases, primarily in the instrumental, may serve as adverbs.

> *türgen-iyer mordobaį* He galloped quickly.
> *mayuį-a ǰobayamuį* He torments fearfully.

491. Converbs may serve as adverbs.

> *dakin irebeį* He came again. (Lit., "repeating," *conv. modale* of *daki-* "to repeat.")
> *či yayakin irebeį* Why did you come? (Lit., "What doing did you come?")

Isolated Words

General Remarks

492. A sentence can be introduced by or include words not governed by any member of the sentence and not serving as subject, predicate, or attribute. Such words do not refer to any member of the sentence and can easily be omitted without any effect upon the sentence as a whole. Such words are comparable, in this respect, to certain conjunctions ("notwithstanding," "yet"), direct address ("Father, give me a book!"), and so on in English.

Direct Address

493. Nouns and pronouns are used in the nominative case in direct address. Nouns are accompanied, in such cases, by the interjection *a* (pronounced *ā*) which is placed after the noun. In old grammars the interjection *a* is erroneously called the vocative suffix, which, in reality, does not exist in Mongolian.

> *qaγan minu a minu üge sonosun soyurq-a* Ah, my Khaghan, deign to listen to my words!
>
> *burqan a* Ah, Buddha!
>
> *či egün-i buu ab* You must not take this! (Lit., "You, do not take this!")

Interjections

494. The interjections are what may be called isolated words.

> *qalaγ qoqoị ǰuru či yayakiγsan buị* Alas, Juru, what have you done?
>
> *ǰ-a či ken buị* Well, who are you?

The Cases

The Nominative

The Subject Designator

495. The nominative is the case of the subject, attribute, and predicate. The subject is either a simple nominative of a declinable part of speech or a nominative with a subject designator. The latter is the pronoun *inu* or *anu*, the particle *ber* (which should not be confused with the instrumental suffix *-bar/-ber*), or the converbs *bolbasu* or *bügesü*. The simple nominative as subject has been discussed in § 441.

496. The subject may be emphasized by the above-mentioned designators. It is always emphasized by one of them, if the word serving as a subject is a part of speech which usually serves as an attribute, e. g., a demonstrative pronoun, a noun expressing a quality (e. g., *sayin* "good"), or a verbal noun. Such words can be easily misunderstood, if they are not followed by a designator, e. g., *ene kümün* without a designator after *ene* is "this man," but with *bolbasu* (*ene bolbasu kümün*) we have a sentence lacking the copula: "This is a man." (Lit., "If it be this—a man.")

The Pronouns *inu* and *anu*

497. The pronouns *inu* "his" and *anu* "their" are the genitive forms of the extinct personal pronouns **i* "he" and **a* "they." They indicate that the person or object in question belongs to the third person.

> *aq-a inu irebeị* His elder brother came.
>
> *blam-a-nar anu quralduba* Their lamas assembled.

These pronouns are frequently used, when the persons or objects in question do not belong, in the direct sense, to anybody. In reality, there is nothing in the world which does not belong to something. There is nothing which stands outside all groups (*sui generis*): sun and moon are parts of the universe, birds and insects belong to the animal kingdom, and so on. The primitive Mongol of ancient times was unable to imagine anything not being part of a group. Therefore, even in cases where ownership was out of the question, he tried to place objects into groups, considering them as belonging to their respective groups, hence the expressions "Their birds go in autumn and return in spring," "Its sun has risen," and so on. Besides, the person or thing indicated by the designator *inu* or *anu* is distinguished from all other similar persons or things, as one or something acting in the manner expressed by its predicate, as distinguished from other persons or things not acting in this manner.

The following examples are classified into two groups: the first group contains examples of sentences with the pronouns *inu* or *anu* in their literal senses with reference to a possessor, and the second group contains examples of sentences with the same pronouns used with no reference to a possessor.

First group

tegün-ü ači inu tegün-eče ülemji nemeyü Its benefit increases (becoming) more than it.

nadur jobalang-un qoor-a inu daki yayun j-e bolqu What will be the evil of suffering to me?

olan qoor-nuyud-i nemegülkü-yin yayča šiltayan inu minu jirükendür mayad büged The only cause of the increase of many evils is certainly in my heart.

buį inu adali-yin tulada nigen bolqu As their existence is similar (they) will be one and the same.

urida bolju bütüjü nögčigsen-eče üleküį inu edüge nadur yayun buį What is to me now the remainder of what had appeared in the past and has ceased to be?

jiryalang-un šiltayan anu nigen nigen-te boluyu Each cause of happiness comes into existence (only) once.

bodisadu-a-nar-un yabudal anu teyimü buį Such are the deeds of the Bodhisattvas.

mongyol-un yajar oron anu yadayadu dalaį-ača neliyed qola bayimuį Mongolia (lit., "the country of the Mongols") is quite far away from the ocean (lit., "the outer sea").

mongyol-un čay ularil anu qayuraį bayimuį The climate of Mongolia is dry.

mongyol yajar-a ayar-un keį inu maši qayuraį bayimuį The air is very dry in Mongolia. (Lit., "The air of the atmosphere is very dry in the Mongolian country.")

Second group

nasu čay-tur tere metü kereg inu uqaju üįledtügeį Through all the span of life such things should be done understandingly.

erkin inu busud-un tusa-yi sedkigdeküį The sublime must think of the profit of the others.

ünen inu ese oldabasu if truth is not to be found

ebül inu maši küįten jun anu maši qalayun amuį Winter is very cold (and) summer is very hot.

Although there is a slight difference between the examples of the two
groups, the use of the pronouns *inu* and *anu* is justified even from the
point of view of their original meaning: *tegün-ü ači inu* "its benefit"
(lit., "its benefit its") and *erkin inu* "the sublime" (lit., "his sublime"),
because the others, not mentioned here, are not sublime and he is the
only sublime among them; hence "his or their sublime."

The sentence *ebül inu maši küiten ǰun anu maši qalayun amui* "Winter
is very cold (and) summer is very hot" contains also the pronouns *inu*
and *anu*. In this sentence winter and summer are opposed to each other
and, therefore, even here the use of the pronouns *inu* and *anu* is justified:
"Of them winter is very cold and of them summer is very hot."

However, the original meanings of *inu* and *anu* are no longer apparent
in all cases and, therefore, they are often omitted, e. g., in this sentence:
ǰobalang-un šiltayan maši olan bolumui "The causes of suffering are very
numerous." This sentence immediately follows, in the same book, the
sentence: *ǰiryalang-un šiltayan anu nigen nigen-te boluyu* "The causes
of happines each come into existence once." In two similar constructions
the designator *anu* is present one time and it is omitted the other time.

The Particle *ber*

498. The first meaning of the particle *ber* is "too" or "even." This often
serves as a designator of the subject.

> *qamiy-a bolqu tere metü buyan ber* Where will there be a virtue like
> that?

> *basa basa nigül-nügüd ber mašida törömüi* Again and again sins
> are born in great numbers.

> *egün-eče yeke mungqay ber ügei bui* There is no greater foolishness
> than this.

> *nadur ken ber ögkü* Who will give me?

> *qamuy tengri-ner asuri-nar ker ber minu dayisun bolbasu ber tede
> ber ayus tamu-yin yal-un dotor-a uduridču oroyul-un ülü čidaqun*
> Even if all deities and Asura became my enemies, they could
> not lead and put me into the fire of the terrible hell.

> *urin tačiyangyui terigüten dayisud-un yar köl terigüten ber ügei buyu*
> There are no hands and feet (nor) anything else of foes such as
> anger and passion.

> *nigül ber ülü bolun buyan-nuyud nemeyü* There is no sin and the
> virtues increase.

> *tediii kü ǰobalang-i üjejü bür-ün tegün-ü tonilqui ber inu ügei bui*
> In consequence of witnessing so many sufferings there is even
> no salvation for him. (Lit., "there is even no salvation of his.")

> *tede bügüde ber nigültü sedkil-eče boluysan buyu* All that happened
> from the sinful thought.

The Converbs *bolbasu* and *bügesü*

499. The converb *bolbasu* "if he becomes" of the verb *bol-* "to become"
and the converb *bügesü* "if he is" of the verb *bü-* "to be" serve as de-

signators of the subject. Sentences such as *mongyol ulus bolbasu ayuu yeke amui* can be translated literally as "If it is Mongolia, it is wide and large." In English idiom the sentence should read: "Mongolia is wide and large."

As remarked above, certain parts of speech usually serve as attributes. Such parts of speech, attributive *par excellence,* are demonstrative pronouns, verbal nouns, and nouns expressing qualities and acting as adjectives in the European languages.

Such expressions as *ene nom, iregsen kümün,* and so on, consist of nouns with attributes: "this book," "the person who has come." The only way of converting these attributes into subjects is to separate the pronoun *ene* "this" or the verbal noun *iregsen* "who has come" from the words *nom* "book" or *kümün* "person" by an element which emphasizes the subject. This is the only possible means of indicating that the words in question serve as subjects. Therefore, in all such cases in the modern language the converbs *bolbasu* and *bügesü* are used. The presence of a converb after the word which, without a converb, would serve as an attribute, and before another word, indicates that the group concerned does not constitute an attributive construction, since no member of a sentence may be placed between an attribute and a word to be modified. In other words, an attribute is always placed immediately before the word to which it refers.

All other designators (*inu, anu,* and *ber*) are subject to the same rules.

> *negüdelčin arad bolbasu üker aduyu qoni imaya ǰerge-yin mal öskeǰü usu belčiger-i dayaǰu negüdel-iyer amiduramui* The nomads (lit., "nomad people") raise cattle, horses, sheep, goats, and other stock, follow water and pasturage, and lead a nomadic life.

> *erkim bayan bolbasu erdem bilig, dumdadu bayan bolbasu eregül sayin, aday bayan bolbasu aduyu mal bui* The highest wealth is science and intellect, the intermediate wealth is health, the lowest wealth is horses and cattle. (A proverb.)

> *qayan qatun bügesü bügüdeger maši bayasbai* The khaghan and the queen were both very glad.

The Genitive

General Remarks

500. The genitive is governed by a noun. A genitive with a postposition serves as an object governed by a verb.

There are three principal kinds of genitive:

a) The attributive genitive
b) The predicative genitive (very rare in Written Mongolian)
c) The genitive with a postposition

I. The Attributive Genitive

501. The attributive genitive (*genitivus attributivus*) acts as an attribute. There are several special cases.

A. Genitivus appositivus

The appositive genitive occurs in proper names similar to the English "the city of New York."

> *ong-un γool* the Ongin River (lit., "the river of Ong," i. e. the river of Wang, Chin. "king")
>
> *tariyatu-yin keyid* the Tariyatu Monastery (lit., "the monastery of Tariyatu")
>
> *terki-yin čaγan naγur* Lake Terkin Chaghan (lit., "the White Lake of Terki")

B. Genitivus possessivus

The possessive genitive indicates the possessor— in the widest sense of the word—of something. There are several kinds of possessive genitive.

a) Genitivus possessoris: this genitive indicates the possessor or owner in the narrow sense of the word.

> *šabi-yin nom* the pupil's book
>
> *aq-a-yin morin* the horse of the elder brother
>
> *bayši-yin ger* the teacher's house
>
> *ečige-yin mal* father's cattle

b) Genitivus subjectivus or genitivus activus: this genitive designates the acting person. From the grammatical point of view, such a genitive is an attribute, but logically it is a subject. The genitivus activus designates the performer of an action and answers the question "whose action?"

The genitive qualifies both nouns and verbal nouns. The latter are always active verbs, but in such constructions they may serve as passive verbs.

The genitive occurs only in attributive constructions, such as "the meat eaten by the dog," but never in such cases as "The meat was eaten by the dog."

> *burqan-u nomlal* Buddha's sermon
>
> *bodisadu-a-nar-un yabudal-nuγud* the deeds of the Bodhisattvas
>
> *činu abuγsan nom* the book taken by you (lit., "your taken book")
>
> *bayši-yin kelegsen üge* the word spoken by the teacher (lit., "the teacher's spoken word")

It is not difficult to discover that all the above constructions can be converted into sentences of which the subject is the present active genitive: "Buddha is teaching," "The teacher spoke a word," and so on.

c) Genitivus objectivus: this genitive (*genitivus objecti* or *genitivus passivus*) designates the object of someone's action, e. g., "worship of the sun": the latter construction can be converted into a sentence with "the sun" as an object (complement): "They are worshipping the sun."

> *miqan-u qudalduγ-a* butcher's shop (lit., "shop of meat")
>
> *modun-u darqan* carpenter (lit., "smith of wood")

nidün-ü emči oculist (lit., "a physician of eyes")
kelen-ü suryayuli school of languages

C. Genitivus qualitatis

Genitivus qualitatis or the qualitative genitive expresses qualities and functions as the adjective in European languages. A special case is the *genitivus quantitatis*, i. e., the genitive of quantity.

eldeb öngge-yin čečeg-nügüd flowers of various colors
olan ǰüịl-ün amitan-nuyud living creatures of many kinds
ǰayun ǰil-ün üy-e a period of a hundred years
qoyar dayun-u yaǰar a distance of two voices (a distance of one voice is the distance the human voice is heard)
yurban ǰil-ün yaǰar a distance of three years' travel

D. Genitivus partitivus

The partitive genitive expresses the whole of which a part is talked about.

teden-ü nigen one of them

This genitive occurs in two other particular cases: in the expression of fractions and in constructions corresponding semantically to the superlative of European languages.

a) Fractions: the denominator is either a numeral with the following word *qubi-yin* (genitive of *qubi* "part") or a genitive of a numeral without *qubi-yin*.

tabun qubi-yin nigen one fifth (lit., "one of five parts")
arban-u nigen qubi one tenth (lit., "one part of ten")

In modern books the idea of percentage is expressed in the same manner.

ǰayun-u qoyar qubi two per cent (lit., "two parts of hundred")

b) Genitivus superlativi: the Mongolian languages have no superlative as a grammatical form. The idea of the highest degree of a quality is expressed by a genitive of a noun (e. g., "man") followed by the basic form of a noun expressing a quality (e. g., "good"). Thus such a construction may literally be translated as "the good of men." Instead of a noun (e. g., "man"), the word *qamuy* "all" may be used: the literal translation of such a construction is "the good of all."

er-e-yin sayin the best of men
qamuy-un yayiqamšiy-tu the most admirable (lit., "the admirable of all")

II. The Predicative Genitive

502. The predicative genitive is a predicate. In Written Mongolian it occurs with a copula.

ene nom minu buị This book is mine.
tere morin geser-ün buyu Is that horse Geser's?

III. The Genitive with Postpositions

503. Many postpositions govern the genitive. Such a genitive together with its postposition is, in turn, governed by a verb and serves as an object.

The following postpositions govern the genitive:

tula for, for the sake of, because of
tölüge for, for the sake of, in order to
tuqaï concerning, about, of (e. g., to speak about or of something)
door-a under
dotor-a in, within
deger-e on
dergede at, by (e. g., at the table, by the table)
inadu on this side of
činadu on that side of
qoyin-a behind
γadan-a out of, outside
qoyorundu between
emün-e in front of, before, etc.

Examples: *tegün-ü tula* for its sake
ger-ün dergede by the house
aγula-yin qoyin-a behind the mountain
tegün-ü tuqaï concerning that

The Dative-Locative

General Remarks

504. The dative-locative, in general, answers the questions "to whom?," "at whom?," "where?," and "whither?" There are also many other meanings in particular cases.

The dative-locative is governed by verbs and nouns.

A. Dativus Commodi atque Incommodi

505. The *dativus commodi* answers the question "to whom?". It is used to indicate the immediate recipient of something, e. g., "He gave the book to the pupil."

The *dativus incommodi* answers the question "for whom?." It is used to indicate the ultimate recipient of something, e. g., "I gave you a book for your son."

eke-degen ögbe He gave to his mother.
qaγan-dur eyin kemen ügülerün He said this to the khaghan.
bi köbegün-degen qatun erimüi I am seeking a wife for my son.
burqan-dur süsüg-teï believing in Buddha (lit., "possessing belief in Buddha")

B. Dativus Finalis

506. The *dativus finalis* is the dative of the purpose. This expresses the ultimate aim of an action.

a) Dativus terminalis: this indicates the aim of an action.

> *usun-dur yabumuị* He goes after water (i. e., to fetch water).
> *yayun-dur irebeị* Why did he come? (lit., "What did he come
> for?")

A particular case is the dative of the *nomen futuri* in *-quị/-küị*. The
dative suffix is here *-a/-e*. Thus the endings of such a form are *-quị-a/
-küị-e*. The meaning of such a form is that of the *converbum finale* or
the Latin *supinum*, i. e., the aim of an action, e. g., "in order to take."

> *abquị-a irebeị* He came to take.
> *bi tegün-i üjeküị-e irebeị* I have come to see him.

b) Dativus translativus: this dative indicates something into which
something is being transformed, e. g., "He was appointed teacher" (Lit.,
"He was appointed to teacher.")

> *tedeger tegün-i sayid-tur songyuba* They elected him minister (Lit.,
> "They elected him to minister.")

C. Dativus Actoris

507. This dative, also called the active dative, indicates the acting person, when the action is expressed by the passive voice of a verb.

> *činu-a-dur bariydaysan qonin* a sheep caught by a wolf
> *dayisun-dur alaydabaị* He was killed by the enemy.

D. Dativus Temporalis

508. The temporal dative (*dativus temporalis* or *dativus temporis*) indicates
the time during or at which an action takes place. This answers the
question "when?"

> *ene sara-yin nigen edür-e* on the first of this month (lit., "on the
> first day of this month")
> *minu baya-dur* when I was a child (lit., "in my little")

A particular case of the temporal dative is the dative-locative of the
nomen futuri or *nomen perfecti*. The former of these verbal nouns indicates an uncompleted action during which an action is or will be performed (e. g., "when he is" or "when he will be here"); the latter indicates the completed past during which the action has been performed
(e. g., "when he did something"). Such constructions act as the Latin
ablativus absolutus or as subordinate temporal clauses in modern European languages.

> *tende irekü-dür* when he comes there (lit., "in the future coming
> there")
> *tegün-ü ükügsen-dür* when he died (lit., "in his past dying")

The person acting is indicated in such constructions by the *genitivus
subjectivus* (*gen. activus*).

E. Locativus

509. The locative answers the questions "where?," "whither?"

a) Locativus allativus-illativus: this locative indicates the place to which someone or something is moving. It answers the question "whither?"

> *qota-dur yabumui̥* He goes to town.
> *usun-dur orobai̥* He entered the water. (Lit., "He entered into the water.")

b) Locativus inessivus: this locative answers the question "in what?" or "within what?"

> *ger-tür sayumui̥* He lives in a house.
> *suryayuli ene bayišing-dur bayimui̥* School is in this building.

c) Locativus adessivus: the adessive locative answers the question "on what?" or "by what?"

> *šibayun modun-u üjügür-tür sayumui̥* The bird sits on the top of the tree.
> *nadur nom ügei̥* I do not have any books. (Lit., "There are no books at *or* by me.")

In Mongolian there is no verb "to have." The idea of "to have" is expressed by the locative with the verb "to be."

> *nadur morin bui̥* I have a horse. (Lit., "There is a horse to me.")

F. Dativus cum Postpositione

510. The only postposition occurring with a dative is *kürtele* "till." By origin this is a converbal form (*converbum terminale* of *kür-* "to reach, to arrive").

> *qota-dur kürtele* till the town

The Genitive-Dative

511. The double genitive-dative case acts as locative.

a) As *allativus* answering the question "whither?"

> *blam-a-yin-dur odba* He went to the lama.

b) As *adessivus* answering the question "at whose?"

> *blam-a-yin-dur sayuju amui̥* He is living at the lama's.

The Accusative

General Remarks

512. The accusative is governed only by transitive verbs. The accusative is the case of the direct complement and is only used to indicate a definite object or person already known to the reader, especially when the person or thing in question is modified by an attribute. On the other hand, certain parts of speech, when serving as a direct complement, are always accusative forms. The accusative is used, in general, in cases in which the definite article in English is used.

10*

Besides, there is a special construction bearing a certain resemblance to the Latin *accusativus cum infinitivo*, another construction resembling the English double accusative, and an *accusativus relativus* explained below.

A. Accusativus Objecti

513. The so-called *accusativus objecti* is the direct complement.

a) Pronouns serving as a direct complement are always accusative forms. They do not occur suffixless.

> *tegün-i üjebe* He saw him.
> *či namayi yaγun-dur dayudabai̯* Why did you call me?

b) Nouns serving as a direct complement and modified by a pronominal attribute are always accusative forms.

> *ene selm-e-yi ab* Take this sabre!
> *tere mori-yi unuba* He rode that horse.

c) The accusative is used, when there is an indication of the possessor of the object concerned.

> *nom-i inu ungšiba* He read his (*ejus*) book.
> *aq-a-yin mori-yi unuba* He rode the horse of the elder brother.

d) The words *bügüde* "all," *bükü* "all," and all numerals summarizing the total amount of the persons or things in question are used in the accusative.

> *bi činu kereg bükün-i bütügesügei̯* I shall fulfil all your needs.
> *tere inu yaγum-a bügüde-yi čidamui̯* He can [do] everything.
> *či nom debter qoyar-i ab* Take the book and the notebook!

e) Proper names serving as a direct complement are put in the accusative.

> *činggis qan-i üjebe* He saw Chinghis Khan.

f) Nouns serving as direct complements are in the accusative, when the person or thing in question was mentioned in a previous context and is supposed to be known to the reader, or when there are any attributes making it distinguishable from other, similar persons or things, or in cases where in English the definite article would be used.

> *tende nigen süme bui̯. süme-yi üjemüi̯ uu* There is a temple. Will you see the temple?

B. Accusativus cum Nomine Verbali

514. The accusative with a verbal noun acts like the English accusative with the infinitive without "to" (e. g., "I saw him come,") or the Latin accusative with the infinitive (e. g., *puto eos vincere*). The only difference is that in Mongolian both the noun and the verbal noun are in the accusative like in Latin constructions such as *Juravit uterque se sine dolo indutias conservaturum.*

> *geser-i yabuqu-yi üjebe* He saw Geser go.
> *tegün-i ükügsen-i medebe* He learned that he had died. (Lit., "He learned him to have died.")

C. Accusativus Relativus

515. *Accusativus relativus* or *relationis* can be translated into English as "concerning someone" or "in reference to someone."

> *čimayi yayu abqu buį kemen qayan asayumuį* The khaghan will ask what you would like to take. (Lit., "The khaghan will ask, referring to you, what will he take.")

D. Accusativus Praedicati

516. The accusative of the predicate is the same as the double accusative in English (e. g., "They proclaimed him emperor") or in Latin (e. g., *Homines caecos reddit cupiditas*). This accusative occurs mainly with the verb *bolya-* "to make" and expresses that into which something is being transformed.

> *qayan inu tere ekener-i qatun-iyan bolyabaį* The khaghan made that woman his wife.
> *tere ulus tegün-i qayan-iyan ergübeį* That people proclaimed him their khaghan.

E. Accusativus Actoris

517. This accusative is the accusative of the person acting and indicates the person acting in verbal-nominal and converbal constructions. The verbal noun or converb is an intransitive verb. The accusative replaces the genitive of the acting person.

> *tegün-i yabuqu-dur* when he goes
> *tegün-i iretele* until he comes

The Suffixless Oblique Case

General Remarks

518. Instead of the accusative with the usual suffixes *-yi* and *-i* a suffixless form coinciding with the nominative is used in certain cases, but this, of course, is not a nominative. This form is used in cases where in English the indefinite article is used or where there is no article at all. This form serves as a direct complement, temporal, etc.

A. As a Direct Complement

519. The suffixless form functions as an accusative in the following cases:

a) If the word in question expresses something not mentioned in the previous context and, therefore, is unknown to the reader; if the word in question has no attribute distinguishing it from other, similar, objects, the direct complement has no suffix.

> *usu uyuqu* to drink water
> *nadur miqa ög* Give me (some) meat!
> *bi mori unuju irebe* I came riding a horse.
> *bi köbegün-degen qatun erijü yabumuį* I go seeking a wife for my son.

b) The direct complement always lacks a suffix in the following expressions, among others:

> *nom ungši-* to read a book
> *bičig biči-* to write letters
> *kele sur-* to learn language
> *mori unu-* to ri:le a horse
> *üniy-e saya-* to milk a cow

B. As Temporal

520. This form expresses time.

> *γurban sar-a yabuqu* to travel three months
> *bi önggeregsen ǰil irebeȶ* I came last year.
> *edür söni ügeȶ yabuqu* to travel day and night
> *bayši irekü ǰil iremüȶ* The teacher will come next year.

C. With a Verbal Noun

521. The suffixless form is sometimes used instead of the accusative with verbal nouns and indicates the person acting (v. § 514).

> *bi kümün yabuqu-yi ese üǰebe* I did not see anybody walk.

D. The Suffixless Form of the Predicate

522. This form functions as *accusativus praedicati* (v. § 516). If the noun of a predicate contains an indication of the possessor, it is an accusative, but, if there is no indication of the possessor, the noun of the predicate is suffixless.

> *tedener tegün-i qayan ergübe* They proclaimed him khaghan.
> *bay-a qural-un terigülegčid nökör amur-i terigün sayid songyuba*
> The Standing Committee of the Small National Assembly elected Comrade Amur prime minister.

E. As Indication of Place

523. The suffixless form indicates the place or the direction of someone's motion.

> *tere γaǰar sayuǰu amuȶ* He is living in that country.
> *bida qota yabumuȶ* We shall go to town.

The Ablative

General Remarks

524. The ablative, in general, indicates the starting point of an action. There are several categories of ablative: *ablativus separativus, abl. temporis, abl. actoris, abl. compensationis, abl. verbi,* and *ablativus cum postpositione.*

A. Ablativus Separativus

525. The separative ablative answers the questions "from whom?" or "from where?" and "from within what?" There are the following particular kinds of this ablative: *ablativus separativus externus, abl. elativus, abl. originis, abl. causae, abl. partitivus, abl. exclusivus*, and *ablativus comparationis*.

a) Ablativus separativus externus: this ablative answers the questions "from whom?" and "from where?" This indicates the person or thing from whom or from what something is moving.

> *qayan-ača abuba* He took from the khaghan.

b) Ablativus elativus: this ablative answers the question "from within what?" It indicates the thing or the place from within which something is coming out.

> *ger-eče yaruba* He came out of the house.

c) Ablativus originis: the ablative of origin indicates the origin of someone or something.

> *qayan-u qatun-ača nigen köbegün töröbei* A son was born of the khaghan's wife.
> *mongyol-ača yaruysan nigen yasun* a tribe of Mongolian origin (lit., "a tribe which came out of the Mongols")

d) Ablativus causae: the ablative of the cause indicates the cause of something.

> *jobalang anu nisvanis-ača bolumui* Suffering comes from attachment to the world.
> *jiryalang buyan-ača bolumui* Happiness comes from virtue.

e) Ablativus partitivus: the partitive ablative indicates objects which are only partially affected by the action.

> *čai-ača uyuba* He drank some tea. (Lit., "He drank from the tea.")
> *yayum-a-ača oyulčaba* He took part in sewing things. (Lit., "He took part in sewing from something.")

f) Ablativus exclusivus: the exclusive ablative occurs in constructions corresponding to the English "besides something" and "except something." This ablative is followed by the word *busu* "another" or *öger-e* "another" or *yadan-a* "outside."

> *tegün-eče yadan-a* besides that
> *yabuqu-ača busu ary-a ügei* There remains nothing but to go. (Lit., "There is no other way out of going.")
> *nigen üker-eče öger-e ed ügei* no other property than one ox

g) Ablativus comparationis: an ablative immediately followed by a noun expressing a quality functions as the comparative in European languages. To be precise we should add that the ablative indicates the person or thing which possesses the inferior quality.

> *nama-ača yeke* bigger than I
> *čima-ača aq-a* older than you (lit., "from you an elder brother")

B. Ablativus Temporis

526. The temporal ablative indicates the time since which an action takes place. This ablative indicates the starting time.

önggeregsen tabun ǰil-eče since the last five year period

maryaši-yin edür-eče ekilen beginning from to-morrow (lit., "beginning from the day of morrow")

C. Ablativus Actoris

527. The ablative of the person acting indicates the originator of an action.

> *qural-ača toɣtayaba* A resolution was passed by (lit., "from") the assembly.

D. Ablativus Compensationis

528. This ablative indicates things serving as compensation for something else, or things in exchange for which other things are to be given. It is to be translated into English by "for . . ."

> *tegün-i mönggün-eče ögbe* He gave it for money.

E. Ablativus Verbi

529. Certain verbs govern the ablative:

ayi- or *ayu-* to be afraid of (someone)
asaɣu- to ask (someone)
iče- to be ashamed of
bari- to take by (e. g., to take by the hand; otherwise *bari-* governs the accusative)
daba- to violate (a law, regulations)
sur- to ask (someone)
uya- to bind to, to tie to something
elgü- to hang on
tata- to pu'l at

F. Postpositions Governing the Ablative

530. The following postpositions govern the ablative:
ɣadan-a besides
qoyiši after
urida before
činaɣši farther from
inaɣši nearer in this direction

The Instrumental

General Remarks

531. The instrumental, in general, indicates the means of performing an action. It answers the question "by means of what?"
There are some particular cases of application of the instrumental. The following kinds of instrumental are recognizable: the "pure" instrumental indicating the tool of an action (*instrumentalis instructivus*), the sociative instrumental (*instrumentalis sociativus*) answering the question

"together with whom?," the instrumental of manner (*instrumentalis modi*) indicating the manner in which an action is performed, and the compensative instrumental (*instrumentalis compensationis*) indicating things as price for other things.

A. Instrumentalis Instructivus

532. The instructive instrumental indicates the tool of an action. This includes the *instrumentalis instrumenti, instr. actoris, instr. materiae, instr. formae, instr. causae & propositi, instr. itineris,* and *instrumentalis cum nominibus opiae atque inopiae.*

a) Instrumentalis instrumenti: this instrumental indicates the means of performing actions (tools, transportation means, etc.).

> *modu-bar čoki-* to beat with a stick
> *süke-ber čabči-* to cleave with an ax
> *köl-iyer giški-* to tread on with the foot
> *ongγoča-bar yabu-* to go by boat
> *temege-ber ǰüge-* to carry by camel (or camel caravan)

b) Instrumentalis actoris: this instrumental indicates the person acting. This is used with both active and passive verbs.

> *qaγan inu ǰarliγ-iyan elči-ber medegülbei* The khaghan made his order known through a messenger.
> *qural-iyar songγuysan* (or *songγuydaysan*) *daruγ-a* the chairman elected by the assembly

c) Instrumentalis materiae: this instrumental indicates the material or stuff of which something is made.

> *modu-bar bariγsan bayišing* a building made of wood
> *altan-iyar kigsen qayirčaγ* a box made of gold

d) Instrumentalis formae: this instrumental indicates the shape in which something is made (in English: "in the shape of").

> *eldeb ǰüil-ün erdenis-iyer beleg kürgebe* He brought gifts in the shape of jewels of various kinds.
> *alta-bar bügelǰiǰü bayiday quluγan-a* a mouse which vomits gold (lit., "vomiting with gold")

e) Instrumentalis causae atque propositi: this instrumental indicates the cause or the aim.

> *kereg-iyer yabu,* to go on business
> *tegün-i medegsen ügei-ber alday-a γarγaba* He made a mistake because he did not know (Lit., "because of not knowing").

The instrumental of a future noun (*nomen futuri*) expresses the aim or the purpose of an action.

> *tegün-i üǰekü-ber irebe* He came in order to see him.
> *čai uγuqu-bar irebe* He came to drink tea.

f) Instrumentalis itineris: this instrumental can be also called *instr. itineris atque loci* and indicates the way of someone's motion or the place over which something is scattered.

ǰam-iyar yabu- to go by road
egüde-ber oro- to enter by the door
aɣularqaɣ ɣaǰar-iyar nutuɣlamui They live scattered in a mountainous country.

g) Instrumentalis cum nomine: this instrumental occurs only with the so-called *nomina opiae & inopiae*, i. e. such as *bayan* "rich," *elbeg* "abundant," and so on, and indicates goods in which someone is rich (or which he lacks).

mal-iyar bayan rich in cattle
eldeb ǰüil-iyer ügei poor in everything

B. Instrumentalis Sociativus

533. The sociative instrumental expresses the idea of companionship with someone or connection with something, answering the question "together with whom?"

manu morin tegün-ü morin-iyar belčimüi Our horse grazes together with his horse.
utaɣan-iyar degdebe He went up together with the smoke.

C. Instrumentalis Temporis

534. This instrumental is a special case of the sociative instrumental. It indicates the time with which an action coincides.

qoyar ǰil-iyer čerig-ün alban-dur oroba He was conscripted for two years. (Lit., "He entered the military service for two years.")

D. Instrumentalis Modi

535. The modal instrumental indicates the manner in which an action is performed. It corresponds sometimes to an adverb in European languages.

tedeger čuɣ-iyar-iyan qariba All of them went back. (Lit., "They went back with their totality.")
türgen-iyer yabumui He goes fast.

E. Instrumentalis Mensurae

536. This is a special case of the instrumental of manner, indicating something in accordance with which an action is performed (in English "according to . . .," "in accordance with . . ." or "after the pattern of . . ..")

bi činu ǰarliɣ-iyar yabumui I shall act according to your order.
či ɣaɣu kelekü bolbasu bi tegüber bolqu If you say anything, I shall behave according to it.

F. Instrumentalis Compensationis

537. This instrumental indicates things regarded as the price of something (English "for . . .").

mal-iyar soli- to exchange for cattle
bi egün-i alta-bar öggümüi I shall give this for gold.

The Comitative

538. The comitative answers the question "together with whom?"

köbegün-lüge jolyalduba He met the boy. (Lit., "He met with the boy.")

tegün-lüge neyileldübe He joined him.

539. The comitative occurs with the following postpositions:

qamtu together with
nigen-e together with
sača simultaneously with
čuy with
selte or *selte-ber* with

The Comitative-Instrumental

540. The double comitative-instrumental case form acts as a simple comitative, i. e., answers the question "with whom?"

qayan-luy-a-bar together with the khaghan
eke-lüge-ber with the mother

541. This double case occurs also with the same postpositions as the simple comitative.

nökör-lüge-ber qamtu together with the friend

Agreement

Agreement of the Attribute

542. As remarked above (§ 455—456), there is no agreement in case. This means that in Mongolian an attribute does not agree as to case with the word to be modified and is the same as English in this respect.

sayin morin-dur to the good horse
öndür ayula-ača from the high mountain

543. In modern Mongolian the attribute usually does not agree in number, either, with the word to be modified.

öndür ayulas high mountains
jegerde morid chestnut-colored horses

544. However, in a few cases the attribute does agree in number even in the modern language.

In the modern language only the demonstrative pronouns *ene* "this" and *tere* "that" agree in number with the word to be modified, but this is not obligatory.

ene kümün this person
ede kümüs these persons
tere kümün that person
tede kümüs those persons

545. In the pre-classical language agreement in number was a more frequent phenomenon and all parts of speech acting as attributes agreed in number with the word to be modified. This refers, however, only to the attributes in the nominative.

> *ede čidküd* these devils
>
> *ǰobaqu kümün* a suffering person, but *ǰobaqun kümün-nügüd* suffering people
>
> *ǰobalangtu eme* a suffering woman, but *ǰobalangtan amitan-nuγud* suffering creatures

546. There was also what is called *constructio ad sensum*. This means that an attribute is in the plural, although the word to be modified is a grammatical singular form but expresses a multitude. (Cf. the English "The Parliament have passed a resolution.")

> *maγun irgen* evil people (*maγun* is a plural of *maγuɪ̈*)

547. As there is no grammatical gender, there cannot be any agreement in gender. However, in the pre-classical language there was something resembling agreement in gender, although it was different from the Latin *congruentia in genere*. In reference to female beings, special words were used.

In the first place the numeral *ǰirin* "two" is to be mentioned.

> *qoyar er-e* two men
>
> *ǰirin qatud* two ladies

In modern Written Mongolian only words indicating the age or the color of female animals take special suffixes making them different from the same words used in reference to male animals.

> *γunan buqa* a three-year-old bull
>
> *γunaǰin üniy-e* a three-year-old cow
>
> *qar-a buqa* a black bull
>
> *qaraγčin üniy-e* a black cow

The Apposition

548. There is no agreement at all.

> *činggis qan-dur* to Chingis Khan

However, if two or more proper names belong to an appellative noun, the latter is put in the plural.

> *nököd amur gendün qoyar-tur* to the comrades Amur and Gendun

549. In the classical and pre-classical language, the appellative is repeated after each proper name and is always a singular form.

> *činggis qan ügedeɪ̈ qan qoyar* both Chingis Khan and Ugedei Khan

The Predicate

550. There is only one form for all persons in the indicative and, therefore, there cannot be agreement in person. As to the imperative and optative forms, some of them are used only in reference to definite persons.

bi yabusuyaį I shall go.

yabuy-a Let us go!

551. In the pre-classical language there is agreement in number with the subject of verbal nouns serving as predicates.

tede jobaqun Those will suffer.

tedeger ükügsed bülüge Those were dead.

The Nominal and Converbal Predicate

General Remarks on the Copula

552. The copula is a part of a nominal, verbal-nominal, or converbal predicate. Sometimes it can be omitted. The copula is either a simple or a compound one.

The Simple Copula

553. The verbs *buį* "is," *bolaį* "is," *bülüge* "was," and all finite forms of the verbs *a-* "to be," *bayi-* "to be," and *bol-* "to become" usually serve as copula.

ene ken buį Who is this?

manu bayši sayin buį Our teacher is good.

ene morin qurdun buį This horse is quick.

jobalang-un šiltayan anu nisvanis buį The cause of sufferings is attachment to the world.

ene sayin bolaį This is good.

činu kereg yaγun bülüge What is your need?

mongγol γajar inu aγudam yeke amuį Mongolia is vast and big.

manu köbegün sayin bayimuį Our son is good.

tere inu sayin bolba He became good.

The Compound Copula

554. A compound copula consists of more than one form of auxiliary verb. Usually it is made up of a converb or a verbal noun and a finite form.

aγsan ajuγu was, had been

aγsan bülüge was, had been

bayiju bayimuį is being

bolqu buį will become

The Descriptive Verbs

555. A descriptive verb is something different from an auxiliary verb. The latter expresses the mere idea of existence or being, and as a copula, it only connects the predicative word with the subject and indicates the time of the predicative relation. A descriptive verb expresses a definite action, e. g., "to go." When united with a converb of another verb and serving together with the latter as a single predicate, it pre-

serves its primary meaning (e. g., "to go") and the adjoining converb
precisely defines the character of the action of the finite form. Suppose
the converb is a form of the verb "to fly." In this event the meaning
of the word group is "to go flying." This means "to fly off" or "to fly
in a direction away from the speaker." On the other hand, if the finite
form means "to come," the word group expresses the idea of "to come
flying," i. e., the idea of flying toward the person speaking. In English
this can be expressed by prepositions, e. g., "to fly on," "to fly out,"
and so on. Other languages have such verbs as, e. g., *adhaereo* "to stick
to," *defero* "to carry down, to remove" (in Latin), etc. Mongolian *abču
oči-* "to take away, to carry away" is more or less the same as Latin
defero.

There are many descriptive verbs. Some of them will be discussed in
connection with the converbs (§ 576).

ire- "to come" indicates that the action is performed in the direction
toward the person speaking: *abču ire-* "to bring" (lit., "to come taking").

oro- "to enter" indicates that a motion is made into the thing concerned:
güiǰü oro- "to run into" (lit., "to enter running").

The Nominal Predicate

556. The nominal predicate is a noun, pronoun, or a numeral. It usually
has a copula which can be omitted.

A. The Nominal Predicate with Copula

manu bayši sayin bui Our teacher is good.
narasun inu modun bui The pine is a tree.
buriyad anu mongγol yasun-u nigen ulus amui The Buriats are a
  people of Mongolian descent.

B. The Nominal Predicate with Copula Omitted

qoyar anu daqutai qoyar anu daqu ügei Two of them have fur
  coats; two of them have no fur coats. (Lit., "Two of them with
  fur coats; two of them without fur coats.") This is a riddle of
  which the solution is: The horns and ears of a cow.
kümün aq-a-tai debel ǰaqatai A person has a superior; a coat has
  a collar. (Lit., "A person with a superior, a coat with a collar.")
  This is a proverb.

The Verbal-Nominal Predicate

General Remarks

557. Verbal nouns act as predicates with a copula. The latter is usually
a finite form of the verbs *a-* "to be," *bayi-* "to be," or the forms *bolai*
"is," *bui* "is," and *bülüge* "was."

Nomen Futuri

558. *Nomen futuri* with the suffix *-qu/-kü* occurs with the copula *amui̯*
"is" or *bayimui̯* "is" and expresses an intention to perform an action.

maryaši yabuqu amui̯ He intends to go to-morrow.

559. With the copula *bui̯ ǰ-a* this verbal noun expresses actions which
probably will take place.

ükükü bui̯ ǰ-a He will probably die.

560. With finite forms of the verb *bol-* "to become" this verbal noun
expresses the beginning of an action.

ungšiqu bolba He started reading.

561. With the copula *bülüge* the future noun serves as the conditional
in the English "He would have done something, (if he had been told to)".

mönggün bui̯ abasu bi qudalduǰu abqu bülüge If there were (any)
       money, I would buy.

562. With the copula *bui̯* the future noun expresses the necessity of
acting.

edüge yabuqu bui̯ Now it is necessary to go.

On the other hand, the future noun occurs with the copula *bui̯* in sentences containing interrogative words.

manu bayši keǰiy-e irekü bui̯ When will our teacher come?
ta qamiy-a yabuqu bui̯ Where will you go?

563. With the negative noun *ügei̯* the future noun is usually employed
without any verbal copula.

manu bayši irekü ügei̯ Our teacher will not come.

Nomen Imperfecti

564. In Written Mongolian this form occurs only with the negatives
ügei̯ "not" and *edüi̯* "not yet."

irege ügei̯ He has not come yet.
irege edüi̯ He has not come yet.

Nomen Perfecti

565. The *nomen perfecti* occurs with the finite forms of the verbs *a-* "to
be" and *bayi-* "to be" and the defective verbs *bui̯* "is," *bolai̯* "is," and
bülüge "was."

iregsen amui̯ He has come.
ükügsen bui̯ He has died.
törögsen bülüge He was born.

566. The *nomen perfecti* with the negative *ügei̯* often lacks a verbal copula.

iregsen ügei̯ He did not come.
ükügsen ügei̯ He was not dead.

567. The *nomen perfecti* occurs often with the copula *aǰuyu* "was" and
such a construction corresponds to the English pluperfect tense.

ükügsen aǰuyu He had died.
iregsen aǰuyu He had come.

Nomen Usus

568. The *nomen usus* expresses, as predicate, a repeated or habitual action. This form occurs with the copula *buį* "is," *büliige* "was," and the finite forms of the verbs *a-* "to be" and *bayi-* "to be."

> *iredeg buį* (or *amuį* or *bayimuį*) He usually comes.
> *iredeg büliige* He used to come.

569. The *nomen usus* with the negative *ügeį* sometimes lacks the verbal copula. The copula is not omitted when the habitual action refers to the past.

> *iredeg ügeį* He usually does not come.
> *iredeg ügeį büliige* He used not to come.

Nomen Actoris

570. The *nomen actoris* seldom occurs as a predicate. With finite forms of the verb *bol-* "to become" this expresses the simulation of an action.

> *umtayči bolba* He pretended to be asleep.
> *ese üjegči bolba* He pretended not to see.

The Converbal Predicate

General Remarks

571. The converbs serve as predicates of complete sentences only with a copula. Without a copula they cannot act as predicates of complete sentences. All converbs do not act as predicates: only the *converbum imperfecti, perfecti,* and *modale* serve as predicates.

The following forms serve as copula: all finite forms of the auxiliary verbs (*a-* "to be," *bayi-* "to be," *bol-* "to become," *buį* "is," *büliige* "was") and all finite forms of descriptive verbs.

Converbs with Auxiliary Verbs

Converbum Imperfecti

572. The *converbum imperfecti* of any verb with a finite form of the auxiliary verbs *a-* "to be," *bayi-* "to be" or the defective verbs *buį* "is" and *büliige* "was" functions in the same manner as the English progressive.

> *yabuju buį* He is going.
> *ungšiju büliige* He was reading.
> *yabuju amuį* He is walking.
> *umtaju abaį* He was sleeping.
> *ungšiju bayimuį* He is reading.

573. The imperfect converb with finite forms of the verb *bol-* "to become" expresses actions which can be or are permitted to be performed.

> *idejü bolumuį* It is possible to eat.
> *tamaki tataju bolumuį* Smoking is allowed.

Converbum Perfecti

574. The perfect converb seldom occurs as a predicate of a complete sentence. With finite forms of the verbs *a-* and *bayi-* "to be" it expresses actions which were begun before the absolute time of the copula and continue to the time of the latter.

yabuγad amuị He is gone. (Lit., "He after having gone he is.")

Converbum Modale

575. The modal converb with *buị* "is" or with finite forms of the verbs *bayi-* and *a-* "to be" expresses continuous actions.

yabun bayimuị He is continually walking.
yabun amuị He is continually walking.
ungšin buị He is continually reading.

Converbs with Descriptive Verbs

576. The imperfect or modal converb is used with descriptive verbs (§ 555) to form predicates expressing combined actions. The finite form expresses the general idea of the action, e. g., "He went," and the converb defines this idea and indicates the manner of its realization, e. g., "flying," "jumping," "riding," etc.: this means that the action of going ("He went") was performed not on foot but by flying (not by pacing but by jumping, not by walking but by riding a horse, respectively). On the other hand, the finite form indicates the time and the direction of the flying (or jumping or riding): as the meaning of the finite form is "He went" the whole group means "He went flying," i. e. "He flew away" or "He flew off" (or "He jumped away" or "He jumped off," "He rode away," respectively). In the same manner the combination "He came flying" expresses the concept that he flew in or he flew in the direction of the person speaking.

As examples of such descriptive verbs the following ones will be given.

a) The verbs *ire-* "to come" and *od-* "to go":
  nisčü irebe He flew in. (He came flying.)
  nisčü odba He flew off. (He went flying.)

b) The verb *yabu-* "to walk":
  egürčü yabu- to carry away (to walk carrying)

c) The verbs *oro-* "to enter" and *γar-* "to walk out, to leave":
  güịịü oroba He ran in. (He entered running.)
  güịịü γaruba He ran out. (He came out running.)

d) The verbs *ab-* "to take" and *ög-* "to give" express an action performed for oneself and for others:
  qudalduju abuba He bought. (He took trading.)
  bičiju abuba He wrote down for himself. (He took writing.)
  qudalduju ögbe He sold. (He gave trading.)
  bičiju ögbe He wrote for other people. (He gave writing.)

e) The verb *orki-* "to throw, to cast" as a descriptive copula indicates
that the action completely affected the object:

> *tegün-i alaǰu orkiba* He killed him. (He threw killing him.)
> *ǰalgiǰu orkiba* He devoured him. (He threw devouring him.)

f) The verbs *ekile-* "to start" and *dügür-* "to finish" indicate the beginning or the end of an action:

> *angnaǰu ekilebe* He started hunting.
> *angnaǰu dügürbe* He finished hunting.

g) The verb *alda-* "to be unable to keep" or "to fail" indicates that an
action was almost performed, but the subject failed to accomplish it:

> *unan aldaba* He almost fell down.
> *güịčen aldaba* He almost overtook him. (He failed overtaking.)

The Predicate of Incomplete Sentences

General Remarks

577. The predicate of juxtaposed incomplete sentences or clauses is a
converb: either an imperfect converb (less usual is *converbum modale*)
or a perfect converb without a copula.

Converbum Imperfecti

578. The imperfect converb expresses actions simultaneous with the
action of the finite verb.

> *negüdelčin arad bolbasu mal öskeǰü negüdel-iyer amiduramuị* The
> nomads raise cattle and live by transhuming.
> *ebügen mal-iyan tayuǰu arban oyotuna egürčü nigen γar-tayan yisün
> salay-a-tu temür uraγa čirčü irebe* The old man came, driving
> his cattle and carrying ten *oyotuna* (*Lagomys*) and dragging with
> one hand an iron hook with nine prongs.

Converbum Modale

579. The *converbum modale* expresses an action which is simultaneous
with the action of the finite verb and usually merges with the latter to
express a single action, although sometimes it expresses an independent
action.

> *tere kümün ber köbegün-i mören-ü ǰaq-a-dur abču yaǰar erüǰü oroγulun
> alabaị* That person took the boy to the river bank, dug the earth,
> and killed him by interring. (Lit., "and killed him interring.")
> *bey-e inu ebedčin-iyer enelün künesün-ečegen qayačaǰu tabun erketen
> inu bayuramuị* His body being tortured by disease, he refuses
> food, and his five senses (i. e., eyesight, hearing, smell, taste,
> and touch) become weak.

Converbum Perfecti

580. The perfect converb expresses an action which takes place before that of the finite verb and, therefore, may be translated as "after doing . . ."

> *tegün-i üjeged ečige inu kilinglejü numu sumun-i abubaį* After seeing him, his father, getting angry, took the bow and arrow.
> *öndüyiged bosču ülü čidanam* He cannot get up after raising himself.
> *mal-iyan dergede sayuyad kelebe* He sat down near his cattle and talked.
> *teden-i nom-dur oroyuluyad yurban jayun ayta-yi abuyad qariju irebe* Having converted them to the religion, he took three hundred geldings and returned.

581. The perfect converb is often followed by the word *sača* "as soon as" and in this event it expresses an action which is immediately followed by that of the finite verb.

> *burqan-dur mörgüged sača tonilba* As soon as he bent before Buddha, he was freed (from his sins).

The Verbal Predicate

General Remarks

582. The verbal predicate is a finite verb. In the following sections both the indicative and imperative (optative) forms will be discussed.

The Indicative Forms

583. The indicative forms express real actions which either were or are or will be performed. There are several indicative forms expressing the present tense. On the other hand, there are several forms expressing the past. But there are no special forms expressing the future. The latter is expressed by the present form.

584. As for the various present or past forms, there is no difference between the time of one present form and that of another. In the same manner, there is no great difference between the time of one past form and that of another. The difference is not in time (i. e., actions which took place long ago or recently) but in the subjective attitude of the person speaking toward the action: actions which, from his point of view, are doubtless facts or actions about which he cannot say anything definite. Thus there is no temporal difference between various present (or past) forms, but only a difference of the point of view of the person speaking and the latter's subjective attitude.

In English we use in such cases supplementary expressions such as "as a matter of fact," "of course," "possibly," "certainly," and so on. In Mongolian some of these nuances are inherent in the verbal form.

The Present

585. The present form ending in *-muị/-müị* or *-nam/-nem* expresses an action which is present or customary or future.

> *nigen ekener ǰimis tegümüị* A woman is picking berries (now).
>
> *negüdelčin arad negüdel-iyer amiduramuị* The nomads live by transhumance (usually or always).
>
> *γobi-yin amitan quduγ-un usun-dur itegemüị* The living beings of the Gobi depend upon the water of wells (usually or always).
>
> *manu bayši maryaši iremüị* Our teacher will come to-morrow (future).

586. The other present form ends in *-yu/-yü*. This, too, expresses an action which is present or customary or future. The difference between this form and the form in *-muị (-nam)* is that the latter is a mere statement of fact ("he comes," "he will come," and so on) while the form ending in *-yu* expresses an action which is a logical conclusion of the previous context.

> *mergen inu učir šiltaγan bügüde-yi medemüị. teneg inu ülü medeǰü osolduyu* The sage knows all circumstances and causes. The fool, not knowing, consequently makes mistakes.
>
> *qar-a noqaị inu bügelǰisün-i idemüị. arsalang inu görüged-ün qaγan bolqu tula teyimü busu buyu* The ordinary (lit., "black") dog eats vomit. The lion, because he is the king of animals, consequently is not so.

587. Usually the form in *-yu* expresses an action which may be considered the opposite of a previous action.

> *ǰirγalang-un šiltaγan inu buyan buị. kilinče-eče ǰobalang anu töröyü* The cause of happiness is virtue, (whereas) suffering issues from sin.

The Past

588. There are three past forms. They end in *-ba* or *-baị, -luγa,* and *-ǰuquị.*

The past form ending in *-ba/-baị* is used with reference to all persons and expresses an action completed in the past. Such an action is considered a mere statement without any particular nuance.

> *qoyar kümün bayišing dotor-a orobaị* Two persons entered the house.
>
> *duu-a soqor-un köbegüd anu oyirad-un ögeled bayatud qoyid kergüd dörben oboγtan bolbaị* The sons of Duua Sokhor became ancestors of the four tribes Ogeled, Baghatud, Khoyid, and Kergud of the Oirats.
>
> *dörben aq-a-nar-taγan ayurlaǰu onon mören ögede γaγčaγar yorčibaị* He became angry with his four brothers and went upstream along the Onon River.
>
> *ǰiγasun šungγun dalaị-yin iruγar odbaị* The fish dived and went to the bottom of the sea.

589. The past form ending in -*ba* (but never in -*baį*) is sometimes used as a concessive converb.

>*ükübe yāba ǰayayan minu medetügeį* Whether I shall die or what will happen (to me) my destiny must know!

590. The past form ending in -*luya* expresses an action of a little longer duration than that expressed by the form ending in -*ba* (or -*baį*) and is considered a fact well known to everyone or witnessed by someone and, therefore, beyond doubt. This form is less common in Modern Mongolian. Sometimes it expresses an action which almost took place or which did not take place at all but the completion of which in the near future is considered so probable that it may be considered as completed in the past.

>*qalay qoqoį tere mayu inu namayi alaluya* Alas, that evil person killed me!
>
>*yučin bayatur anu ükülüge* His thirty heroes died.
>
>*či tegün-i ese üǰelüü* Did not you see him?

591. The past form in -*ǰuquį* expresses completed, but unexpected actions. Such actions took place long before all the other actions of the context and the person speaking is somewhat surprised when discovering this. This form is not used with reference to the first person of the singular or plural.

>*ger dotor-a-ača tabiyad čerig yarčuquį* About fifty soldiers had come out of the house.
>
>*tere bide-yin ulus qotalayar ǰöbšiyeldün ene ber iǰayurtan-u köbegün aǰuyu kemeldüged* That people of the Bide said, while discussing it in its entity, that he turned out to be a scion of noblemen.
>
>*erte urida enedkeg-ün emün-e eteged nigen yaǰar-tur er-e em-e qoyar aysan aǰuyu* Formerly there were in a country south of India a man and a woman.

The Imperative Forms

592. The imperative and all other related forms such as the voluntative, optative, and so on, express actions which, in reality, do not take place. Whereas the indicative forms express actions which either take place in the present or have taken place in the past and are assertions of such actions as real happenings, the imperative forms express actions which are to be performed by persons so ordered. In the same manner, the optative forms express actions which do not take place, but are considered desirable.

593. The imperative of the second person expresses an order to perform an action. This is the shortest form of the verb and has no ending.

>*či ende sayu* Sit down here!

The Mongolian imperative sentence usually has a subject which here is the person addressed by the speaker. In Latin or in other European languages imperative sentences usually do not have any syntactic subject as the idea of the person acting is inherent in the imperative.

594. The benedictive also is an imperative form, but this does not express an order but rather a polite request. This form is used with reference to a single person, who cannot be addressed with the pronoun "thou," and also with reference to a group of persons.

> *manu ger-tür oroytun* Please enter our house!

595. The imperative of the third person expresses an order to perform an action, with reference to an absent person: there is a speaker and a listener but the real performer of the action may be absent and is supposed to learn about the order of the person speaking through the listener. This form is used in both singular and plural.

> *tere kümün iretügeį* Let that person come! (or "That person must come!", or "That person may come!")

The Voluntative

596. The voluntative expresses the wish to perform the action concerned. The voluntative of the first person of the singular expresses the wish of the speaker to act and may be translated as "I want to . . .," "let me . . ." or "I will . . ."

> *bi odsuyaį* I will go!

597. The voluntative of the first person of the plural denotes a wish expressed by several persons, although sometimes this is used instead of the optative of the first person of the singular.

> *edüge bida ger-tegen qariy-a* Now let us return home!

The Optative

598. The optative of all persons expresses a wish expressed by someone. Usually this form expresses a futile desire which will never be fulfilled and, therefore, has a shade of sadness.

> *bi tegün-i üĵegeseį* Ah, if I could see him!

The Dubitative

599. The dubitative expresses the idea of fear that the action concerned may, contrary to all expectations, take place. This form is used with reference to all persons.

> *yeke süįd boluyuĵaį* A great disaster may occur!, Let a great disaster not occur!

600. The imperative, voluntative, and optative forms are used with the prohibitive particle *buu*, sometimes with the colloquial *bitegeį*.

> *buu ire* Do not come!
> *buu odsuyaį* I will not go!
> *buu iretügeį* He must not come!

Genera Verbi

General Remarks

601. In Written Mongolian there are the following voices or *genera verbi:* the active, factitive, passive, reciprocal, and co-operative.

The Active Voice

602. The subject of an active verb is the person acting. This means that the action is performed by the subject while, for example, the subject of a passive verb does not perform any actions, but undergoes the action of another person.

Active verbs can, for example, be a predicate. Such sentences do not always have a grammatical subject. The latter may be missing when the person acting is mentioned in the previous context and, therefore, is known.

603. In Written Mongolian, active verbs may also replace passive verbs. For instance, the perfect noun (*nomen perfecti*) of the verb *ükü-* "to die," *ükügsen* "dead," may never function as a passive verb, but the same verbal noun of the verb *ungši-* "to read" may so function: e. g., *ungšiysan kümün* is "a person who read" and *ungšiysan nom* is "a book which was read." It is obvious that the active or passive function of such verbs results only from the meaning of the noun which it qualifies: a person cannot be read and, therefore, *ungšiysan kümün* cannot be understood as "a person who was read;" on the other hand, a book cannot read and, therefore, *ungšiysan nom* cannot be understood as "a book which read." It is obvious that the active voice acts as passive only in cases in which the grammatical subject by its nature cannot perform but can only undergo a certain action.

Therefore, active verbs never have a passive function, when the sentence contains only one word which, under various circumstances, can function both as an actor and a passive object of someone's action. Thus *alaysan kümün* can, in this construction, mean only "a person who killed" (i. e., "killer") and cannot be understood as "a killed person." But if the same construction is enlarged by another word expressing something which, under various circumstances, can function both as actor and object of someone's action, the sense of the construction changes and the verb acquires a passive function. The additional word is always, in such constructions, a genitive of any declinable part of speech. Thus the construction *dayisun-u alaysan kümün* means "a person killed by the enemy" (lit., "the enemy's killed person"). The same passive function is also found in the construction *noqai-yin idegsen miqan* "the meat eaten by the dog" (lit., "the dog's eaten meat"). It may be added that in Written Mongolian in such cases, it is always the active voice that is used and never the passive.

The general rule is, that verbal nouns of active verbs, serving as attributes and preceded by a genitive, always have the function of a passive voice.

činu-a-yin idegsen qonin a sheep eaten by the wolf
šabi-yin ungšiysan nom a book read by the pupil
manu sayuysan ger the house inhabited by us
bayši-yin oluysan nom the book found by the teacher

On the other hand, the same constructions with verbs expressing actions which cannot be undertaken by anybody never have a passive meaning, e. g., *minu ükügsen ekener* "my wife, who died."

Is should be pointed out that this has nothing to do with the transitiveness or intransitiveness of the verbs concerned, because even intransitive verbs, which have no direct object, can function as passive verbs, e. g., *minu kebtegsen yajar* "the place in which I was lying": it is not "the place which was lying" but "the place in which I was lying."

This explains why the terms transitive and intransitive have not been used in this section.

The Passive Voice

604. The grammatical subject of a passive verb is, from the logical point of view, not the subject but the object of someone's action. The person really acting is not the grammatical subject, from the logical point of view. Thus in passive sentences the logical and syntactical categories do not coincide.

The logical subject of a passive sentence is a dative-locative, the *dativus actoris*.

qonin činu-a-dur bariydaba The sheep was caught by the wolf.

605. The passive voice is used relatively rarely and, as remarked above, in many cases the idea of a passive action is expressed by the active voice. This takes place primarily in attributive constructions. In the latter, the verba. noun is in an active form and the logical subject is in the genitive. The verbal noun may also be in a passive form and, as remarked above, the logical subject in such cases is a dative-locative. Thus the following constructions, being absolutely different from the syntactical point of view are, nevertheless, equivalent from the point of view of their sense and, therefore, interchangeable:

noqai̯-dur idegdegsen miqan the meat eaten by the dog = *noqai̯-yin idegsen miqan*

dayisun-dur alaydaysan kümün a person killed by the enemy = *dayisun-u alaysan kümün*

It should be pointed out that the construction *noqai̯-yin idegsen miqan* cannot be understood as "dog meat which was eaten" (by someone), because this requires a different word order: *idegsen noqai̯-yin miqan*.

As remarked above, instead of the passive voice, the active voice may be employed in attributive constructions. This is not so, however, in predicative constructions. The predicate is always a passive verb, if the action concerned is a passive one. Thus the construction *činu-a bariydaba* "The wolf was caught," cannot be replaced by anything else.

606. It is commonly known that in English the passive voice is also used in such sentences as "I was told" or "He was given a book" which are impossible in Latin, French, German, and many other languages. In Written Mongolian there occur constructions resembling such English expressions. They are used primarily in attributive constructions, e. g., *γar oytaluγdaγsan kümün* "a person whose hand was cut off" or "a person cut in respect of his hand." In this construction the verbal noun *oytaluγdaγsan* "cut" is an attribute of *kümün* "person" and literally this means "a person who was cut." This may be illustrated better by the following English sentences: "I was amputated my legs," "I was made a surgical operation." Although in common English speech such sentences are impossible, they do not differ much from "I was told a very sad story" or "The pupil was given a new book." Thus the Mongolian sentence given above may be literally translated as "a person who was cut his hand off." In such Mongolian expressions the verbal noun is usually a passive verb. Yet, in a few rare cases, the verbal noun may be an active verb, although the latter would mean that the man himself cut off his hand. To avoid misunderstandings, in such cases the Mongols use the reflexive-possessive suffix or the genitive of the personal pronoun of the third person *inu:* *γar-iyan oytaluγsan kümün* "a person who cut off his own hand" and *γar inu oytaluγsan kümün* "a person whose hand was cut off." In the latter construction the word *inu* indicates that the person performing the cutting (although the person acting is not expressed grammatically) did not cut his own hand (*suus*), but his (*ejus*) hand, whereas in the first construction the person performing the action had his own hand as object.

> *ed abtaγsan* (passive) *kümün* a person whose property was taken away (lit., "a property taken person")
>
> *ed inu quriyan abuγsan kümün* a person whose property was confiscated (lit., "a person confiscated in respect of his property")
>
> *ed-iyen quriyan abuγsan kümün* a person who confiscated his own property (from the point of view of logic this sentence, of course, does not make any sense).

607. The passive also expresses the idea of the necessity to act. This is the case of the future noun (*nomen futuri*) with the ending *-qui* (only this and never *-qu*) of the passive verb.

> *tere inu eyin uqaγdaqui* That is to be understood in this manner.
>
> *amitan bügüde buyan kigdekün* (plural of *kigdeküi*) All living beings must exercise virtue.

608. The passive voice also expresses actions caused by a subject unknown or unmentioned in the sentence.

> *čečeg-ün qur-a oroγuluγdaba* A rain of flowers was rained down.

In this sentence the verb *oroγuluγda-* is a passive of the factitive *oroγul-* "to cause to rain" which is derived from *oro-* "to rain." Therefore, the literal translation should be "a rain of flowers was caused to rain." The rain was sent by someone who was, of course, a god or a ghost.

The Factitive Verb

609. The factitive expresses the idea of causing an action. There are many verbs which cannot govern a direct object, e. g. *ükü-* "to die" or *kebte-* "to lie down." Yet the factitive of such verbs governs the accusative.

tegün-i ükügülbe He let him (or caused him to) die.

tegün-i kebtegülbe He let him lie, or He laid him.

610. Verbs which are intransitive become transitive when put in the factitive. This means that the factitive of such verbs does not express the idea of ordering to or letting act, but the idea of actions such as "to send," "to lay," "to raise," and so on, although in literal translation such factitive verbs mean "to let go," "to let lie," "to let rise," and so on.

Intransitive	Transitive
oro- to enter, to go in	*oroɣul-* to let in, to lead in
yabu- to walk, to go	*yabuɣul-* to send
sayu- to sit down	*sayulɣa-* to set, to plant
bayi- to stand, to be	*bayiɣul-* to found
bol- to become	*bolɣa-* to do, to make
ɣar- to go out	*ɣarɣa-* to take out, to lead out

611. Verbs which are transitive become factitive *par excellence*. This means that the factitive of such verbs expresses the idea of letting act or ordering to act.

ungši- to read	*ungšiɣul-* to order to read
biči- to write	*bičigül-* to let write

612. The factitive of an intransitive verb has only one direct object.

bi tegün-i oroɣulba I let him in.

mangɣus tegün-i ükügülbe Mangus killed him. (Lit., "Let him die.")

613. The factitive of transitive verbs has two direct objects: one expressing the person ordered to act and another expressing the object of the latter's action.

bi tegün-i nom ungšiɣulba I let him read a book.

qaɣan inu tüšimel-i čerig-iyen abču iregülbe The khaghan let the minister bring his army.

614. The person performing the action of a transitive verb in the factitive can also be expressed by a dative-locative. In such cases the factitive has a slightly different meaning. In such constructions the factitive does not express an order but, on the contrary, the idea of the helplessness of the grammatical subject to prevent the action. Thus, in the sentence *bi tegün-i nom ungšiyulba* "I let him read a book," it was I who purposely let or ordered him to read, but, if we replace the accusative *tegün-i* with the dative-locative, I become not the person who ordered him to read but the person who could not help letting him read. This can be illustrated by the following examples:

bi noqai-yi miqa idegülbe I let the dog eat meat (i. e., I purposely gave the dog meat).

bi miqan-i noqaı̣-dur idegülbe I could not help letting the dog eat the meat (i. e., I did not give it to the dog but the dog itself took it and I was unable to prevent it from doing so).

The Reciprocal Verb

615. Reciprocal verbs express mutual actions. Therefore, a reciprocal verb presumes at least two persons acting. The latter are expressed in the subjects or in the subject and the indirect object. The latter is, in such cases, a comitative.

qoyar quča mörgüldübe Two rams butt each other.
bayatur inu tere dayisun-luy-a barilduba The hero wrestled with that foe.

616. It is obvious that transitive verbs may occur in the reciprocal form, since logically each of the persons acting is an object of the action of the other person acting. Yet even intransitive verbs sometimes occur in this form, principally in the language of popular books. These do not express the idea of a reciprocal action, but the idea of an action performed in a co-operative manner.

tedener ebdereldübe They quarreled: *ebdereldü-*, reciprocal of *ebdere-* to fall to pieces

This explains the origin of many formally reciprocal verbs, such as *bayildu-* "to struggle, to make war" from *bayi-* "to stand" (originally *bayildu-* meant "to stand against each other"), *kereldü-* "to quarrel" from a no longer extant verb **kere-*, etc.

The Co-operative Verb

617. Co-operative verbs express the idea of participation in the actions concerned. These verbs may be derived both from transitive and intransitive stems.

čaı̣ uyulčamuı̣ He drinks tea (with other people).
šabi-nar ungšilčamuı̣ The pupils are reading together.

Many co-operative verbs lost their immediate connection with the meaning of the primary stem and became new words.

sayulča- to be present (at a meeting, lit., "to sit with others"— *sayu-* to sit)

Accumulation of Voice Suffixes

618. A verbal stem may take more than one mark of voice: a reciprocal verb may take the suffix of a factitive, a passive may take the same factitive suffix, and so on.

barilduyul- to let wrestle
idegdegül- to let be eaten
idelčegül- to let participate in eating

bayiyuluyda- to be founded
idegdegülügde- to be let be eaten
yabuyuluyda- to be sent
barilčayul- to let participate in catching

Interrogative Sentences

General Remarks

619. There are two kinds of interrogative sentences: 1. that in which
the interrogation refers to the whole sentence (e. g., "Will our teacher
come?") and 2. that in which the interrogation refers only to a single
word (e. g., "When will he come?").
Sentences of the former category are interrogative sentences in general,
and those of the latter category are sentences containing special interrogative words. The predicate in interrogative sentences is either a
nominal or a verbal one. The latter is in an indicative form.

Sentences Generally Interrogative

620. The predicate of such sentences always takes the interrogative
particle *uu.* The latter is on the copula, or, in a predicate without a
copula, on the predicative word.

Nominal Predicate

621. The predicate has a copula which may be omitted.

> *ta sayin bayimuị uu* or *ta sayin uu* How are you? (Lit., "Are you
> well?")

Verbal Predicate

622. The verbal predicate in sentences generally interrogative takes the
interrogative particle *uu.*

> *bi čimadur ese kelelüü* Did I not tell you?
> *ta mongyol kele medemüü* Do you know Mongolian?

Converbal Predicate

623. In converbal predicates it is the copula which takes the interrogative
particle.

> *ta sayin yabuju bayimuị uu* Are you travelling well? (i. e., "Do
> you have a good journey?")

Sentences with Interrogative Words

General Remarks

624. Sentences partly interrogative contain interrogative words, such
as "who," "when," "where," and so on. The latter are either pronouns,
adverbs, or interrogative verbs (e. g., *yayaki-* "to do what?").
In such sentences the predicate does not take an interrogative particle.

Nominal Predicate

625. The nominal predicate of a sentence containing an interrogative word usually occurs with the copula *buį.*

či qamiɣ-a-ača iregsen buį From where did you come?
či ken qaɣan-u albatu buį What khaghan's subject are you?
či yaɣun abqu buį What will you take?
ta keǰiy-e iregsen buį When did you come?

Verbal Predicate

626. The verbal predicate of a sentence containing an interrogative word does not take an interrogative particle. It does not differ in its form from the predicate of a simple statement.

či qamiɣ-a-ača irebeį From where did you come?
či yaɣun abumuį What will you take?
bi yaɣakimuį What am I to do?

Converbal Predicate

627. The converbal predicate of a sentence partly interrogative (i. e., containing an interrogative word) has a copula which is a finite form either of an auxiliary verb or of a descriptive verb.

tere kümün qamiɣ-a saɣuǰu amuį Where does that person live?
yambar šibaɣun nisčü irebeį What bird flew here?

Rhetorical Interrogation

628. A question may be a real one, asked to get necessary information, but it may also be a rhetorical one. Such rhetorical questions, in reality, are not questions at all, but affirmative statements only made in the form of a question. Such sentences are more or less the same as such English sentences as "Certainly, you know. Do you not?" in which the question implies that the person speaking does not doubt that the interlocutor knows what the situation is.

In such sentences the colloquial *biši* or the Written Mongolian *busu* with the interrogative particle *uu* is used.

či minu ekener bišüü (or *bišiuu*) Are you not my wife?
činggis qaɣan minu eǰen busu uu Is not Chingis Khaghan my master?

Disjunctive Interrogative Sentences

629. Disjunctive interrogative sentences contain a double interrogation. Such sentences suppose an alternative, e. g., "Will you take this or that?". The disjunctive interrogative sentences consist of two juxtaposed interrogative sentences and each of them has a separate predicate of its own. Conjunctions are not used, except for a construction which may pass as one containing a conjunction (see § 630).

či abumuį uu bi abumuį uu Will you take or shall I take? (Lit.,
"Will you take? Shall I take?")

ende bayimuu tende bayimuu Is it here or is it there? (Lit., "Is it
here? Is it there?")

630. The second of the juxtaposed interrogative sentences mentioned in
§ 629 may begin with the negative *esebesü* which is in origin a conditional converb of the negative verb **ese-* "not to be" (see § 638).

geser amidu buyu esebesü ükügsen buyu Is Geser alive or has he
died? (Lit., "Is Geser alive? If not, has he died?")

Negatives

General Remarks

631. Nouns and verbs take different negatives. The negatives with nouns
are *ügeį* and *busu*.

The Negative *ügeį*

632. The word *ügeį* is a noun and may be declined. Its primary meaning
is "absence."

Since all nouns may act as a predicate, the negative *ügeį*, too, may serve
as a predicate, with or without the copula.

ende usun ügeį There is no water here.
nadur mönggün ügeį buį I have no money.

633. A noun followed by *ügeį* expresses the same as English nouns
ending in *-less*.

usu ügeį γaǰar a waterless country
mal ügeį yadayu kümün a poor man having no cattle

634. The negative *ügeį* occurs with the verbal nouns and serves as the
negative "not."

suruγsan inu dalaį suruγ-a ügeį inu balaį One who has studied is
an ocean; one who has not studied is blind.

manu bayši iregsen ügeį (or *iregsen ügeį amuį*) Our teacher did
not come.

635. The negative *ügeį* referring to a pair of words means the same as
the English "as well ... and ..."

ǰun ebül ügeį summer and winter
edür söni ügeį yabuba He went day and night.

The Negative *busu*

636. While the negative *ügeį* expresses the mere idea of absence or non-
existence of something, the negative *busu* indicates that the object
concerned, although existing or present, is not what it is believed to be.
In other words, this is the same as the English "not ... but ..."
The negative *busu* is, in origin, a pronoun meaning "another."

modun busu not a tree but ...
ene bolbasu ǰiγasun busu buį This is not a fish.

The Negative *ese*

637. The negative *ese* is used only with verbs. It is placed before the verb.

This negative is used with all indicative forms, with the so-called *nomen perfecti, converbum conditionale*, and *converbum concessivum*.

> *manu bayši ese irebe* Our teacher did not come.
> *ese iregsen kümün* a person who did not come
> *ta ese irebesü* if you will not come
> *ese irebečü* although he will not come

638. The negative *ese* is a fossilized verb and a few forms still exist. Its forms are used as adverbs such as the English "nevertheless," "otherwise," and so on.

> Nomen futuri *esekü* or not (referring to future actions): *yabuqu esekü* to go or not
> Nomen perfecti *esegsen* or not (referring to past actions): *iregsen esegsen-i ülü medemüï* It is unknown whether he came or not. (Lit., "One does not known the coming or not.")
> Past tense *esebe* or not: *ükübeiüi esebeiüi* Did he die or did he not?
> Converbum conditionale *esebesü* if not, otherwise: *esebesü bi absuyaï* Otherwise I shall take (it).
> Converbum successivum *eseküle* otherwise: *eseküle ene ǰorily-a-yi güïčedkeǰü bolqu ügeï* Otherwise it will not be possible to achieve this aim.
> Converbum concessivum *esebečü* in spite of, nevertheless: *esebečü bi abčiramuï* And even so, I shall bring (it), or Nevertheless, I shall bring (it).

The Negative *ülü*

639. The negative *ülü* is used with verbal forms and also is placed before the latter.

It occurs with all indicative forms, with the verbal nouns of the future and the actor (*nomen futuri, nomen actoris*), and with all converbs except for the *converbum conditionale* and *concessivum*.

> *šabi ülü medemüï* The pupil does not know.
> *ülü irekü činu yaγun buï* What does your not coming mean?
> *ülü medeǰü* not knowing

The Prohibitive Particles

640. There are two prohibitive particles: *buu* and *bitegeï*. The latter is a colloquial form. Both are used with imperative and optative forms and with the dubitative.

These particles are placed before the verbal forms concerned.

> *buu ire* Do not come!
> *buu iretügeï* He must not come!
> *buu medegeseï* Ah, if he did not know!

The Nominal Constructions

General Remarks

641. The predicate of a completed sentence is a finite verb and the person acting is expressed by the subject, which is a nominative. A sentence may relate to another sentence in the same manner as a single word relates to the rest of the sentence: a sentence may serve as a subject of the whole, as an object, and so on. In such cases a sentence becomes a nominal construction which is nothing other than an enlarged member of a sentence.

Thus, instead of a simple subject expressed by a single word, a sentence may have a subject expressed by a group of words, e. g., instead of "The premature death of our friend caused grief among us" there may be "What our teacher had told us about the premature death of our friend caused grief among us," where "What our teacher had told us about the premature death of our friend" is an enlarged subject of the whole.

A sentence, to become a nominal construction, loses its predicate and replaces it with a verbal noun (*nomen verbale*). The latter takes all the suffixes of that member of the sentence of which it has to play the role. This means that the verbal noun is followed by the designator of the subject (e. g., *inu, anu, bolbasu*, and so on), if it has to serve as subject of the whole, or it takes the ending of the appropriate oblique case, if it has to serve as an object, and so on.

Such a nominal construction has neither a grammatical predicate nor a grammatical subject. Therefore, these terms (subject, predicate) will be avoided. Instead, the terms "action" and "actor" will be used.

Nominal Constructions as Subjects

642. In such nominal constructions the actor is expressed by a genitive (*genitivus actoris*) or a nominative. The action is expressed by a verbal noun which has all the grammatical characteristics of a grammatical subject: it is a nominative and is followed by a subject designator.

> *tere kümün-ü kelegsen inu ünen buį* What that man said is true.
>
> *mongγol yasutan-u uy iǰayur-un tuqaį bičigsen inu edüge udal ügeį neyitelegden γarumuį* What was written about the origin of the Mongol tribes will be published soon.

643. A special case is a nominal construction of which the actor is expressed by an interrogative pronoun. Such constructions, seen from the point of view of their meaning, correspond to relative subordinate sentences of the European languages.

> *tegün-i ken deyilügsen inu abumuį* He who has vanquished will take it.

Nominal Constructions as Attributes

644. Nominal constructions serving as attributes consist of a verbal noun (with an object, attribute, etc.). The verbal noun is a nominative. The actor is expressed by a genitive (*genitivus actoris*).

> *bi tegün-ü ǰokiyan bičigsen nom ungšimuį* I am reading a book written by him.
>
> *manu bayši-yin mandur kelegsen üge ünen aǰuyu* The words spoken to us by our teacher turned out to be true.

645. In nominal constructions serving as attributes the passive voice may be replaced by the active. The actor is expressed in passive constructions by the dative-locative (*dativus actoris*), while it is in the genitive (*genitivus actoris*) when the active voice is used.

> *noqaį-dur idegdegsen miqan* the meat eaten by the dog
>
> *bayši-yin bičigsen bičig* a letter written by the teacher

Nominal Constructions as Objects

General Remarks

646. Nominal constructions may serve as objects. In such constructions the action is expressed by an oblique case of a verbal noun. The oblique case is the same as that of an object represented by a single word. It may be accompanied by a postposition.

Nominal Constructions in the Genitive

647. A nominal construction in the genitive serving as an object occurs only with postpositions.

> *bi erdem surquį-yin tulada suryayuli-dur orobaį* I entered school with the purpose of studying science.
>
> *bida tanu bayši-yin ükügsen-ü tuqaį medegülügsen-i küliyen abuba* We received the message about the death of your teacher.

Nominal Constructions in the Accusative

648. Nominal constructions in the accusative serve as direct objects. The actor is put in the genitive.

> *bi tegün-ü bičigsen-i ese ungšiba* I did not read what he had written.
>
> *bi qota-ača ger-tegen bučaǰu iregsen-iyen medegülümüį* I am telling of my return home from town.

649. A special case is the accusative with a verbal noun corresponding to the Latin *accusativus cum infinitivo*. Here both the actor and the action are put in the accusative (see § 514).

> *geser-i yabuqu-yi üǰebe* He saw Geser go.

650. When the actor of the nominal construction is independent of the grammatical subject of the whole sentence, the action is put in the simple accusative, but when the actor of the nominal construction coincides with the subject, the action is put in the accusative with the reflexive-possessive suffix.

> *edüge bi tandur činggis qayan-u tuqaį bičigsen-i ilegemüį* Now I am sending you what was written about Chingis Khan.
>
> *edüge bi tandur činggis qayan-u tuqaį bičigsen-iyen ilegemüį* Now I am sending you what I wrote about Chingis Khan.

Nominal Constructions in the Dative-Locative

651. Nominal constructions in the dative-locative correspond, in meaning, to temporal subordinate clauses of European languages and to the Latin *ablativus absolutus*. They are translated into English as "When the person concerned did (or will do) something . . ."

The action of such constructions is expressed by a verbal noun in the dative-locative. When the actor of the construction is the same as the grammatical subject of the whole period, the action is indicated by a dative-locative with the reflexive-possessive suffix.

The actor is put in the genitive (or in relatively rare cases, under the influence of the Colloquial, in the *accusativus actoris*, see § 517), when he is not the same as the subject of the whole sentence.

> The actor in the accusative:
>
> *manu nökör-i qota-dur irekü-dür tegün-ü olan tanil bayiɣsan aǰuɣu* When our friend came to town, there were many acquaintances of his there.
>
> The actor in the genitive:
>
> *manu nökör-ün irekü-dür bida bügüde mašida bayasba* When our friend came, all of us were very glad.
>
> The actor is the subject of the whole sentence:
>
> *bi qota-dur irekü-degen suryaɣuli-dur oromui̯* When I come to town, I shall enter school.

Nominal Constructions in the Ablative

652. Nominal constructions in the ablative function in the same manner as a simple ablative object. According to the various meanings of the ablative such constructions may be regarded as *ablativus exclusivus, ablativus comparativus*, etc.

The action is put in the ablative, and the actor, if he is not the same as the subject of the whole sentence, in the genitive (and rarely in the accusative).

> *kilinče üi̯leddügsen-eče eldeb maɣu ǰobalang bui̯ boluɣsan amui̯* In consequence of sins having been committed, various grave sufferings came into existence.
>
> *činggis qan-u ügei̯ boluɣsan-ača qoyiši ügedei̯ qan inu qaɣan ergügde-ǰüküi̯* After the death of Chingis Khan, Ugedei Khan was elected emperor.

Nominal Constructions in the Instrumental

653. Nominal constructions in the instrumental usually act as causal subordinate clauses of European languages and, therefore, may be translated as "because of . . . ," "in consequence of . . . ," or "by doing so . . ."

> *mongɣol yasutan-u dotor-a eb ügei̯ boluɣsan-iɣar teden-ü küčün anu neng bayuraǰuqui̯* In consequence of internal discord among the Mongolian tribes, their power declined still more.

eldeb ǰüịl-ün buruγu arγ-a kemǰiy-e-nügüd-i yabuγuluγsan-iyar eyimü süịd boluγsan buị In consequence of taking various wrong measures, such a disaster arose.

Nominal Constructions in the Comitative

654. Nominal constructions in the comitative express events simultaneous with the action of the predicate of the whole sentence. They may be translated into English as "simultaneously with . . ."

ür čayiquị-luγ-a qamtu mordoba He started with the break of dawn. (Lit., He started together with the dawning of the dawn.)

tere inu kitad ulus-un qubisqal-un manduquị-luγ-a tokiyalduba That coincided with the rise of the Chinese revolution.

Order of Nominal Constructions

655. Nominal constructions are members of a sentence and they differ from simple members only in that they are groups of words while simple members are single words. Therefore, a nominal construction occupies the same place in a sentence as a simple member. This means that a nominal construction serving as a subject occupies the usual place of the subject, one serving as an object occupies the usual place of an object, and so on.

The usual order of words in sentences is: a—s—a—o—p, where a is attribute, s is subject, o is object, and p is predicate.

If we replace the symbols of simple members with symbols for nominal constructions serving as the members concerned, the formula is as follows: A—S—A—O—P, where A is an attributive nominal construction, S is a nominal construction serving as a subject, O is a nominal construction serving as an object, and P is a predicative nominal construction with a copula. Of course, in reality, there are very few sentences of which all the members are nominal constructions. Usually only one or two members represent such groups of words while the remaining members are simple ones, e. g., a—s—O—p or S—a—O—p, and so on.

The Converbal Constructions

General Remarks

656. The imperfect, modal, and perfect converbs act as predicates of incomplete juxtaposed sentences or as parts of the main predicate.

negüdelčin arad bolbasu üker aduγu qoni imaγ-a ǰerge-yin mal öskeǰü usu belčiger-i daγaǰu negüdel-iyer amiduramuị Nomad people, raising cattle, horses, sheep, goats, and other animals, and following water and pastures, exist by transhumance.

bi ungšiǰu sayumuị I am sitting and reading.

657. Most of the remaining converbs are, from the historical point of view, fossilized forms of oblique cases of various verbal nouns, some

of which no longer exist as such. Since nominal constructions may act
as certain members of a sentence, it is obvious that fossilized forms of
original verbal nouns, too, must be able to act in a similar manner. Indeed, there are such groups of words in which the idea of an action is
expressed by a converb.

Historical Survey of Some Converbal Forms

658. As remarked in § 657, many converbs are fossilized forms of oblique
cases of verbal nouns.

The *converbum finale* ending in *-r-a* is the dative-locative (suffix *-a*) of
a noun ending in *-r* (cf. *amur* "peace, rest" from *amu-* "to rest"). Originally such forms answered the same question as the dative-locative, e. g.,
ider-e now "in order to eat"—formerly "to the eating" or "toward the
eating." It should be remarked that this converb corresponds, from the
point of view of meaning, to the dative-locative in *-a* of the *nomen
futuri* in *-qui̯*, e. g., *sayur-a = sayuqui̯-a* "in order to sit."

The same can be said of the *converbum praeparativum* in *-r-un*. The
latter was originally a genitive (suff. *-un*) of a noun ending in *-r* (cf.
supra). Thus, *amitan-i jobayulur-un kilinče üi̯leddügsen amui̯* "He committed sins by causing sufferings to living beings," originally was "He
committed sins of tormenting living beings." It should be added,
however, that the genitive served in Ancient Mongolian or in Common
Altaic both as genitive and instrumental.

The *converbum terminale* ending in *-tala*, e. g., *ükütele* "until he dies,"
was originally a dative-locative (with the suffix *-a*) of nouns ending in
-tal (cf. *surtal* "doctrine" from *sur-* "to learn"). Thus, *ükütele* "until he
dies" was originally "till the death" or "to the death."

The *converbum abtemporale* (suffix *-ysayar*) is a fossilized instrumental
of the *nomen perfecti*. The ancient instrumental suffix *-yar* still exists as
the ending of certain adverbs, e. g. *yayčayar* "alone, solely," *manayar*
"tomorrow," and so on. Thus, *abuysayar* now means "since he took,"
but originally it meant "through having taken."

The *converbum contemporale* with the ending *-mayča* is a fossilized *casus
aequativus* (with the ancient suffix *-ča* related to the ablative suffix) of
a deverbal noun ending in *-may* (e. g., *qayurmay* "fraud" from *qayur-*
"to deceive").

Thus the forms of many converbs are fossilized oblique cases of verbal
or deverbal nouns. Consequently, they do not differ in principle from
living oblique cases of existing verbal nouns. Indeed, constructions with
such converbs act in a manner similar to nominal constructions.

The idea of the action is expressed in such constructions by converbs.
The actor is subject to the same rules as the actor of a nominal construction.

659. The actor is expressed in converbal constructions by the nominative
or genitive (or even accusative), if the subject of the whole sentence does
not coincide with the actor. Yet this is not obligatory and the nominative
can be used in all cases.

boroγan ürlüge boltala oroǰu abaį It rained till morning. (Lit., "Rain was falling until morning came.")

nökör-i oromayča bügüdeger mendücilebe As soon as the friend came in, all of them welcomed him.

mongγol arad ulus bayiγuluγdaγsaγar qorin ǰil bolba Twenty years have elapsed since the Mongolian People's Republic was established.

Converbum Terminale

660. Constructions with the *converbum terminale* express: 1. events during which the action of the main predicate takes place and 2. events before which the action of the predicate takes place. In the latter case the converbum terminale indicates the time limit of the main action: "till . . .," "until . . .," "so that . . ."

dorǰi tür küliyeǰü saγutala mönö buriyad morin terge abčiraba "While Dorji sat for a while, waiting, the same Buriat brought a horse car.

noyitan modu-yi nočotala qayuraį modu-yi quγurtala ǰodoǰu bayiba He beat until the wet stick caught fire and the dry stick splintered.

Converbum Abtemporale

661. The *converbum abtemporale* is the opposite of the *converbum terminale*. While the latter indicates the time limit of an action in the future (until . . .), this indicates the time limit in the past (since). Such converbal constructions indicate that the action of the predicate of the whole sentence starts from the beginning of the action of the converb and may last during the whole time during which the latter takes place. Therefore, the *converbum abtemporale* may be translated as "since someone did something" or "while someone was doing something."

manu surγaγuli angq-a bayiγuluγdaγsayar tabun ǰil bolba Five years have elapsed since our school was established.

tendeče nököd inu kereg-ün učir-a ende tende saγuγsaγar qoyar sar-a ilegü ǰam yabuǰu sayi qota-dur kürčü irebeį Afterwards his friends, living here and there because of business, travelled more than two months and have just arrived in town.

Converbum Contemporale

662. The *converbum contemporale* expresses an action which takes place simultaneously with the beginning of the main action. Such converbal constructions may be translated as "as soon as he did something . . ." or "immediately as . . ."

nigen dabaγ-a dabamaγča nigen aγudam ködüge tala bayimuį As soon as they pass the summit, there will be a vast steppe.

Converbum Conditionale

663. The action of the *converbum conditionale* is the condition making the main action possible. Therefore, this converb is to be translated as "if . . ." On the other hand, this converb indicates an action at the time of which the main action takes place, and, in this case, it may be translated as "when something took place . . ."

The general rule is that this converb expresses a condition (if . . .) when the main verb is a present (or future) tense. When the main verb is a past tense, the converb expresses the time at which the main action takes place (when . . .)

> *kümün ama-yin toγ-a-yi kedün mingγ-a kürtele olan ese bolγabasu mal-un aǰil-i tuγil-dur kürtele bolbasuraγulun kögǰigülǰü čidaqu ügei bui* If the size of the population is not increased by several thousand, it will be impossible to develop the cattle husbandry to the ultimate goal.

> *ene ǰorilγ-a-yi güičedkekü abasu manu aǰu aqui kögǰiǰü bolumui* If this task is solved, our economy will develop.

> *tendeče tedeger nököd inu ǰüg ǰüg-eče modun-u dergede quraγad üǰebesü busud ber bürin aǰuγu, emči-yin köbegün ügei* Thereafter, when those friends of his gathered by the forest and looked, all the others were present, but the son of the physician was not.

664. The *converbum conditionale* is often followed by the particle *ele*, which does not change the meaning.

> *tere γaǰar-a iregsen abasu ele nököd inu ügei aǰuγu* When he came to that place his friends, as it turned out, had not been there.

665. When the predicate of the whole sentence has a negative, the converbum conditionale is followed by the particle *ber* and, in such cases, it expresses an action in spite of which the main action takes place (although . . .). But in positive sentences the particle *ber* does not change the meaning of the converb.

> *amusuγai kemen sedkibesü ber amur ügei amui* And even if he longs for rest, there will be no rest, or Although he longs for rest, there is no rest.

> *tere γaǰar-a kürčü üǰebesü ber nököd inu tende quraγad bürin aǰuγu* When he arrived at that place and looked, his friends had assembled and were all there.

Converbum Successivum

666. This colloquial form ending in *-qula/-küle* (pronounced in Khalkha as *-xlā/-xlē*) functions in Written Mongolian as the *converbum conditionale*.

> *edüge darui arγ-a kemǰiy-e-nügüd-i ese abqula tere dutaγdal-nuγud-i usadqaǰu čidaqu ügei bui* If measures are not taken immediately, it will be impossible to remove those defects.

Converbum Concessivum

667. The *converbum concessivum* expresses an action in spite of which the main action of the predicate takes place. This converb is translated as "although . . . ," "in spite of . . ."

> *čayan čerig-i qamiy-a bayiquị-yi ǰüg büri-eče eribečü oytu üǰegdekü ügeị bayiba* Although they were looking everywhere for the White Army, it was not seen at all.

668. The particle *ču* in the ending *-baču* is sometimes written separately and may be placed before the verbal form.

> *tegün-i ču abuba gem ügeị* Never mind if he did take it.

Converbum Finale

669. The *converbum finale* acts as the supine in Latin and expresses the aim of the action of the predicate. Therefore, it can be translated as "in order to . . .'

> *tegün-i abur-a irebeị* He came to take him.

670. The converbum finale was originally a dative-locative of the verbal noun ending in *-r*. It preserves its original meaning in pre-classical texts.

> *ükür-e oyiratuba* He was near death.

Converbum Praeparativum

671. The *converbum praeparativum* is originally the genitive of a noun ending in *-r*. In texts of the pre-classical period it expresses the cause of the action of the predicate of the whole sentence.

> *amitan-i ǰobayulur-un nigül-i üịleddümüị* He commits sin in tormenting living beings. (Lit., "He commits the sin of tormenting living beings.")

672. In the classical and modern language this converb is rarely used; the verbs *ügüle-* "to speak," *sedki-* "to think," and *üǰe-* "to see" are among the few which occur in this form.

> *tegün-i qayan üǰeǰü bürün sayin čirai-tu-yin minu ebedčin yeke bolbaị kemebeị* When the khaghan looked he said: "The illness of my Beautiful-Faced One has become grave."

Direct and Indirect Discourse

673. Sentences expressing direct discourse usually occupy the place between the subject and the predicate of the whole sentence, being linked to the predicate by the *converbum modale* of the verb *keme-* (or *geme-*) "to say," i. e., *kemen* or *gemen* "saying." In other words, the direct discourse is inserted into a sentence. It is not always good, from the point of view of the English style, to translate direct discourse as

such. Frequently direct discourse is translated as indirect. In such cases,
the converb *kemen* (or *gemen*) "saying" is replaced in the translation
by "that."

> *nökör maryaši iresügei kemen ügülebe* The friend said he would
> come tomorrow. (Lit., The friend told saying, "I shall come
> tomorrow.")

674. When the verb "to tell" or "to say" is a *converbum praeparativum*
it is placed before direct discourse. But even in this event the direct
discourse is followed by *kemen* (or *gemen*) and the latter by a finite form
of a *verbum dicendi*.

> *qayan ügüler-ün a köbegün minu a či tere morin-i buu unu kemen*
> (or *gemen*) *kelebe* When the khaghan spoke, he said (lit., "spoke
> saying,") "Ah, my son, do not ride that horse!"

675. The converb *kemen* (or *gemen*) may be replaced by a finite form of
the verb *keme-* (*geme-*). In this event any other *verbum dicendi* is not
necessary.

> *nökör bi maryaši iresügei kemebei* The friend said: "I shall come
> tomorrow."

676. All verbs of thinking, seeing, hearing, saying, and so on (i. e., *verba
cogitandi, sentiendi, dicendi*, etc.), are linked with the sentence expressing
the result of any of these actions by the use of *kemen* in the same manner
as in direct discourse.

> *tere inu maryaši iremüi kemen sedkibe* He thought that he would
> come tomorrow.

677. Indirect discourse is expressed in the same manner. In such constructions the converb *kemen* (*gemen*) functions as the English conjunction "that."

> *edüge tere mayad iremüi kemen bičigsen-i ungšibai* He read a written
> statement that he would certainly come now.

678. The subject of a construction indicating indirect discourse may be
expressed by an *accusativus relationis* (see § 515).

> *qayan tegün-i iretügei kemen ǰarliy bolba* The khaghan ordered him
> to come.

679. The object of someone's perception may be expressed by an *accusativus cum nomine verbali* (see § 514).

> *qayan inu tegün-i irekü-yi üjebe* The khaghan saw him come.

680. The converbal form *kemen* (*gemen*) is often used, in cases when there
is no speech at all, to serve as the English conjunction "that" or "in
order to." The verb indicating the aim of someone's action is either a
form of the direct discourse or a *nomen futuri*.

> *bi suryayuli-dur erdem sursuyai kemen orobai* I entered school in
> order to study. (Lit., I entered school saying, "I shall study
> science.")
>
> *bi suryayuli-dur erdem surqu kemen orobai* I entered school in order
> to study. (Lit., I entered school saying, "To study science.")

Particles

General Remarks

681. Particles do not affect the forms of words. In this respect they are different from postpositions. Their role is to contribute additional emotional shades of meaning to the basic idea expressed by the words concerned. Some particles follow and others precede the word to which they refer.

The Particle *ber*

682. This particle is placed after the word to which it refers. It is used as a mark of the grammatical subject.

bi ber mörgün namančilamui̯ I am praying and making a bow.

683. The particle *ber* is often used in antitheses and in such cases it may be translated as "but."

mergen inu učir šiltayan bügüde-yi medemüi̯, mungqay ber teyimü busu bui̯ The sage knows what the matter is (lit., knows all the causes and circumstances) but the fool is not so.

684. The particle *ber* repeated after two or more words serves as a conjunction and may be translated as "as well as . . ."

kümün amitan ber bayasču tngri-ner ber bayasču luus-un qayad ber uyaraba People as well as living beings rejoiced and the deities rejoiced and the kings of the *Nāga* (dragons) were touched.

685. Interrogative pronouns with the particle *ber* are indefinite pronouns.

ali ber whoever
ken ber whoever
yayun ber whatever.

686. Indefinite pronouns with the particle *ber* in negative sentences are negative indefinite pronouns.

ken ber ese üi̯ebe Nobody saw.
nadur yayun ber ügei̯ I have nothing.

687. The converbum conditionale with the particle *ber* serves sometimes as *converbum concessivum* (see § 665).

emči-yi abčirabasu ber manu bayši edegekü ügei̯ Even if we bring a physician, our teacher will not recover.
qarabasu ber ǰam ügei̯ bolqu Even if one seeks, there will be no road.

The Particle *ču*

688. The particle *ču*, too, is placed after the word to which it refers. Its function is similar to that of the particle *ber*. It means often "also, too". It is not used as a mark of the subject nor is it used in antitheses.

689. The particle *ču* after any word has the same meaning as the English "also" or "too."

bi ču tegün-i medemüi̯ I also know it.
bi tende ču yabuqu sanayatai̯ amui̯ I intend also to go there.

690. The particle *ču* repeated after two or more words may be translated as "as well as . . ."

> *tende modun ču buį ǰimis ču buį sayin čečeg-nügüd ču buį* There are trees as well as fruits and beautiful flowers.

691. The particle *ču* repeated after two or more words in a sentence with a negative predicate may be translated as "neither . . . nor . . ."

> *tere inu üǰebesü ekener inu ču ügeį keüked inu ču ügeį aǰuyu* When he looked, there were neither his wife nor his children.

692. Interrogative pronouns with the particles *ču* are indefinite. In negative sentences, they serve as negative indefinite pronouns.

> *alin ču* whosoever
> *ken ču* whosoever
> *yaγun ču* whatsoever
> *ken ču ese irebe* Nobody came.
> *tende yaγun ču ügeį buį* There is nothing.

693. The past tense ending in *-ba* with the particle *ču* is the *converbum concessivum*. The particle may be placed before the verb.

> *mangγus irebečü namayi olǰu ese čidamuį* Even if the Mangus comes, he will not be able to find me.
> *tere ču ükübe bi tegün-i eriǰü očisuyaį* Even if he died, I would go and seek him.

694. The imperative of the third person of the auxiliary verb *a-* "to be" and *bol-* "to become" with the particle *ču* may be translated into English with the conjunctive "even if it be . . ."

> *nadur morin keregteį buį. maγu ču atuγaį bi absuyaį* I need a horse. I shall take it even if it be a bad one.

The Particle ǰ-a

695. The particle *ǰ-a*, always written with the final letter for *ǰ* and separately from its vowel, is placed after the word to which it refers.
This particle expresses doubt and is translated as "perhaps," "maybe." It occurs with the present tense ending in *-muį* (or sometimes *-m*) and also with the defective verb *buį*.
The present tense with this particle is a potential (*potentialis*) which may be translated "it is possible that . . .," "perhaps . . ."

> *tngri ečige minu medemüį ǰ-a* Probably my father, Heaven, knows.
> *tere inu maryaši irekü buį ǰ-a* He will, perhaps, come tomorrow.
> *tere inu edüge tende buį ǰ-a* He is now, perhaps, there.

The Particle kü

696. The particle *kü*, in emphatic pronunciation *kö*, stresses the meaning of the word to which it refers. This particle is also placed after the word to which it refers.

> *tere kü kümün* precisely that man, that man indeed
> *ulaγan baγatur qotan-a očimuį kü* I am really going to Ulan Bator.

The Particle *a*

697. The particle *a* or *a-a*, placed after the word to which it refers, is used in addressing people.

    köbegün minu a Ah, my son!

The Particle *ele*

698. The particle *ele*, sometimes *le* or *la* under the influence of the colloquial language, generalizes the meaning of the word to which it refers. It is placed after the word concerned.

    sayin ele keüked good girls in general
    tere ele čaγ-tur at that very time.

699. This particle joins the *converbum conditionale* without changing its meaning (see § 664).

    tere γaǰar-a iregsen abasu ele nököd inu ügei aǰuγu When he came to that place, his friends, as it turned out, had not been there.

The Particle *da*

700. This is a colloquial particle and serves to emphasize the meaning of the word to which it refers. It is placed after the word concerned.

    boluna da (colloquial instead of *bolumui ǰ-a*) It will be.

Index

The figures refer to the §§